Sugar rusn

Manchester University Press

INSCRIPTIONS

Series editors
Des Fitzgerald and Amy Hinterberger
Editorial advisory board
Vivette García Deister, National Autonomous University of Mexico
John Gardner, Monash University, Australia
Maja Horst, Technical University of Denmark
Robert Kirk, Manchester, UK
Stéphanie Loyd, Laval University, Canada
Alice Mah, Warwick University, UK
Deboleena Roy, Emory University, USA
Hallam Stevens, Nanyang Technological University, Singapore
Niki Vermeulen, Edinburgh, UK
Megan Warin, Adelaide University, Australia
Malte Ziewitz, Cornell University, USA

Since the very earliest studies of scientific communities, we have known that texts and worlds are bound together. One of the most important ways to stabilise, organise and grow a laboratory, a group of scholars, even an entire intellectual community, is to write things down. As for science, so for the social studies of science: Inscriptions is a space for writing, recording and inscribing the most exciting current work in sociological and anthropological – and any related – studies of science.

The series foregrounds theoretically innovative and empirically rich interdisciplinary work that is emerging in the UK and internationally. It is self-consciously hospitable in terms of its approach to discipline (all areas of social sciences are considered), topic (we are interested in all scientific objects, including biomedical objects) and scale (books will include both fine-grained case studies and broad accounts of scientific cultures).

For readers, the series signals a new generation of scholarship captured in monograph form – tracking and analysing how science moves through our societies, cultures and lives. Employing innovative methodologies for investigating changing worlds, it is home to compelling new accounts of how science, technology, biomedicine and the environment translate and transform our social lives.

Previously published titles

Trust in the system: Research Ethics Committees and the regulation of biomedical research   Adam Hedgecoe
Embodiment and everyday cyborgs: Technologies that alter subjectivity   Gill Haddow
Personalised cancer medicine: Future crafting in the genomic era   Anne Kerr *et al.*
The elephant and the dragon in contemporary life sciences: A call for decolonising global governance   Joy Y. Zhang & Saheli Datta Burton

Sugar rush

Science, politics and the demonisation of fatness

Karen Throsby

Manchester University Press

Copyright © Karen Throsby 2023

The right of Karen Throsby to be identified as the author of this work has been asserted in accordance with the Copyright, Designs and Patents Act 1988.

Published by Manchester University Press
Oxford Road, Manchester M13 9PL
www.manchesteruniversitypress.co.uk

British Library Cataloguing-in-Publication Data
A catalogue record for this book is available from the British Library

ISBN 978 1 5261 5154 4 hardback
ISBN 978 1 5261 5155 1 paperback

First published 2023

The publisher has no responsibility for the persistence or accuracy of URLs for any external or third-party internet websites referred to in this book, and does not guarantee that any content on such websites is, or will remain, accurate or appropriate.

Typeset
by Cheshire Typesetting Ltd, Cuddington, Cheshire
Printed in Great Britain
by Bell & Bain Ltd, Glasgow

For Pam Throsby

Contents

List of figures

Acknowledgements

A single-authored book is always indebted to many.

The research for this book was conducted with the support of a Leverhulme Trust Research Fellowship in 2017–18 (REF-2017–382), which gave me the time and space to fully immerse myself in the world of anti-sugar. The book also includes material from four publications, and I am grateful for permission to reproduce content from these publications in revised form. Chapter 2 includes material first published in Karen Throsby, 'Pure, white and deadly: sugar addiction and the cultivation of urgency', *Food, Culture and Society* 23 no. 1 (2020): 11–29, copyright © 2019 Association for the Study of Food and Society, available online: https://www.tandfonline.com/10.1080/15528014.2019.1679547. Chapter 4 incorporates material from Karen Throsby, 'Giving up sugar and the inequalities of abstinence', *Sociology of Health and Illness* 40, no. 6 (2018): 954–968, copyright © 2018 Foundation for the Sociology of Health & Illness. The Introduction draws on both Karen Throsby, 'Sweetening the "war on obesity"', in *Routledge Handbook of Critical Obesity Studies*, ed. M. Gard, D. Powell and J. Tenorio (London: Routledge, 2022), and on Karen Throsby, 'But you're not defending sugar, are you?', in *Difficult Conversations: A Feminist Dialogue*, ed. R. Ryan-Flood, I. Crowhurst and L. James-Hawkins (London: Routledge, 2023), both reproduced with permission of The Licensor through PLSclear.

Over the five years from the start of this project to its culmination in this book, I have enjoyed the support of colleagues in the School of

Acknowledgements

Sociology and Social Policy at the University of Leeds and in the Centre for Interdisciplinary Gender Studies (CIGS). Colleagues from our regular Writing Together Tuesdays also kept me going when it felt like I was getting nowhere. Kim Allen, Joanne Greenhalgh, Ruth Holliday, Greg Hollin, Ana Manzano, Jessica Martin, Sam Murray, Maud Perrier, Nick Piper, Jayne Raisborough, Celia Roberts, Elaine Swan, Megan Warin and many others have asked critical questions, listened to presentations, read draft chapters and given endless encouragement; their willingness to have their ears bent about sugar over several years was fundamental to bringing this project to fruition. I have also been invited to present my research at conferences and seminars both in the UK and overseas, which has given me the chance to refine my thinking and make new connections. These opportunities are too many to list, but each one was an important step in keeping the book project moving forward. The team at Manchester University Press, and particularly Tom Dark, have been hugely supportive in the face of my struggles to complete the book on time. I am enormously grateful for their patience.

And thank you to Peter. For everything, always.

Introduction

We live in a time of profound uncertainty and anxiety around food. Food is not only a necessity for survival, but also fulfils multiple, and often conflicting, social roles: it is a site of pleasure and conviviality; a locus of familial tension and conflict; a source of everyday labour; a marker of identity; an axis of inequality; and a domain of fear, anxiety and shame. We worry about what food is safe to eat, what it might do to our bodies and what it might make others think of us.[1] We must be on guard against foods that might make us, or those we care for, acutely or chronically ill or that mark us out as failed citizens for whose poor choices everyone must pay. For some, the primary relationship with food is its absence or scarcity, with hunger in the UK skyrocketing as austerity measures slowly dismantle the safety net of the welfare state and as the hardships of the pandemic and a cost of living crisis bite unevenly.[2] For others, the privileges of time and money create spaces for 'foodie' identities, accruing social and cultural capital via their discerning, adventurous palates and local and environmental investments.[3] Food sits at the heart of a vast global, transnational industrial complex built upon classed, raced and gendered global inequalities, but is experienced at a profoundly personal, domestic and local level as we go about our daily lives, purchasing and preparing food to nourish and sustain ourselves and those for whom we care. As such, food is endlessly multiple, uncertain and contingent. As food sociologist Sarah Bowen and colleagues observe, 'food is never just food'.[4]

But despite all this uncertainty and multiplicity, food is also characterised by (always provisional) certainties. At any given time, particular
foods are sedimented in dietary advice, marketing and the popular imagination in binary terms; they are 'good' or 'bad', 'healthy' or 'unhealthy'.
The unabashed or inadvertent consumption of 'unhealthy' food carries the stain of the failed citizenship of the ill-informed, undisciplined
(over)consumer whose lifestyle failures will lead inexorably to expensive
chronic diseases and a wasted life of unproductivity. And in the face of
these poor dietary choices, confidently proscriptive and prescriptive
public health and nutritional science wisdoms around food set out to
educate and persuade us to change our habits and behaviours in line
with the prevailing certainties of the moment. Meanwhile, popular self-
help books happily enter the dietary fray, offering up neatly packaged
formulas for negotiating a pathway through dietary uncertainty with
the promise of a healthier, leaner and longer life. In this way, the confident certainties of food are inextricable from its endless uncertainties,
creating a 'nutritional cacophony',[5] with each prescription attempting
to solidify the unpredictably shifting ground of the prevailing dietary
knowledges and practices.

This book focuses on a contemporary food whose risk to health is
widely treated as beyond dispute and in need of urgent redress, but
which is also replete with uncertainty: sugar. After years of primacy
as public enemy number one in public health campaigns, dietary fat
is increasingly being supplanted by sugar, which is held culpable for
rising levels of obesity and a catalogue of associated expensive and
chronic non-communicable diseases (NCDs). Sugar reduction has been
the subject of national and international policy,[6] with predictable ros-
ters of proposed and implemented interventions including the taxation
of sweetened fizzy drinks, limiting sales of sugary foods in locations
such as hospitals and schools, reformulation initiatives and attempts
to control advertising, particularly to children. The anti-sugar campaigning organisation Action on Sugar was launched in January 2014
with the headline-grabbing claim that 'sugar is the new tobacco'[7] – a
soundbite that tarred sugar with the brush of carcinogenic addiction that

characterises contemporary understandings of smoking.[8] Meanwhile, public health campaigns in the UK such as Change4Life use social marketing techniques to urge consumers to be 'Sugar Smart' and to exchange sugary foods for low-sugar alternatives.[9] The alarm surrounding sugar has opened up a burgeoning market for popular science tracts, TV and film documentaries, autobiographies and self-help guides, all dedicated to sounding the alarm and persuading people to quit the white stuff. Amid urgent calls that something must be done, in the second and third decades of the twenty-first century, we can be in no doubt of the 'wrongness' of sugar.

Sugar has a long and often traumatic history, which reaches into its present. Sugar travelled from India to the Mediterranean and to the privileged tables of Europe's medieval nobility.[10] Anthropologist Sidney Mintz famously mapped out its nineteenth-century transition from extravagant luxury to a dietary staple of the new industrial proletariat, which made 'a busy life seem less so' and eased the transitions back and forth between work and rest.[11] He argued that sugar altered work patterns, eating habits and modern diets, declaring that 'the first sweetened cup of hot tea to be drunk by an English worker was a significant historical event, because it prefigured the transformation of an entire society, a total remaking of its economic and social basis'.[12]

The history of sugar's consumption also cannot be separated from its roots in, and dependence on, the slave trade, with millions of people forcibly transported from Africa to South America, the Caribbean and North America to a life of brutal enslaved labour in the sugar cane fields. Beginning in the seventeenth century and continuing through to the abolition of slavery in the nineteenth century, the sugar trade brought enrichment to a privileged few and dislocated and killed millions. Even after abolition, the importing of indentured labour sustained the exploitative foundations of the industry, including Chinese, Japanese, Koreans and Filipinos in Hawaii, Indians in the Caribbean and the Indian Ocean, and South Pacific Islanders in Australia.[13] As well as producing these enforced global demographic shifts and their enduring inequalities, sugar's colonial legacy also lives on through the industry's rapacious consumption and devastation of natural resources and land, including the violent displacement of indigenous people.[14] Sugar has, indeed, 'changed the world',[15] although it might be more accurate to argue that it is colonialism and capitalism, rather than sugar *per se*, that have wreaked such misery.

Contemporary concerns around sugar rarely invoke these damaging legacies of inequality and exploitation, focusing instead on the dietary ubiquity of sugar and its perceived threat to health. This conviction finds solidity in the second of the certainties that are the concern of this book: that obesity is a catastrophic affront to health that has expensive, but avoidable, consequences for individual wellbeing, productivity and the resourcing of public services. Sugar is heavily implicated in this looming catastrophe.

The contemporary 'war on obesity' has its origins at the turn of the twenty-first century, when concerns about fatness were packaged up in a perfect storm of anxieties about personal responsibility, rising health care costs, and threats to security and productivity. This built upon decades (and centuries) of concern about, and derogation of, the fat body,[16] but found new life amid fears of unseen threats to national security and in neoliberal demands that individuals take responsibility for their own selves, bodies and futures. Like sugar, obesity has been the subject of multiple policy interventions at the national and international level,[17] with no fewer than fourteen new policies in the UK between 1992 and 2020.[18] In spite of sociologist Michael Gard's predictions that the 'obesity epidemic' is entering its terminal phase,[19] the war on obesity continues apace, constantly revivifying itself through the discovery of new emergencies and blameworthy culprits.[20] Like sugar, obesity is the target of policy pronouncements, popular science books, media coverage, documentaries, confessional accounts and uncountable self-help and advice books, all invoking the catastrophe of obesity and the urgent need for a sustained war against it. The wrongness of obesity, like sugar, sits securely beyond contestation in popular, biomedical and policy discourse. If we can agree on nothing else, we are assured, we can agree that both obesity and sugar are problems about which something must (and can) be done.

Despite the received wisdom of the wrongness of obesity, its certainties as an avoidable personal and public health catastrophe have not entirely escaped criticism. As discussed in more detail in Chapter 2, voices from fat activism and from the interdisciplinary field of fat studies have advanced a range of critiques of the assumptions and practices of the targeting of fat bodies. These critiques also dovetail with those from critical food studies, which highlight the ways in which the singular focus on obesity obscures the vast inequalities in relation to food quality and access. They also highlight the repressive effects of expert-led attempts to distil the complexities of the food–body relationship into decontextualised and universalised dietary prescriptions without consideration of the socioeconomic priorities and challenges that inform food decisions.[21] These intersecting bodies of work also join critical voices challenging both the notion of 'health' itself as a 'transparent, universal good'[22] and of obesity as self-evidently incompatible with health.[23] Nevertheless, these critical voices are difficult to hear above the roar of the war on obesity and its constant need for reinvention.

Until very recently, dietary fat was seen as the primary agent of obesity, as well as heart disease and other chronic illnesses commonly associated with fatness. The targeting of fat, particularly in relation to cardiovascular disease (CVD), rose to prominence in the mid-twentieth century, driven by the work of American physiologist Ancel Keys, whose long-standing interest in the relationship between diet and health increasingly focused on the role of saturated fat in CVD – a health issue which was thrust into the public spotlight in 1955, when President Eisenhower suffered a heart attack. This culminated in the launch in 1958 of the Seven Countries Study – a longitudinal epidemiological study across populations and regions of the relationships between diet, lifestyle, CVD and stroke.[24] *Time Magazine* featured Keys on its front cover in January 1961, and the accompanying article – 'Medicine: the fat of the land' – set out Keys' core arguments that Americans eat too much in general and specifically, they consume too much saturated fat, leading to increased risk of CVD.[25] The article showcases Keys' own parsimonious lifestyle, including a lunch of 'a sardine sandwich, an olive, a cooky [sic] and a glass of skim milk' followed by a nap of precisely ten minutes. Keys and his wife, Margaret, went on to publish two best-selling cookery books advocating the health-producing properties of a low-fat, Mediterranean diet, and his research paved the way for nutritional guidelines for decades to come, although these were not without bitter contestation. Biochemist George Mann, for example, drew on his own studies in the 1950s of the traditional Masai diet of meat, blood and milk to challenge the claims of what he later called 'the heart mafia', who he felt had sidelined him professionally and wrecked his career.[26] This is addressed in more detail in Chapter 1, but what these fat-versus-sugar debates share is the use of the fat body not only as a commonplace proxy for NCDs, but also as a moral threat. As the *Time Magazine* article notes, Keys had undisguised contempt for fat bodies, describing them as 'disgusting'. This reflects the familiar pattern of the thin cloaking of moral judgements about fat bodies in discourses of health that, as I will argue throughout this book, also characterises the attack on sugar.

One of the challenges inherent in efforts to reduce dietary saturated fat is its role in providing palatability and texture to food, meaning that a replacement was required. Sugar filled this role perfectly, improving 'mouth feel' and flavour, as well as acting as a preservative. Consequently, its presence in everyday foods increased as the fat content fell. As the war on obesity lost steam in the wake of its failure to achieve its own stated goals of sustainable population-level falls in obesity rates, sugar, already increasingly prevalent in packaged and processed foods, found itself increasingly in the firing line. For some, sugar had been the root problem all along, sidelined by the focus on fat;[27] for others, it was a missing piece in the complex puzzle of obesity that had been overlooked in the intense focus on fat.[28] Either way, the link between sugar and obesity became increasingly sedimented, and the war on obesity had a new enemy to fight. This is not to argue that the connection hadn't previously been made, and the high demand among (mostly female) consumers for artificial sweeteners since the 1950s demonstrates a sustained link in the public and commercial imagination between sugar and weight.[29] But in its most recent moment in the spotlight, sugar is being figured not simply as *a* cause of obesity, but as *the* cause. Consequently, while public health messages about sugar are always about more than obesity – including, for example, dental decay – obesity remains the primary lens through which the problem of sugar is viewed. In this way, to talk about sugar is always to talk about obesity, and to talk about obesity is, in the current moment at least, to talk about sugar. *Sugar Rush*, then, begins from the question: what are the social meanings and practices of sugar in the context of the war on obesity?

What's new about sugar?

While in many ways sugar can be understood as picking up the role of dietary nemesis where fat left off, this is not a consecutive shift from one to the next, but rather is embedded in a series of nutritional and dietary continuities.[30] First, as discussed above, even the most ardent low-fat dietary prescriptions maintain suspicion towards sugar and its 'empty' calories. Conversely, contemporary mainstream dietary advice remains determinedly committed to limiting consumption of saturated fat, even while emphasising the need to reduce sugar. This continuity was illustrated in 2016 when members of the National Obesity Forum (NOF) released a report entitled *Eat Fat, Cut the Carbs and Avoid Snacking to Reverse Obesity and Type 2 Diabetes*.[31] The report adhered closely to the logics of the low-carbohydrate-high-fat (LCHF) dietary movement, disputing a causative relation between saturated fat and heart disease, advocating complete abstinence from sugar and pointing accusatory fingers at the food industry for corrupting nutritional science in the interests of financial gain. Experts lined up to decry the report, which was described in a *British Medical Journal* editorial as 'oversimplistic' and 'flawed in its assumptions'.[32] It was dismissed as 'irresponsible' by Public Health England and as 'extremely dangerous' by the British Dietetic Association.[33] Several NOF members resigned in protest both at the content of the report and at the lack of consultation leading up to its release.[34] Regardless of the specific rights and wrongs of the claims being made, this highlights the ways in which sugar and fat always circulate in relation to each other, rather than as exclusively consecutive threats. They occupy the same anti-obesity territory, characterised by a hostility to fatness and urgent calls for action.

A second continuity can be seen in the embeddedness of the attack on sugar in the nutritionist paradigm; that is, it relies on 'a reductive *focus* [sic] on the nutrient composition of foods as the means for understanding their healthfulness, as well as by reductive *interpretation* [sic] of the role of these nutrients in bodily health'.[35] In the late nineteenth and early twentieth centuries, malnutrition was the primary driver of attempts to quantify the nutritional content of foods, but by the middle of the twentieth century, concerns had shifted towards excess consumption, leading to the development of what food politics scholar Gyorgy Scrinis calls 'the era of good-and-bad nutrition'.[36] This led to the creation of single-nutrient proscriptions against particular foods, which he argues rely on 'the decontextualization, simplification and exaggeration of the role of nutrients in determining bodily health'.[37] This dietary binary of good/bad foods characterises both low-fat advice and the attack on sugar, with consumers urged to meticulously monitor grams of fat or the number of teaspoons or cubes of sugar they are consuming to the exclusion of questions of food quality, the social context of consumption and the combination of foods with which the problematised nutrient is consumed. This is particularly pertinent in the case of sugar, which is rarely consumed in isolation and yet is the focus of a sustained single-nutrient reduction campaign. This ongoing dislocation of sugar from the context of consumption is a core concern of *Sugar Rush*.

But despite these continuities evident in the rush to sugar, it is also a crisis of its time. This is particularly evident in relation to changing understandings of the body characterised by an intensifying focus at the molecular level. According to sociologist Nikolas Rose, the molecularisation of the body marks a departure from molar conceptualisations 'at the scale of limbs, organs, tissues, flows of blood, hormones and so forth', looking instead towards molecules such as DNA to define human difference.[38] This informs future-oriented understandings of bodies at risk and in need of health-maximising intervention. This is not to argue that biomedicine and healthcare no longer operate on the molar scale; in fact, according to Rose, this is how most people continue to imagine and act upon their bodies. This is particularly the case for obesity, for example, where internal and external body fat, clogged arteries and damaged organs serve under the clinical gaze as the visible evidence of the health-damaging effects of bodily excess. However, obesity is also increasingly conceptualised as a metabolic disorder – that is, as a disorder of 'the biological processes by which bodies metabolize nutrients derived from food' and which can be diagnosed only via an 'aggregation of clinical and laboratory measurements'.[39]

The turn to sugar aligns comfortably with this molecularisation. Unlike the action of fat which is easily (albeit reductively) imagined settling on the body as fat in visible ways ('a moment on the lips, a lifetime on the hips'), sugar is understood as acting in the body in ways that are largely invisible to human observation without the mediation of technologies of measurement and their associated biomarkers. This invisibility also exacerbates the invidiousness of the risk that attaches so easily to the consumption of sugar: anybody can be at risk, regardless of body size, and not know it. As popular anti-sugar author Robert Lustig warns menacingly: 'You think you are safe? You are SO screwed. And you don't even know it.'[40] This invisible threat to health is also compounded by the invisibility of sugar itself, which is conceptualised within anti-sugar discourse as 'hidden' in everyday processed foods and therefore requiring constant vigilance (see Chapter 3).

The second way in which the rush to blame sugar can be understood as a crisis of its time is through the intensification of the moralisation of health, or what cultural studies scholar Robert Crawford described as 'healthism'.[41] While the imperative to health can be understood as one of the continuities of the attack on sugar, Crawford argues that the early twenty-first century saw an intensification of this health consciousness and the moral imperative to 'achieve' health and manage risk. The ubiquity of mass media, the commercialisation of health products and services, the growth of technologies for detecting risk factors (including those at the molecular level) and the rise of personalised biosensing technologies to facilitate the ongoing monitoring of those factors all converge to aggravate insecurities around health. At the same time, this reinforces the conviction that health can (and should) be accomplished through the exercise of individual responsibility and self-control. This intensification provides fertile ground for the attack on sugar, which is increasingly imagined as devoid of nutritional or health-giving properties, replete with risk and within the remit of the individual to remove from the diet.

The final factor that marks that the contemporary nature of the attack on sugar in the UK is its coincidence with the implementation of austerity measures under the Conservative–Liberal Democrat coalition government (2010–15). These measures were in response to the 2008 financial crisis, and were consolidated in the 2012 Welfare Reform Act, which entrenched a raft of public spending cuts targeting the most disadvantaged sections of society. As discussed in more detail in Chapter 7, austerity provides a key piece of context through which the rush to blame sugar has taken hold, particularly via intensifying narratives of irresponsible overconsumption (of sugar, of public resources). Conversely, the attack on sugar, particularly in its repudiation of the fat body, shores up the figure of the abject Other who is central to securing public consent for the unequal cruelties of austerity.[42] This is not to argue that austerity caused the attack on sugar (or vice versa), but rather to suggest that austerity and the rush to blame sugar constitute mutually reinforcing and sustaining discourses that have allowed each other to flourish.

This combination of competing and coincident nutritionist conceptualisations of food and health, the molecularisation of the body, the proliferation of risk, the intensifying imperative to health, and a social and political climate of escalating intolerance towards those most readily painted as undeserving of public support all provide fertile ground for anxieties around sugar. This makes sugar simultaneously more of the same, particularly in relation to the repudiation of the fat body, and also a crisis of its time. With this in mind, *Sugar Rush* investigates the social life of sugar, exploring its contemporary meanings and practices (including those of its repudiation) in the context of a war on obesity and asking what is at stake in the multiple (and often competing) understandings of sugar's wrongness, what gets lost along the way and with what effects.

Researching sugar

The core of this project lies in a dataset of 556 newspaper articles dating from January 2013 to August 2020, gathered from nine UK newspapers, including a mix of tabloids and broadsheets in both daily and Sunday iterations.[43] The articles were selected using the Nexis database, beginning with an initial headline search for 'sugar' from 2000 to 2018 and focusing on articles of over 500 words. The search results were then filtered manually to exclude irrelevant articles such as recipes, the extensive coverage of businessman and TV personality Alan Sugar, and the metaphorical uses of sugar ('a spoonful of sugar ...') commonly found in business or political reporting that did not relate directly to sugar's intensifying public health infamy. The initial search from 2000 to 2018 garnered 640 articles. These were very unevenly spread, with coverage escalating significantly from 2013 and peaking in 2016 (when Chancellor George Osborne announced plans to introduce the Soft Drinks Industry Levy or 'sugar tax') (see Figure 0.1). This provided the parameters for what I initially planned to be the final dataset (2013–18) – a collection of 496 articles covering a neat chronological arc from the rise of sugar as the primary object of dietary concern to the 2016 announcement of the sugar tax and concluding with its implementation in 2018.

As is the way with research, however, things didn't quite proceed to plan, and as the analysis and writing inched slowly forwards during 2019, based on the original 2013–2018 dataset, the arrival of 2020 brought with it the COVID-19 pandemic – a public health catastrophe from which the world is still reeling as I am finalising this book at the beginning of 2022. By the end of March 2020, and after a period of fatal indecisiveness, the UK was locked down, and the book had to take a back seat as I found myself consumed with the task of adjusting my work and private lives to this scary and uncertain new reality. But as I struggled my way back to the task of book-writing, there was an unmistakable bubbling up of

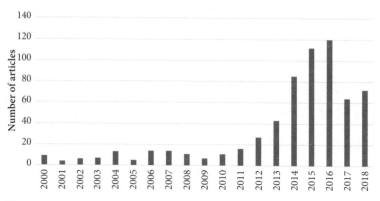

Figure 0.1 Newspaper coverage of sugar, 2000–18

anti-obesity rhetoric, particularly in the context of claims that those who are obese face specific and heightened risks from the virus. On 5 April 2020, UK Prime Minister Boris Johnson, who had earlier boasted about fearlessly shaking hands with infected hospital patients, was admitted to hospital suffering from COVID-19, spending a short time in intensive care before finally being discharged on 12 April. He later attributed the severity of his illness to his weight, further fuelling the anti-obesity fires and laying the foundations for the launch of a new anti-obesity campaign in late July in which sugar, inevitably, featured heavily. The book contains further discussion of these events and the context that they provide for the social life of sugar, but for now, it is enough to say that by the launch of the campaign, it was already clear that a book about the social life of sugar would be gapingly incomplete without some consideration of these extraordinary events. So I returned to the Nexis database and, using the same search terms and approach, I added a further sixty articles from January 2019 to August 2020, to a total of 556 for the entire dataset (see Figure 0.2).

This end date of August 2020 comes with the caveat that the boundaries of any study of the social life of sugar will always be arbitrary, especially since the war on obesity endures through a process of endless revivification, reinstating familiar ideas in novel ways that make sense in that particular social, cultural and political moment. Thus there is an endless temptation

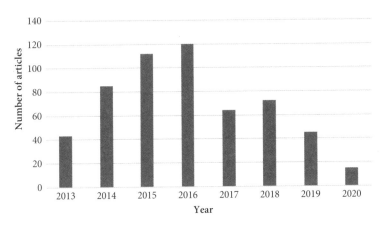

Figure 0.2 Newspaper coverage of sugar, 2013 – August 2020

to look just a little further, and a little further, to see what happens next. But book deadlines are not so open-ended, so the line was drawn.

As shown in Figure 0.3, the articles were spread unevenly across the nine newspapers. This unevenness of coverage extends not only to the quantity and frequency of reporting, but also the nature of that reporting. For example, broadsheet coverage, and particularly that in *The Guardian*, engaged extensively with debates surrounding regulation and taxation, exploring obesity as a matter of societal rather than individual responsibility.[44] As discussed in Chapter 8, this is one strategy for avoiding the overt blaming of individuals. However, as I argue throughout the book, individual responsibility still looms large, even in these ostensibly societal accounts. Tabloid coverage, on the other hand, focused on personal stories and dietary advice columns, as well as strongly worded editorials and commentaries, particularly about the sugar tax.[45]

Using the qualitative data analysis software NVivo, each article was assigned an over-arching theme (e.g. regulation, addiction, hidden, inequality) and then coded in detail according to the key discourses, concepts, events, practices, knowledges, debates, individuals and organisations that were identified through multiple re-readings

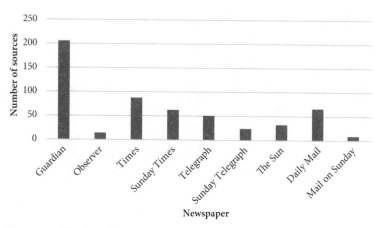

Figure 0.3 Number of sources per newspaper

as constituting the social life of sugar in the news. This coded data was analysed by looking beyond what is said to how meaning is constructed and to what intended and unintended effects. In this way, I treat language as social and active, as a site of power and always political, thinking simultaneously about the context in which it is made meaningful and considering its social consequences.

In working through and with the data, the book seeks out what I have called 'sugar talk'. This is a borrowing from Rebecca Jordan-Young and Katrina Karkazis, who coin the term 'T talk' in their study of testosterone to describe 'the web of direct claims and indirect associations that circulate around testosterone both as a material substance and as a multivalent cultural symbol', weaving 'folklore into science' to validate cultural beliefs about masculinity and the binarised sexed body.[46] They argue that T talk cements the notion that testosterone and oestrogen are respective male and female sex hormones; that it obfuscates any need for demonstrable empirical detail about testosterone's function; that it codes testosterone as natural and biological, giving the veneer of science to anecdote; and that it animates testosterone, rendering it a 'willful character'.[47] I have appropriated their approach of 'looking for the T talk' here in pursuit of sugar's social life, seeking out the sugar talk that constitutes and solidifies the prevailing narratives of sugar (and all while avoiding the obvious 'sweet talk' pun).

This newspaper data and analysis sit at the heart of this book, but while newspapers are an important source of health information, and especially in relation to the obesity epidemic, I am not suggesting a straightforwardly causative relationship between newspaper reporting and individual choices, beliefs and behaviours. Instead, the book asks what different articulations and enactments of sugar are made imaginable or necessary through the newspaper coverage, and what their intended and unintended effects are.

While the news media is a significant site of dietary health information, it is by no means the only one. In recognition of this, I gathered research papers, press releases, popular science tracts, websites, autobiographical accounts, TV shows and documentary films, dietary lifestyle guides and policy documents that had triggered or been cited in the newspaper reporting, and these were added to the dataset. These were supplemented by additional texts that were either encountered incidentally or, in the case of popular science tracts and dietary lifestyle and self-help guides, by selecting the most popular and most-reviewed texts on online bookstores or, pre-pandemic, visiting large bookshops to see what was displayed on the shelves.[48] Although there is considerable slippage between the two, I excluded recipe books, focusing instead on texts that set out a substantial rationale for the dietary lifestyle they are advocating and that offer advice on how to achieve that dietary change. While the newspaper data draws on UK publications, this wider array of anti-sugar texts has a much more international reach, with strong representation from the US, where concern around sugar finds much common ground with that in the UK. This assemblage of texts constitutes the dataset on which *Sugar Rush* draws.

But you're not defending sugar, are you?

Writing about their experiences of researching testosterone, Jordan-Young and Karkazis recall the 'emotional force' of people's responses, 'asking us urgent questions or making definitive statements about how it affects them in daily life'.[49] The same can be said for sugar, which regularly prompts two key responses. The first of these is sugar confessions, where people offer up unprompted confessions of their own helplessness in the face of sugary foods, describing themselves as addicts or as having a sweet tooth. At conferences and events where I have presented my research, they apologise for eating biscuits or cakes in front of me and promise to do better tomorrow. In these moments of heightened food anxiety, my own consumption also comes under scrutiny. As a vegan, I am rarely able to consume the sweet snacks at events, but where I am known as someone working on sugar, my non-consumption is repeatedly read as sugar avoidance, with the unspoken (or sometimes spoken) suspicion that this is somehow in tension with my critical take on the attack on sugar. It is an assumption that is difficult to refute without opening up the fresh can of worms that is public veganism and its killjoy potential.[50] The mundane surveillance of the self and others that bubbles quickly to the surface in relation to sugar reflects the everyday struggles with food that many people, and especially women, experience and the easy way in which guilt, shame and worry about food and bodies trickle into everyday conversation and sociality.

The second key response is the alarmed question: 'But you're not defending sugar, are you?' Or in another manifestation of the same impulse: 'But it *is* bad for you, isn't it?' The questions reflect the desire for consensus about the wrongness of sugar. Without that consensus, conversations around the troubling social inequalities and problematic assumptions about fat bodies that lie at the heart of this book struggle to proceed, and I find myself constantly pressed to concede the wrongness of sugar in exchange for engagement with my critical analysis of sugar's fraught social life. Jordan-Young and Karkazis see the emotionally forceful responses they encountered as resulting from testosterone being something that people know about 'in ways that involve a lot of shared information (right or wrong) as well as their own bodily or personal experiences'.[51] They argue that this creates layers of ideas and talk which solidify over time into closely held certainties. The same can be said of sugar, whose high-stakes wrongness has become sedimented across multiple intersecting domains to the point where it has become impossible to begin a conversation about it without first positioning it firmly on the losing side of the healthy/unhealthy and good/bad food binaries. Within this binary framing, asking critical questions about the attack on sugar can only ever be understood as coming to its defence, and my refusal to join the chorus of voices denouncing sugar risks placing me in dangerous alignment with the forces of Big Sugar. Health sociologist Emma Rich and colleagues encountered a similar impasse in their critical engagements with physical cultures and the stigmatisation of fat bodies, finding themselves repeatedly challenged with the loaded question: 'But don't you care about children?' Given their commitment to enhancing individual health and wellbeing, particularly among marginalised groups, they observe with pointed understatement that 'something is lost in translation'.[52]

Consequently, one of the challenges that I have faced in writing this book is finding ways to articulate my critical position without sounding as though I am either shilling for Big Soda, whose public demonisation currently exceeds even that of sugar itself, or denying the materiality of the multiple ways in which bodies and sugar interact. It is a tricky impasse to navigate. How can I challenge the prevailing assumptions of the straightforwardly causative and problematic relationship between sugar and the fat body while still acknowledging that sugar is embodied in materially and socially significant ways? The question 'But you're not defending sugar, are you?', then, signals the need to find a language to express this critique in a context where the terms of the debate are already firmly entrenched in ways that attempt to head that critique off at the pass.

If I were to concede to the terms of the debate, I would argue that as much as any food can be categorised as good or bad, sugar is not especially healthful, but that nutricentric approaches to food – that is, approaches that measure food by its nutrient properties and imagined health effects alone – cannot begin to capture food's social meanings and values. As sociologist Brenda Beagan and colleagues argue in their insightful analysis of how families come to eat in the way that they do, 'eating isn't just swallowing food'.[53] Good/bad evaluations of food miss the pleasures and sociality of cooking and eating, as well as imposing a classed and future-oriented vision of health that ignores what might be necessary to secure health in the present (see Chapter 8). Specifically in relation to sugar, they disregard as dysfunctional the deliciousness of sweetness and its fond associations for many with the giving and receiving of love and care or as a source of comfort in otherwise straitened circumstances. If forced to engage with debates about the health status of sugar, I would argue that the demonisation of sugar as irretrievably health-damaging on the scale of tobacco is contradicted by the fact that, apart from the most zealous of anti-sugar advocates, the moderate consumption of sugar is treated as legitimate. This comes with the caveat, though, that this legitimacy is always closely circumscribed by class, with middle-class 'treats' given exceptional approval that is not granted to foods associated with working-class consumption. Consequently, I would argue that the case for the specific and unique harms of sugar is fundamentally flawed by its dislocation from the social world in which food is consumed and is embodied.

But while questions about the harmfulness of sugar are addressed in the book, these are not the conversations that I want to engage in most directly. Instead, *Sugar Rush* raises fundamental questions about whether sugar and health is the right conversation for us to be having in the first place and asks what other conversations the desire for consensus around the health-damaging properties of sugar might be distracting us from. Thus the aim of the book is never to intervene in, proscribe or prescribe individual eating behaviours or to pass judgement on particular foods. Instead, the book asks what work sugar (and its repudiation) is performing in the social domain, and in whose interests; and it explores what the singular focus on sugar obscures and what inequalities it facilitates. These are questions that can be asked and answered only by stepping outside the good/bad binary into which sugar is persistently corralled; this is the challenge that *Sugar Rush* takes on.

A note about the text

Before briefly setting out the chapter outlines, I wanted to add some explanation of my approach to the presentation of the book. First, the articles collected from the Nexis database are from the print issues of the newspapers, but where possible, I have traced the online versions and included those details in the reference information to facilitate easy access for readers. The print and online versions are not always identical, with online versions often published the day before the print copy, and sometimes with a different headline or with content and headlines being revised in multiple online iterations. Where the two versions are broadly comparable and with only non-significant differences, I have referenced the online version to make it easier for readers to follow up on sources. However, historical content is not available online for some articles, and in these cases, I have referenced the original print version only.

And secondly, one of the problems of writing a book that challenges received wisdoms is the constant need to refuse the closure of meaning around key terms. Consequently, the temptation is to signal the problematisation of key terms with 'scare quotes'; for example, both 'the war on obesity' and the 'obesity epidemic' are commonly used terms, but by invoking militarism and contagion, they escalate the sense of urgency and quickly shift the focus of attack from fatness to people who are fat. However, in a book like this, where chains of received knowledges come under interrogation, this can create a flurry of scare quotes that litter the text, irritating the reader and neutralising the critical effects of the punctuation through overuse. In each case, I have used scare quotes to introduce challenges to those terms, but do not use them throughout. I trust the reader to keep in mind my scepticism in relation to the common usages of those terms, even if they don't agree with it, for the sake of an uncluttered page (even while arguing that we need more 'clutter' in the ways we think about sugar).

Book outline

The first two chapters of the book explore the ways in which the near-ubiquitous agreement that sugar *is* a problem obscures the ways in which multiple and competing understandings of the nature of that problem are in circulation. Chapter 1 ('What's wrong with sugar?') looks at two contrasting approaches: the first understands sugar as a source of empty calories that disrupts energy balance to cultivate fatness; and the second sees sugar as uniquely toxic, creating metabolic chaos. However, as discussed in Chapter 2 ('Hanging together'), although these appear inimical to one another, they manage to hang together in pursuit of their shared investment in sugar reduction. The chapter argues that this is achieved via three key discourses: (1) the obesity epidemic; (2) addiction; and (3) nostalgia for a lost past. I argue that these provide a lowest-common-denominator platform from which to pursue their anti-sugar efforts. Together these opening chapters of the book lead to the conclusion that although 'What's wrong with sugar?' is a good starting point, especially for a book about sugar, it may be the wrong question all along, since the primary concern in sugar's social life is not what it does in the body but how it gets there and how its consumption can be reduced. This aspect of sugar's social life is the focus of the remainder of the book.

Chapters 3 and 4 take up this challenge. Chapter 3 ('Hidden') addresses the common understanding of sugar as both hidden and actively hiding in the everyday food supply, tricking consumers into accidental overconsumption. Focusing on the popular media device of the 'hidden-sugar shock' exposé, the chapter explores the ways in which consumers are encouraged to become sugar detectives, but how even the most diligent attempts to contain food within the healthy/unhealthy binary are unsustainable. Chapter 4 ('Giving up sugar') continues this theme, focusing on popular self-help books on how to give up sugar. The chapter argues that the work of giving up sugar is an act of self-making; it is a testimony to the determination of the individual to take responsibility for health. In doing so, they can distance themselves from the feckless overconsuming Other against whom their own successes can be measured.

Chapters 5 and 6 move away from this focus on individual self-making, broadening the frame to consider the social life of sugar in film and policy. Chapter 5 ('Entertaining sugar') focuses on two documentary films: Jamie Oliver's TV documentary *Jamie's Sugar Rush* and Damien Gameau's feature-length film *That Sugar Film*. Offering up a much wider canvas than the world of self-help, the films both traverse familiar and exotic environments to demonstrate the wrongness both of sugar and of those who overconsume it. Positioning themselves as amiable non-expert experts, Oliver and Gameau communicate to their viewers a way of being in the world that lionises individual acts as a vehicle for change, necessarily smoothing over the social and health inequalities that they encounter along the way. Chapter 6 ('Taxing sugar') focuses specifically on the debates leading up to, and following, the introduction of the sugar tax in the UK, which is a central issue in the narrative arc of the social life of sugar in the second decade of the twenty-first century. The chapter argues that the decision to introduce a tax marks sugar out as a problem about which something must be done and that as a result, the very fact of the tax becomes more important than its effects. The tax constitutes a shift from voluntarism to the regulatory 'big stick', constituting a change not only in the relationship between governments and industry, but also between industry and the consumers on whom their living depends.

Chapters 7 and 8 return to look more closely at a recurring theme through the book: the strategic pushing into the background of the wider social, economic and political context within which the attack on sugar has come to make sense. Chapter 7 ('Sweetening austerity') argues that the co-occurring rise in newspaper reporting about sugar and the introduction of austerity measures in the UK are connected not in a relationship of cause and effect, but rather through mutual endorsement, with each providing fertile ground for the other. This mutuality highlights the ways in which, regardless of claims that giving up sugar is a radical act, its reality is profoundly conservative, holding in place prevailing relations of power and privilege, as well as the vast inequalities on which they rely. Chapter 8 ('The inequalities of sugar') picks up this theme, exploring the ways in which social inequalities are not so much erased by sugar talk, but rather are mobilised strategically and one-dimensionally to signify ignorance, indolence, a lack of self-discipline and excessive vulnerability to the allure of sugar. Focusing on discourses of race, gender and class, I argue that these inequalities are selectively (in)visible in the data; they are simultaneously absent and present, with the everyday lived experiences of the most disadvantaged sublimated to their discursive roles as the abject Other against which successful elite, white neoliberal citizenship can be measured. The chapter concludes that leaving the articulation of the problem of sugar to those best positioned to accrue status by giving it up solidifies rather than challenges those inequalities.

The concluding chapter draws together the key themes of the book to argue that for all its maverick and revolutionary claims, the anti-sugar domain is ultimately governed by a politics of despair that reaffirms rather than disrupts social relations of power. In the face of complexity, sugar becomes the one thing that can be done, but privileging sugar as a problem to be solved makes sugar reduction an end in itself. It is an act of foreclosure rather than a first step. Beginning from the understanding that the definition of a problem determines what will count as its resolution, I argue that questions about sugar's place in our diets are not only impossible to answer straightforwardly but are also the wrong questions to be asking. Instead, the conclusion considers alternative starting points that refuse the comforting singularity of the attack on sugar but carry greater possibilities for social justice.

1

What's wrong with sugar?

'We are eating too much sugar and it is bad for our health'

In 2015, Public Health England (PHE) released heavily trailed and controversially delayed guidance on sugar reduction. The opening sentence declared: 'we are eating too much sugar and it is bad for our health'.[1] The guidance revised the upper limits of recommended sugar consumption from 10% of total dietary energy to 5%. The campaign Change4Life, funded by the National Health Service (NHS), subsequently translated this into the more legible unit of the 'sugar cube', prescribing no more than five cubes for 4–6-year-olds, no more than six cubes for 7–10-year-olds and no more than seven cubes for those aged over 10.[2] The PHE document declares that in 'meeting these recommendations within 10 years we would not only improve an individual's quality of life but could save the NHS, based on a conservative estimate, £500m a year', adding that 'any significant progress to reduce sugar intake would yield benefits'.[3]

In making the claim that 'we are eating too much sugar', a universal and known problem is asserted.[4] It assumes that the reader knows how 'it is bad for our health', although just in case, the rest of the paragraph offers a summary by way of reminder:

Consuming too many foods and drinks high in sugar can lead to weight gain and related health problems, as well as tooth decay. Almost 25% of adults, 10% of 4 to 6 year olds and 19% of 10 to 11 year olds in England are obese, with significant numbers also being overweight. Treating obesity and its consequences alone currently costs the NHS £5.1 bn every year.[5]

In this summary, the processes through which sugar produces these negative effects are left unsaid, and the linear causal relationship between sugar consumption and expensive illness is confidently asserted; it is a warning rather than an explanation. The harmfulness of sugar, to use sociologist John Law's term, has been placed 'beyond the limits of contestability';[6] it doesn't even need explaining because it has already been placed beyond dispute. As such, it can become the subject of urgent imperatives; it is a known problem about which something must be done.

The PHE's opening claim functions as an act of problem closure; that is, where the definition of a problem frames the subsequent research and interventions in ways that align with socially acceptable solutions.[7] This forestalls any alternative conceptualisations of the problem. In short, if the problem is that 'we are eating too much sugar and it is bad for our health', then the solution to the problem of ill-health is to find ways to reduce sugar consumption. The discursive closure of the problem means that the social, environmental and economic inequalities in which sugar consumption and its associated health problems are embedded drift quietly into the background. One effect of this is to obscure the ways in which sugar is many different things in different contexts. For example, the sugar in a traditional family birthday cake or woven into acts of caring in times of comfort and difficulty is different from that in a policy document that measures it out in calories and (absent) nutrients or in research that seeks to quantify its metabolic and hormonal (dys)regulatory effects.[8] Furthermore, while there is near-unanimous agreement that sugar is a known problem – that it is 'bad for our health' in ways which have pronounced financial and human costs – this unanimity conceals the fact that there is a distinct lack of consensus about what kind of problem sugar is; about how it is bad for health. This lack of unanimity matters because, as American sociologist Abigail Saguy observes in relation to fatness, different ways of framing a problem imply different courses of action, each of which has social consequences in terms of what they bring into the foreground and what gets pushed aside.[9] As a result, the claim that 'we are eating too much sugar and it is bad for our health' acts as a unifying statement that forecloses questions and obscures uncertainties to create a platform for socially and politically palatable action (e.g. focusing on individual sugar consumption).

This chapter interrogates the solidified wrongness of sugar, arguing that the treatment of the problem of sugar as self-evident gives misplaced singularity to entangled multiple realities, commitments and agendas. I begin by setting out two key discourses of sugar's wrongness that, superficially at least, are irreconcilable: (1) sugar as empty; and (2) sugar as toxic. The chapter argues that while the discourse of sugar as empty rests on received wisdoms that require little explanation, understandings of sugar as toxic go against those mainstream understandings, necessitating detailed and categorical explanations via high-profile advocates who can cultivate sufficient authority to challenge dietary orthodoxy. The two competing explanations of the problem of sugar rest on different models of metabolism and in many ways appear irreconcilable. Indeed, those arguing for sugar as uniquely toxic actively distance themselves from the nutritional mainstream as corrupted by the food industry and peddling false truths for profit. However, as discussed in Chapter 2, the two approaches hang together, and in the end, the claim that 'we are eating too much sugar and it is bad for our health' acts as a lowest-common-denominator conviction which tethers multiple agendas and commitments together with its sugar-centric focus. In short, for all the protestations to the contrary, the two competing perspectives have more in common than first impressions suggest.

'The emptiest of empty calories'

One of the most common accusations towards sugar is that it is empty; that is, that it provides energy without nutritional benefit. In a food landscape increasingly characterised by demands for foods to be nutritionally functional and for energy (calories) to be restricted, this calorific emptiness marks out sugar as a target for reduction. This is the mainstream position that dominates anti-sugar discourse, policy and practice. The guidelines on sugar consumption published by the World Health

Organization (WHO) in 2015 exemplify this: 'There is increasing concern that intake of free sugars – particularly in the form of sugar-sweetened beverages – increases overall energy intake and may reduce the intake of foods containing more nutritionally adequate calories, leading to an unhealthy diet, weight gain and increased NCDs [non-communicable diseases].'[10] Taken from the opening page of the report, this statement establishes sugar as a twofold assault on the body. First, it increases energy intake, with the specific mention of sugary drinks, or what nutrition and public health expert Marion Nestle calls 'candy in liquid form'.[11] This highlights the nature of those calories from sugar as both additional and unnecessary. It then draws a straight line from energy intake to weight gain to NCDs without needing to elaborate on the mechanisms through which these consequences are produced. The second assault on the body comes in the form of an opportunity cost, with sugary foods supplanting more nutritionally dense ones. This is the dominant discourse of the problem of sugar: its empty calories make you fat, which makes you ill.

Neither the PHE nor the WHO reports use the term 'empty' to describe sugar, focusing instead on excess calories or energy intake, but the newspaper coverage offers a more vernacular account of the same argument. For example, in the first of a series of articles encouraging readers to quit sugar, wellness advocate Calvary Avansino advises readers to avoid anything ending in 'ose' (e.g. glucose, fructose), including white table sugar (sucrose), explaining that: 'Like all sugars, it has absolutely no nutritional value – no proteins, no essential fats, no vitamins or minerals. These 'oses' are the emptiest of empty calories. It's just pure, refined energy. It contains a whole bunch of calories and nothing else.'[12] Energy can be forgiven only if it brings other nutrients along with it. As the 'emptiest of empty calories', sugar has no other nutritional contribution to make and is therefore irredeemable. Elsewhere, it is described as 'dead calories'[13] or as an 'anti-nutrient'.[14] It is, according to personal trainer to the stars and wellness coach James Duigan, 'a nuclear fat bomb exploding all over your body'.[15]

The articulation of the problem of sugar as one of emptiness exemplifies what Gyorgy Scrinis describes as nutritionism (as discussed in the

Introduction above).[16] He argues that our contemporary understanding of food, both scientifically and politically, is characterised by a reductive focus on nutrient content and the drawing of direct cause-and-effect relationships between specific nutrients and health in ways that over-simplify, decontextualise and exaggerate those relationships. Within the nutritionist paradigm, under the scrutiny of the nutritional gaze and endorsed by a myth of nutritional precision (that we can know how much of nutrient X we need to achieve health outcome Y), food can be evaluated only by its nutritional properties or the absence of them. For example, in June 2013, the *Daily Mail* published an article by journalist Polly Dunbar about her attempts to quit sugar. In common with this genre of article, Dunbar's struggles are interspersed with commentary from experts whom she consults along the way, including nutritionist Dr Sam Christie, who advises: 'Unrefined food contains more nutrients to protect our health, fewer empty calories and allows us to avoid peaks and troughs in blood sugar, keeping our moods and energy-levels stable.'[17] Scrinis cites 'empty calories' as a prime example of what he calls 'nutrispeak', arguing that it serves as a nutritional euphemism for low-quality, highly processed food.[18] Christie's celebration of 'unrefined foods' performs a similar euphemistic function, this time standing for high quality, unprocessed foods, which in turn serve as a proxy for sugar-free/low-sugar.

The invocation of sugar as empty of nutrition but replete with calories places the sugar-as-empty discourse firmly within the logics of energy balance, whereby the balance of calories consumed and expended determines weight loss or gain. This also locates the problem of sugar within the anti-obesity domain, where energy balance reigns supreme in mainstream explanations of fatness and is embodied in the unshakeable weight loss demands to 'eat less, exercise more'. This is exemplified in the 2015 report by the UK's Scientific and Advisory Committee on Nutrition (SACN) *Carbohydrates and Health*, which offers a familiar calories-in-calories-out account of weight gain: 'Obesity occurs when energy intake from food and drink consumption is greater than energy expenditure through the body's metabolism and physical activity over a prolonged period, resulting in the accumulation of excess body fat.'[19] The same paragraph acknowledges the 'many complex behavioural and societal factors that combine to contribute to the causes of obesity', including 'people's latent biological susceptibility interacting with a changing environment that includes more sedentary lifestyles and increased dietary abundance'. But even these qualifications rest firmly on the principle of energy balance, with overconsumption of unspent calories (for whatever reason) lying at the heart of the problem.

This logic is embedded in the SACN and PHE reports that together frame sugar reduction policy in the UK, particularly in relation to the recommendation that the consumption of free sugars should not exceed 5% of total dietary energy (compared with the previous limit of 10%). PHE's adoption of the 5% limit is explained at length in a separate document – *Why 5%?*[20] – which was issued alongside the main report, *Sugar Reduction: The Evidence for Action.*[21] The explanation is elaborate but is worth retelling to demonstrate the competing modes of approximation and self-conscious precision that are necessary to give credibility to the conveniently round 5% recommendation.

The foundation for the targeting of sugar as path to reduced energy consumption is based on an SACN meta-analysis of eleven trials which concluded that relative changes in sugar intake result in corresponding relative changes in energy intake, with one unit change in percentage energy consumed as sugars equating to an approximately 19 kcal change in energy intake.[22] Having established this principle, the next task was to establish the total desired reduction, which was quantified by drawing on a 2011 statement by the specially convened Calorie Reduction Expert Group, which recommended a reduction of 100 kcal per person per day.[23] This statement was premised on the conviction that 'if the rate at which the population is gaining weight is known, then the rate at which body energy is being accumulated and the degree of positive energy balance that produced the weight (and energy) gain can be calculated'. The Expert Group adopted a methodology used by obesity researcher James Hill and colleagues in a US study, which also recommended a reduction of 100 kcal per person per day.[24] Drawing on Health Survey for England figures for twenty-to-forty-year-olds from 1999 to 2009, the Calorie Reduction Expert Group concluded that there had been a median weight gain of 6.2 kg over ten years, which it equates to an excess of 16 kcal per day, while at the 90th percentile, gains of 9 kg equated to 24 kcal per day excess. These estimates of excess energy intake are lower than those for the US population because of the slower pace of weight gain among the English population, but even while acknowledging this, the Expert Group nevertheless settled on Hill and colleagues' recommended reduction of 100 kcal per person per day. This, it argued, would 'address energy imbalance and also lead to a moderate degree of weight loss for some individuals'. PHE then calculated that if a 100 kcal reduction is required, and if one percentage point reduction in the consumption of sugars equates to 19 kcal fewer, then a 5 percentage point reduction in sugar consumption is required (from 10% to 5%).

The path to the target reductions of 100 kcal per person per day and from 10% to 5% of total dietary energy intake is circuitous and riven with tension between performances of precision and multiple uncertainties and approximations. Hill and colleagues acknowledge that their model is '[...] theoretical and involves several assumptions';[25] less charitably, Scrinis describes their 2003 paper as a 'back-of-the-envelope calculation'.[26] Nevertheless, the conveniently round and legible figures of 100 kcal and 5% are solidified via this entangled chain of studies and reports, transforming through increasingly reductive and confident restatement into incontestable and self-evident truths.

The demonstrative precision and strategic rounding of the calculations stand in contrast to the WHO guidelines, released a few months before the SACN report.[27] The WHO report shares the 5% recommendation but is more circumspect about the possibility of establishing a threshold based on energy intake and weight. Indeed, one of the report's conclusions is the outstanding need 'to assess thresholds above which consumption of free sugars increases the risk of unhealthy weight gain, obesity and other NCDs'.[28] However, while specific thresholds remain elusive, the report determines that 'Increasing or decreasing free sugars is associated with parallel changes in body weight and the relationship is present regardless of the level of intake of free sugars. The excess body weight associated with free sugars intake results from excess energy intake.'[29] Thus the need for a precise figure is subordinated to this foundational premise, rooted in the energy balance paradigm, with reduction in general remaining the guiding principle. Instead, for the WHO, studies of dental harm provide the basis for the recommended reduction to 5% of total dietary intake, although even this recommendation is marked as only conditional (as opposed to the strong recommendation for the existing 10% limit). The designation as conditional signals 'uncertainty about the balance of benefits versus harms or when the anticipated benefits are small'.[30] The recommendation that sugars should constitute no more than 5% of total dietary energy, then, has gained a solidity not specifically borne out by the evidence, and has been arrived at via multiple and somewhat tortuous paths. Nevertheless, it finds purchase in the logics of energy balance and the urgent appetite for change that surrounds the problem of sugar. All that matters is that sugar consumption (with the empty calories it brings along) is being reduced.

The SACN's announcement of the recommended reduction in sugar consumption from 10% to 5% of total dietary intake was the trigger for extensive debate in the press about a tax on sugary drinks (see Chapter 6). The tax was also a core recommendation of a British Medical Association (BMA) report, *Food for Thought*, on healthy diet promotion for children and young people that was released the same month,[31] and the two documents combined to stir up debate. The BMA report spoke directly to the need to reduce sugar consumption, particularly from sugary drinks in their role as the archetypical empty calories. But while debates raged about the sugar tax, the 5% recommendation itself was received with equanimity in the press (although with less enthusiasm by the food industry), with reporting focusing in the first instance on translating the 5% figure into meaningful measures rather than questioning the revised limits themselves. For example, *The Guardian* explained that 'for those aged 11 and over, the 5% figures equate to 30 g or seven sugar cubes',[32] while *The Sun* informed readers that 'new research suggests men and women should consume no more than SEVEN teaspoons – the amount in a can of fizzy drink – and for kids under 11 it's FIVE teaspoons'.[33] The use of everyday units to make abstract quantities of sugar legible is discussed in more detail in Chapter 3, but here we see a tangle of percentages, grams, cubes, teaspoons and the 'can of fizzy drink' (a ubiquitous unit of sugar consumption) mobilised to make sense of the new recommendations. By September 2015, the recommendations were sufficiently established for *The Guardian* to publish advice to teachers on how to communicate the new limits successfully, including familiar pedagogic strategies such as measuring out the amounts of sugar in popular snacks and displaying the wrappers alongside the equivalent number of sugar cubes.[34]

One reason for the calm acceptance of the new limits was that they aligned comfortably with claims about sugar that were already widely accepted. The conviction that 'we are eating too much sugar and it is bad for our health' was uncontroversial, and by extension, so was the recommendation to consume less, regardless of the precise calculations. The effect of the new limits, then, was not scepticism or resistance, but the intensification of those default meanings and the growing urgency around the problem of sugar. For example, the capitalised numbers of teaspoons in above extract from *The Sun* – 'SEVEN teaspoons' – lend drama and urgency to the new recommended limits, which the PHE's *Why 5%?* report acknowledges will be 'challenging to achieve', necessitating a diet that 'is not representative of the average diet eaten in the UK'.[35] The revised limits also extend the distance between current and recommended levels of consumption, amplifying the problem at hand. For example, drawing on the 2008–2012 National Diet and Nutrition Survey, PHE reported that the current average total dietary intake of sugars for adults (aged 19–25) was 11.5%, rising to 14.7% for children and 15.4% for teenagers.[36] Consequently, the lowering of the acceptable limits from 10% to 5% of total dietary intake increases both the percentage of the population consuming sugar to excess and the degree of that excess. The effect is reminiscent of the 1998 decision by the US National Institutes of Health (NIH) to lower the body mass index (BMI) threshold for 'overweight' from 27.8 for men and 27.3 for women to 25 for both men and women, despite warnings by the WHO about the limitations of BMI as a predictor of individual health. As a result of the move, 29 million Americans became overweight overnight.[37] In the same way, under the harsh light of the new guidelines, the problem of sugar and its dangerously empty calories is suddenly much worse than we thought.

Neither Hill's research, nor the Calorie Reduction Expert Group's recommendations, nor the BMA *Food for Thought* report relate specifically to sugar, but even those reports directly targeting sugar are primarily about energy intake rather than sugar intake *per se*. It is the calorific emptiness of sugar that makes it a promising target for energy reduction rather than anything inherently harmful in sugar itself (with the exception of potential dental impacts). The PHE report *Why 5%?*, for example, notes that the reduction of 100 kcal per person per day doesn't necessarily have to come entirely from sugar reduction, which is just 'one approach to lowering the average total dietary energy intake of the population'; it also notes that 'SACN also acknowledges that there is nothing specific about the effect of sugars when energy intake is held constant, apart from where dental caries is concerned'.[38] The calorific emptiness of sugar, therefore, constitutes a prime site of energy economies rather than a distinct source of harm in its own right.

This locates these sugar reduction efforts within a model of metabolism that sociologist Hannah Landecker observes held sway in the nineteenth and early twentieth centuries, but which also continues to dominate contemporary explanations of obesity.[39] She argues that during the nineteenth century, what came to be called 'metabolism' transformed from the conviction that food turns into building materials for the body towards a theory of energy conversion. This theory gained further purchase with early twentieth-century research into the role of vitamins and other essential nutrients in the catalysing of particular reactions within cells.[40] Through these developments, alongside the rise of biochemistry, the workings of what nineteenth-century biologist Thomas Huxley called 'the single inward laboratory' were elaborated in increasing detail.[41] Within this paradigm, even while one person's metabolism may be faster or slower than another's, metabolism is fundamentally the same for everyone. It was seen as operating in predictable ways to convert food into energy and nourish the body. In line with this model, food is the same for everyone, either as fuel or as individual nutrients, which can be metabolised to give energy and build tissue. Food is treated as the sum of its molecular parts, each of which is substitutable since the body will simply break food down into its components anyway. In this way, sugar is a prime target for energy savings because of its calorific emptiness, but an equivalent reduction in energy intake by reducing other foods would have the same effect.

This energy balance model of metabolism is exemplified by the work of US chemist Wilbur Atwater, whose experiments in calorimetry in the late nineteenth and early twentieth centuries helped to elevate the calorie to what Scrinis describes as a 'metanutrient', providing a single value against which all foods, and all nutrients, can be measured.[42] Atwater used calorimeter technologies – what communications scholar Jessica Mudry describes as 'a cornerstone technology for the applications of science to human food'[43] – in order to 'regulate appetite by reason'.[44] In line with both the principles of scientific management and his temperance roots, Atwater argued that more expensive or flavoursome foods were not necessarily the most economical or healthful. By subordinating questions of taste or preference to the quantifiable logics of energy in (food) and energy out (labour), Atwater argued that the consumption of scientifically calibrated meals that could meet nutritional requirements at minimal cost was essential to tackling poverty.[45]

Mudry argues that this seeking of 'numeric regularity'[46] is not simply a way of describing food, but rather 'refigures food by making real new qualities of foods and suggesting that those qualities are the most important'.[47] This is reflected in the ubiquitous contemporary exhortations to count calories as a means of 'knowing' the food that we eat, or to count grams, spoons or cubes of sugar as a proxy for those (empty) calories. The framing of measurable nutritional qualities as intrinsic to foods also positions the burgeoning field of nutritional science not only as an empirical science but also as what public health scholar John Coveney describes as 'a spiritual discipline'. This pits pleasure and the sensuous against rationality and empiricism and renders 'poor' food choices both 'irrational and morally questionable'.[48] This moral framing is evidenced by the widespread interest in Atwater's work, which had obvious appeal not only to industrialists invested in managing workers' wage demands, but also to social reformers and philanthropists for the ways in which his work 'married the empirical aspects of nutritional science to the social and moral aims of economy'.[49]

In a contemporary example of this, in July 2020, after UK Prime Minister Boris Johnson launched an anti-obesity campaign in the wake of his hospitalisation with COVID-19,[50] the Health and Social Care Secretary, Matt Hancock, declared that if everyone in the UK lost five pounds this would save the NHS £100m.[51] This echoed the announcement in 2001 by the US Health and Human Services Secretary, Tommy G. Thompson, that 'all Americans – as their patriotic duty – [should] lose 10 pounds'.[52] The moral failure that attaches to individual choices that are coded as economically and socially costly is clear. As a result, the nutritional quantification of food choices serves as a means not only of measuring the quality of food, but also of judging the quality of the eaters themselves. (Over)consuming the empty calories of sugar is positioned as a similarly measurable failure.

Energy balance is a familiar target of critiques from the field of critical fat studies, which has pointed to the uncertain evidence base for many of its assumptions. Australian sociologists Michael Gard and Jan Wright, for example, highlight the ways in which obesity science texts mingle certainty and uncertainty via claims which have self-evident appeal but which are not supported by the studies themselves. Drawing on studies of the impact of exercise (energy out) on weight, they argue that in spite of determined claims of a predictable relationship between energy expenditure and body weight, there is a marked lack of direct evidence to support the assumption that the body operates in a predictably machine-like way, particularly once experiments are taken out of short-term, controlled laboratory settings and into everyday life.[53] They also highlight the ways in which unknowns are positioned as not yet known in ways that resist disruption of the foundational principle of energy balance. In this framing, the answer awaits discovery, firmly holding in place the undemonstrated starting premise that exercise protects against obesity; we just don't know (yet) how much.

In a similar way, the WHO guidance on sugar reduction highlights the need for further research to assess the thresholds at which sugar consumption leads to weight gain and ill-health, holding in place the absolute certainty of this causative relationship and its future discoverability.[54] This highlights the problem closure exercised by the energy paradigm, and typifies the empty calories discourse. Gard and Wright conclude that these uncertain certainties 'suggest that conclusive evidence may not be a particularly important factor in deciding what scientists hold to be true',[55] arguing instead that 'the dire predictions and sheer intensity of "obesity talk" has more to do with preconceived moral and ideological beliefs about fatness than a sober assessment of existing evidence'.[56] The same can be said for sugar, whose characterisation within the energy balance paradigm as a dangerously empty source of calories leaves no space for alternative explanations or lines of enquiry, and whose consumption constitutes a moral failure to protect public services.

Sweet poison

The discourse of sugar's emptiness dominates mainstream anti-sugar rhetorics, policy and practice, but a competing account of the problem of sugar has risen (or more accurately, resurged) to prominence in parallel with sugar's growing dietary infamy: the conviction that sugar is not simply a source of excess energy without nutritional benefit, but is actively toxic. From this perspective, sugar is a 'sweet poison';[57] it is the 'Professor Moriarty of this story'.[58] For science journalist and enthusiastic anti-sugar advocate Gary Taubes, all sugars have 'unique physiological, metabolic and endocrinological (i.e. hormonal) effects in the body that directly trigger [diabetes and obesity]'.[59] Unlike the empty calories discourse, which positions sugar as one source of calories among many (albeit one that is especially energy dense and without compensatory nutritional benefits), the sugar-as-toxic discourse identifies sugar as a specific threat to health that intervenes in the body's regulatory systems to inflict long-term harm. While the empty calories argument has been rendered so self-evident as to require little explanation, sugar-as-toxic is a contested counter-discourse. As such, it demands careful explanation in order to be understandable to an audience already accustomed to accounts of sugar as calorifically empty. To achieve this, authoritative voices are required, and in particular, those of people who are able to align themselves with the authority granted by science and to act as its translators. These authors are evangelical in their anti-sugar zeal, embracing their role as iconoclasts in the face of energy balance orthodoxy.[60]

This section draws primarily on the work of three such popular authors. The first is Australian David Gillespie, author of *Sweet Poison: Why Sugar Makes Us Fat*.[61] Gillespie is a non-scientist, former corporate lawyer and (self-)entrepreneur who has published books on food, schooling, workplace psychology and, most recently, children and the addictive dangers of screen time.[62] His website quotes a *Courier Mail* description of him as 'a polymath, an old-fashioned Renaissance man, who finds few things dull and everything else interesting'.[63] His self-narrative is not one of established scientific expertise but instead presents him as a truth-seeking myth-buster. In *Sweet Poison*, which is credited on his website as driving the contemporary wave of sugar awareness in Australia, he takes pride in being 'one of those people who can't leave a problem alone',[64] educating himself about the science in his quest for understanding. In 2013, *The Times* described him as engaging his 'lawyer brain' in order to read and render accessible 'thousands of scientific papers about sugar and its effects'.[65] In the absence of professional scientific expertise or qualifications, his role as evangelical translator also gains additional endorsement from experiential knowledge based on his own significant weight loss after giving up sugar. In 2010, he published the follow-up self-help book *The Sweet Poison Quit Plan*, which focuses on sugar addiction and includes a combination of a popular science account of sugar addiction and techniques and recipes for quitting.[66]

He has also published numerous recipe books and shopping guides as part of the *Sweet Poison* brand and is a regular talking head in anti-sugar documentaries (including Damon Gameau's *That Sugar Film*, which is discussed in detail in Chapter 5).

The second author is US science journalist Gary Taubes. Taubes is the author of a trilogy of weighty popular science books written across a decade and homing steadily in on sugar: *Good Calories, Bad Calories, Why We Get Fat and What to Do about It* and *The Case Against Sugar*.[67] This latter was the subject of extensive UK newspaper coverage on its 2017 release, arriving at a time of peak interest in sugar following the 2016 announcement of the sugar tax but before its implementation in 2018. In January 2017, following the book's launch, *The Sunday Times* described Taubes as having studied physics at Harvard before changing track to study journalism at Columbia.[68] His training in physics, we are told, taught him 'how the scientific method should work – doubt, testing, retesting, peer review and above all, not fooling yourself'. The article tells us that his first two books – *Nobel Dreams* and *Bad Science*[69] – demonstrated his 'formidable and relentless talent for research'; a review in *The Observer* described him as 'like a terrier with a bone'.[70] As a self-described 'compulsive reporter', he then turned his attention to nutritional science as a field which 'seemed to be a mess beneath its surface confidence'. In this way, Taubes' authority is secured, firstly, through his early training in physics, but secondly, and perhaps more importantly, through his journalistic credentials, which enable him to lay claim to the kind of dogged truth-seeking that is required to distinguish between legitimate and illegitimate scientific claims. Unlike Gillespie's work, Taubes' trilogy eschews personal revelations or experiential narratives of conversion, adopting instead a posture of neutral translator and exposer of silenced scientific truths. However, he departs from this mode in his most recent book, *The Case for Keto: The Truth about Low-Carb, High-Fat Eating*, which is a self-described 'work of journalism masquerading as a self-help book' and includes information about his own dietary preferences and allegiances to boost the persuasiveness of the case.[71]

The final author I focus on in this section is US paediatric endocrinologist and popular science author Robert Lustig. Lustig is the author of *Fat Chance: The Hidden Truth about Sugar, Obesity and Disease*, which was widely reported in the UK press on its release in 2014, enabling the book to both generate and capitalise on the escalating interest in sugar. He is also the star of a 2009 YouTube video, 'Sugar: the bitter truth'.[72] This is a recording of a presentation he gave to medical students at the University of California, San Francisco, accumulating over 12 million views by the end of 2020. Since the release of *Fat Chance*, he has published *The Fat Chance Cookbook* with chef Cindy Gershen, who lost 100 lb following his dietary recommendations,[73] before adjusting direction to publish *The Hacking of the American Mind: The Science behind the Corporate Takeover of Our Bodies and Brains*.[74] The book argues that everyday forms of consumption from sugary drinks to mobile phones are addictive by design, tricking our brains into confusing pleasure for happiness. Lustig's most recent book, *Metabolical*, focuses on the harms of highly processed food through the same lenses of addiction and food industry malfeasance that have informed his oeuvre.[75]

As a practising physician, Lustig wields his scientific credentials with confidence, insisting: 'My reputation in the field is built on the science. It's also my protection against those who would try to discredit me [...] Indeed, it's the only reason I haven't been discredited yet. And I won't be, because I stick to the science. Now and forever.'[76] He also fervently affirms his own neutrality, insisting that 'I am not a pawn of the food industry or a mouthpiece for any organisation', highlighting that, unlike other authors writing about obesity, he doesn't have a product line 'designed to enrich my bank account'.[77] This is a claim that is perhaps undermined by his subsequent cookbook, but it works discursively to position him as a campaigner motivated by uncontaminated, objectively knowable scientific truths. Lustig is a popular figure in the newspaper reporting on sugar.[78] This is in part because of the authority that his medical credentials bring, but also because of high levels of public recognition (for example, as a result of the YouTube video) and his uncompromising and often colourful use of language, which make for good copy and punchy soundbites.

This section explores the sugar-as-toxic discourse by drawing on the published work and pronouncements in the press of Gilliespie, Taubes and Lustig. I have chosen to focus on these three, first, because they are commonly cited sources in the news articles. Second, their popular science books provide sustained accounts of the problem of sugar, rather than the more prolific self-help publishing domain, which focuses on tips, techniques and recipes for quitting sugar with the occasional sidebar venture into 'the science' (see Chapter 4 for more discussion of this genre). Thus Gillespie, Taubes and Lustig are all targeting perceived information deficits; their texts assume that once readers know these truths, wrapped in the authority of science, their dietary behaviours will change. Their texts therefore offer insight into the discursive construction of the problem of sugar, both in response to and distinct from the mainstream sugar-as-empty discourse. And finally, their books share a specific focus on sugar. This differentiates them from the proliferating genre of popular science and self-help texts advocating low-carbohydrate, high-fat (LCHF) diets (or paleo or keto diets), with which they share considerable common ground (and which Taubes' most recent book explores), but which reach beyond sugar specifically to carbohydrates more generally.[79] These texts are discussed further in the next chapter and in Chapter 8, but the primary focus for now remains on the work of these three authors as a jumping-off point for these wider discussions.

The story of sugar's toxicity begins from the premise that a calorie is never simply a calorie, and that not only aren't all carbs equal and interchangeable, but neither are all sugars. In particular, fructose, which constitutes 50% of table sugar and 55% of high-fructose corn syrup, is placed at the heart of the problem.[80] Lustig calls fructose the 'Darth Vader of the Empire, beckoning you to the dark side of this sordid tale'.[81] The threat posed by fructose lies in the ways it is processed in the body. As Taubes explained in a feature in the *Daily Mail* in January 2017 following the release of his book:'Unlike other carbs, fructose is mostly processed in the liver, where it is turned into fat and seems to trigger a sequence of events that eventually leads to cells becoming resistant to insulin.'[82] This leads to a chain of disruptions whereby increased amounts of insulin are required to enable cells to use the glucose in the bloodstream for energy. This is seen as triggering a cascade of health problems associated with a cluster of biomarkers that have together come to be understood as metabolic syndrome: hyperinsulinemia, low glucose tolerance, dyslipidaemia, hypertension and obesity. Collectively, these are associated with chronic diseases such as type 2 diabetes and coronary heart disease, as well as a host of other NCDs. It is worth noting, however, that the precise mechanisms described in these accounts remain unclear: fructose 'seems to trigger' effects, according to Taubes, but the 'how' remains uncertain. As Michelle Murphy observes in her study of sick building syndrome, this uncertainty is integral to the contested diagnostic category of a syndrome, which is recognised 'only as a constellation of symptoms, not by an underlying mechanism'.[83] As Ryan Hatch argues in his study of the racial politics of metabolic syndrome, it is labelled a syndrome 'precisely because it is an aggregation of clinical and laboratory measurements that has not yet reached designation as a disease'.[84] Nevertheless, sugar-as-toxic advocates proceed with evangelical conviction that, as Lustig declared in an article in *The Guardian* in 2015, 'the science is in'.[85] As he observes in *Fat Chance* with a typically rhetorical flourish: 'Face it, we've been "frucked".'[86] This reproduces the same combination of uncertainty and certainty that Gard and Wright identify as characteristic of obesity science, but the counter-normative sugar-as-toxic position demands that certainty wins out; its critical response to the dominant empty calories discourse can never be 'Yes, but …' but, rather, a confident 'It's not that, it's this … .'

These accounts of the problem of sugar rest on a very different model of metabolism from the empty calories discourse. US sociologist Hannah Landecker calls this 'post-industrial metabolism': that is, a metabolic understanding that, she argues, is as historically and culturally specific to the twenty-first century as energy conversion was to the nineteenth and early twentieth centuries (and which she acknowledges still lives on in contemporary anti-obesity rhetorics and practice).[87] Under this new post-industrial metabolism, the same foods will be metabolised differently, with cultures of eating shaping metabolic capacities not only in individuals, but also across generations. As she notes, food is no longer simply seen as broken down in the 'inward laboratory'; it also builds the laboratory. Food, she argues, has the capacity 'to set the conditions of its future reception'.[88] These changes occur at the epigenetic level (that is, at the level of gene expression) transforming the potential of genes to be expressed, resulting in bodies which all regulate and process food differently. This is a marked departure from earlier constructions of metabolism as singular, knowable and predictable across bodies. This new metabolism, she argues, is regulatory rather than energetic, and 'constituted by a dynamic web of cellular signals'.[89] This is visible in accounts of sugar as toxic, with sugar (and particularly fructose) described as setting off cascades of hormonal disruption, disturbing signals of satiety and appetite control and creating catastrophic, if slow, dysregulation of the body's systems with devastating long-term health consequences. As Taubes argues in *The Case Against Sugar*, 'It's a kind of homeostatic disruption in which regulatory systems throughout the body are misbehaving with slow, chronic, pathological consequences everywhere.'[90] The slow invisibility of this regulatory disruption in *all* bodies is central to its perceived threat, recalling Lustig's typically colourful warning against the complacency of slimness: 'You think you're safe? You are SO screwed. And you don't even know it.'[91]

It is a threat that extends not only across the lifetime of the individual, but also across generations. As discussed above, from a post-industrial metabolic perspective, the food we eat sets the conditions of its future reception, leaving an imprint on bodily processes that is heritable across generations. This is captured in the Barker hypothesis, which proposed that adverse conditions in early development, and particularly at certain stages of gestation, can lead to permanent physiological and metabolic changes that have detrimental health consequences, exacerbating social inequalities and limiting life chances.[92] This is exemplified by the enduring effects of the 1944–45 Dutch Hunger Winter, where those *in utero*

41

during the famine, and particularly during early gestation, had higher levels of obesity and metabolic and cardiovascular disease as adults than those gestated outside the famine.[93] These inter-generational impacts of food (or its absence) are referenced by both Lustig and Taubes, although the frame is narrowed to maternal behaviours in ways that amplify maternal responsibility. For example, Taubes notes that sugars 'do their damage over years and decades, and perhaps even from generation to generation', and that 'mothers will pass the problem down to their children'.[94] Or as Lustig insists bluntly, in the face of a 'hostile uterine environment', we should: 'Fix the mother. Fix the offspring.'[95] This misses the potential of the Barker hypothesis to 'evince complex understandings that span biology, social positionality, place and generation',[96] and instead maintains a fixation on sugar that is wilfully blind to the social and cultural environments, with all their constitutive inequalities, within which sugar consumption takes place and which shape the body and its processes.

From this perspective, the commitment to an understanding of metabolic systems and networks as transformed by sugar is strategically half-hearted and never extended to its logical conclusion; if sugar can exact those changes, then so can uncountable other known and unknown exposures. As a result, the body is rendered dangerously porous to sugar and its metabolically disruptive capacities, but not to the many other environmental exposures that also disrupt the boundaries between the organism and the environment.[97] And even where other impacts are acknowledged, the risks posed by sugar overshadow other possibilities. Lustig, for example, in a chapter on 'Environmental "obesogens"', lists multiple environmental exposures that impact upon fatness, noting, 'even though the exposure might end, the damage appears to last forever'.[98] However, these are quickly set aside as matters for governmental regulation, returning instead to 'the most ubiquitous toxin of them all: fructose, the Evil Queen/Witch of this story, peddling the poison we just can't get enough of'.[99]

This matters because specific dietary restrictions make sense only where particular foods can be identified as the only problem. If we see sugar (or any other food) as just one disruptive exposure among many, the solutions extend far beyond giving up sugar (and beyond food). But where sugar is seen as uniquely toxic, mainstream recommendations of (highly constrained) moderation can never be enough, and abstention is the only possible solution. The distinction between moderation and abstention, then, constitutes a key point of divergence between the sugar-as-empty and sugar-as-toxic discourses, although what constitutes abstention remains a point of debate within the sugar-as-toxic domain, ranging from eschewing fructose alone to avoiding all sugars or all carbohydrates. This lack of internal consensus occurs not least because, as with all diet and self-help books, each anti-sugar advocate must carve out their own niche in a crowded field to be marketable.

But regardless of these internal differences, the sugar-as-toxic proselytisers maintain a determined differentiation between themselves and the dietary mainstream's commitment to energy balance. This includes the rejection of the nutritional science on which mainstream dietary advice relies, which is seen as corrupted by the forces of Big Sugar in cahoots with vested political interests. The case of British physiologist and nutritionist John Yudkin is a touchstone for concerns about the untrustworthiness of dietary norms that see sugar as just another source of calories, albeit empty ones, rather than as uniquely harmful. As discussed briefly in the Introduction, from the 1960s onwards, under the sway of research by American epidemiologist Ancel Keys, dietary fat was implicated in coronary heart disease. Its subsequent demonisation was taken up enthusiastically by policymakers and the food industry, for whom the sale of low-fat products presented new opportunities for profit. At the same time, Yudkin was developing research which identified sugar, and especially fructose, as the primary culprit in coronary heart disease (CHD) and many other diseases, culminating in his 1972 book *Pure, White and Deadly*.[100] The book argued that 'if only a small fraction of what is already known about the effects of sugar were to be revealed in relation to any other material used as a food additive, that material would promptly be banned'.[101] As discussed later in this book, this is a common theme in contemporary sugar-as-toxic discourse, with sugar figured as a food contaminant rather than a nutrient.

Both Yudkin's book and the author himself were sidelined and disparaged, including by Keys himself, who described Yudkin's ideas as a 'mountain of nonsense'.[102] As Lustig observes, following the incorporation of low-fat diets into the US dietary guidelines in the 1980s, 'Keys delivered the knockout punch and won the food fight, while Yudkin was thrown under the bus.'[103] In the revised 2012 edition of the book, Yudkin describes the forceful and career-damaging attacks on his research that *Pure, White and Deadly* generated, ranging from the loss of professional opportunities to his derogation in print. For example, in 1979, a bulletin published by the World Sugar Research Organisation, under the headline 'For your dustbin', noted that *Pure, White and Deadly* falling out of print was a loss to readers of science fiction.[104] The book's final paragraph observes: 'It is difficult to avoid the conclusion that [the silencing of the book] is the result of the vigorous, continuing and expanding activities of the sugar interests.'[105]

For sugar-as-toxic advocates, as well as low-carb evangelists more widely, Yudkin stands as a martyr to the cause – a brave iconoclast who paid the price of professional marginalisation and disdain for speaking heretical truths. In his introduction to the 2012 edition of *Pure, White and Deadly*, Lustig describes the book as 'a prophecy' written by a man who 'preached in the wilderness'.[106] His acolytes identify as the silenced apostates of dietary orthodoxy, taking overt pride in going against the dietary grain and describing themselves as heretics, disciples and mavericks who are not afraid to speak dietary truths to power. This connects directly to their self-definitions and credentialism as set out earlier in this chapter.

However, in their wielding of a pure and disinterested science to support evangelistic claims, they are often more scientistic than scientific in their sugar talk. In their unauthorised biography of testosterone, Rebecca Jordan-Young and Katrina Karkazis argue that scientism involves 'the elevation of scientific values, evidence and authority above all others – even as it paradoxically obviates the need for evidence'; it marks forms of authority 'in which something is a "fact" or is "scientific" because a scientist says it is, not because it meets any particular criterion of method'.[107] This is modelled in Lustig's claims in the introduction to *Fat Chance* that 'there is not one statement made in this entire book that can't be backed up by hard science'.[108] It is a boldly scientistic claim that smooths over the constantly evolving and contested nature of scientific knowledge. It also sits awkwardly alongside his own recognition that the book includes several 'fits of speculation', each under the heading 'Deconstructing Darwin', where he lets his 'imagination run wild' to try and locate obesity within evolutionary processes.[109]

This defiant confidence can be understood as an example of what sociologist Steven Epstein calls 'credibility struggles', where credibility 'describes the capacity of claims-makers to enrol supporters behind their arguments, legitimate those arguments as authoritative knowledge, and present themselves as the sort of people who can voice the truth'.[110] Furthermore, as Mikko Jauho notes in his study of low-carb dieters' narratives of science, these displays of scientistic confidence are an invitation to readers themselves to gain command of the scientific idiom.[111] In this way, readers are invited not simply to follow, but also to acquire (and display) competence along the way. For example, Taubes describes his earlier anti-sugar text, *Why We Get Fat and What to Do about It*, as a 'thinkers' manifesto' which readers are promised will 'arm you with the necessary information and logic to take your health and well-being into your own hands'.[112]

Battle cries herald the struggle. 'Let the food fight begin', declares Gillespie at the end of *Sweet Poison*;[113] and 'Time to cry out', concludes Lustig in *Fat Chance*.[114] In an article in *The Guardian* in July 2017, journalist Giles Fraser described his own dietary conversion following a heart attack and a diagnosis of type 2 diabetes. 'Sugar is poison', he declares, noting his own significant weight loss after cutting out sugar and carbs: 'It's not a diet – I hate diets. It's a form of protest. The scales have fallen from my eyes.'[115] The sugar-as-toxic discourse, then, is not simply a less compromising version of energy-balance justifications for sugar reduction, but is, rather, explicitly claimed as a radical departure from it.

Conclusion

In this opening chapter, I have argued that the wrongness of sugar as an understood and urgent problem appears unproblematically singular; it is a costly threat to health about which something must be done. However, there is a lack of consensus about the nature of that problem. To illustrate this, I have explored two different explanations of sugar's encounter with the body. The first of these is the mainstream approach which sees sugar as the source of empty calories, creating a positive energy balance without other nutritional benefits. The second is a counter-discourse which positions sugar as actively toxic, dysregulating the body's fat storage and hormonal systems to create far-reaching metabolic disorder. These two rely on different understandings of metabolism and are in many ways inimical to each other, with mainstream anti-sugar advocacy suspicious of the absolutism of claims that sugar is toxic, and the sugar-as-toxic advocates seeing the dietary mainstream as intractably wedded by vested interests and corrupt science to a dietary model that is doomed to fail.

And yet ... the two hang together, with comments from representatives from Action on Sugar or PHE, both of which are firmly committed to sugar as a problem of empty calories, frequently appearing without rupture in newspaper reporting alongside those from staunch sugar-as-toxic advocates such as Gillespie, Lustig and Taubes. The next chapter explores the ways in which these apparently incompatible approaches find common ground.

2

Hanging together

'The obvious place to start was obesity'

In *Sweet Poison*, Gillespie describes his research journey to establish the relationship between non-communicable diseases (NCDs) and fructose, declaring: 'The obvious place to start was obesity. It's the unequivocal sign that something is going wrong with our body.'[1] For Gillespie, whatever other uncertainties are yet to be resolved, no space can be left for the reader to dispute this claim of bodily disfunction. He also notes the extensive media coverage of obesity, adding that 'rather than rely on the hype, I wanted to sort out exactly how fat we were all getting and how fast'. The only questions are how fat and how fast; the rest can treated as known and ready to be acted on.

In the previous chapter, I explored two different ways in which the problem of sugar has been conceptualised: sugar as empty and sugar as toxic. I argued that these two appear irreconcilable and especially that the logics of sugar as toxic depend on establishing an unbridgeable distance from mainstream dietary logics of energy balance. And yet they hang together, solidifying the problem of sugar and smoothing out the differences by resting on common denominators that enable them to occupy the same spaces. Obesity is a prime example of this, serving as an 'unequivocal sign' that all is not well; Gillespie's claim insists that whatever else we might disagree on, we can all agree on this.

In this chapter, I focus on three core discourses through which this consensus is cultivated: (1) the obesity epidemic; (2) sugar as addictive;

and (3) nostalgia for a lost dietary past. These operate collectively in ways that are simultaneously bounded and expansive, maintaining a tight focus on sugar (over)consumption while expansively accommodating multiple uncertainties and contradictions. This facilitates a lowest common denominator consensus about sugar as a known problem about which something must (and can) be done.

The crisis of obesity

It was almost impossible to find newspaper articles about sugar that didn't mention obesity. The conviction that obesity is an urgent health crisis against which a war must be fought is a ubiquitous feature of health reporting in general and reporting of sugar specifically. Sugar's complicity in the crisis is treated as incontestable, regardless of how the problem of sugar is understood. Without a war on obesity, there would be no sustained attack on sugar, and the unacceptability of the fat body runs rampant through anti-sugar rhetoric, policy and practice. Now over twenty years old, the war on obesity is unable to warrant its core empirical claims and has been a notable failure when measured against its own goals of sustained population-level weight reduction.[2] Nevertheless, the wrongness of obesity has achieved near-unassailable status, and its relationship with sugar solidifies easily without requiring agreement on the precise nature of the threat that either sugar or obesity pose.

Across the materials analysed as part of this research, from policy documents to self-help books to newspaper coverage, obesity is ubiquitously presented as *a bad thing*. For example, in *The Daily Telegraph* in December 2014, journalist Victoria Lambert wrote a lengthy piece setting out the case for sugar as toxic, including interviews with both Robert Lustig and David Gillespie. She offers this dire warning:

> [Obesity] rates continue to rise: currently 26% of Britons are obese, half of us are overweight. This is a mighty problem: direct costs caused by obesity are now estimated to be £5.1 bn per year. Obesity is associated with cardiovascular risk and with cancer, disability during old age, decreased

life expectancy and serious chronic conditions such as type 2 diabetes, osteoarthritis and hypertension.[3]

In this short extract, Lambert reproduces three common themes of contemporary obesity discourse: first, constantly escalating obesity rates; second, the healthcare costs of obesity; and third, the listing of the health and social consequences of obesity.

'... rates continue to rise'

One of the most common features of obesity discourse is its ominous predictions of endlessly escalating obesity rates that foretell a problem that will only get worse if not stopped in its tracks. However, the reality is less dramatic and might otherwise be seen as cause for optimism. For example, according to figures from the 2018 Health Survey for England, while mean rates of overweight and obesity rose steadily between 1993 and 2001 (from 53 to 62%), from 2002 to 2018, rates remained relatively stable, fluctuating between 62 and 64%. This pattern is broadly mirrored by obesity rates alone (see Figure 2.1):[4]

Writing in 2011 about US obesity data, sociologist Michael Gard observes a similar contrast between evidence of a largely stable situation

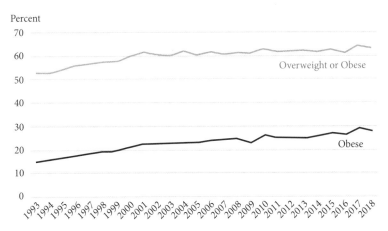

Figure 2.1 UK overweight and obesity prevalence from 1993 to 2018

and the crisis-filled tone of obesity rhetoric.[5] He argues that the power of the obesity epidemic 'rests on warnings about the future – a future in which more and more people are expected to become unacceptably fat'.[6] The focus on sugar gives renewed urgency to these claims, and in this way, the spectre of an unchecked, sugar-fuelled crisis spiralling out of control keeps the war on obesity alive. This is even while, as Gard argues, 'the most credible component of the alarmists' case – unambiguously climbing obesity rates – is now also crumbling'.[7] This future-orientation also aligns easily with warning of sugar wreaking unseen metabolic havoc in the present that will make itself known over years or even decades.

Bankrupting the NHS

The second familiar anti-obesity theme mobilised by Lambert is the costs it is presumed to bear, particularly in relation to healthcare. In the UK, this commonly takes the form of demands to 'protect the NHS [National Health Service]' – a mantra that also dominated the UK's pandemic public health messaging – and Lambert illustrates the threat with estimated costs of £5.1 billion per year. This estimate recurs across the newspaper data and in policy documents. For example, we also encounter it in the opening section of the Public Health England (PHE) guidance on sugar reduction, which claims that 'Treating obesity and its consequences alone currently costs the NHS £5.1bn every year.'[8] This claim comes from a 2011 study by population health researcher Peter Scarborough and colleagues, who estimated the costs accrued to the NHS as a result of poor diet, physical inactivity, smoking, alcohol and overweight/obesity.[9] The figure of £5.1 billion is a combination of costs associated with poor diet, physical activity and obesity and joins a parade of wildly divergent, headline-grabbing predictions designed to animate the war on obesity. For example, in 2002, the House of Commons Health Select Committee estimated the direct and indirect costs of overweight and obesity at approximately £7 billion.[10] This figure was then taken up as a baseline in the landmark Foresight Report, which projected that by 2050, direct NHS costs attributable to overweight and obesity would reach £9.7 billion, with an overall total cost of £49.9 billion annually.[11]

Gard observes the striking way in which 'big, round and highly contestable numbers are blithely deployed in public discussions of health',[12] claiming that these are rhetorical rather than literal, 'floating free from science, in order to have an effect on readers and listeners'.[13] They are 'rhetorical viruses', which can be endlessly recycled, 'mutating but keeping their essential structure'.[14] The £5.1 billion figure operates in exactly this way, passing easily from context to context, inciting urgency and fear through repetition. This incitement also bears an additional implicit message: that this looming crisis is preventable because the fat body is malleable and by embracing informed individual responsibility, it can (and should) be restored to 'healthy' slimness. This is demonstrated by the title of the paper from which the £5.1 billion estimate originates: 'The economic burden of ill health due to diet, physical inactivity, smoking, alcohol and obesity in the UK: an update to 2006–7 NHS costs'. By including obesity alongside 'lifestyle' risk factors (smoking, drinking, inactivity), and by describing it as a burden, fatness is positioned not as a bodily state but as a (deviant) behaviour. This directs attention away from the political choices on which public services like the NHS depend and onto individual ones, denying the legitimacy of fat people's claims on public resources.

This assumption of the malleability of the fat body was made explicit in July 2020, when the UK government launched its policy paper: *Tackling Obesity: Empowering Adults and Children to Live Healthier Lives*.[15] The new policy paper was triggered by claims of links between mortality from COVID-19 and obesity and followed Prime Minister Boris Johnson's public blaming of his own encounter with the virus on his weight. The paper observes that obesity is more common in deprived areas than in wealthy ones, that minority-ethnic populations are 'susceptible' to obesity-related diseases and that 'black, Asian and minority ethnic populations and those living in deprived areas are at greater risk of dying from COVID-19'. It explains that 'excess weight is one of the few modifiable factors for COVID-19 and so supporting people to achieve a healthy weight will be crucial to seeing people fit and well as we move forward'.

This is problematic in two key ways. First, the assumption that weight is modifiable is a common-sense claim in that we know that body weights change (and can, to some extent, be changed). But the assumption of the easy and purposeful reduction of body weight flies in the face of the evidence that sustainable weight loss remains elusive for the vast majority of those engaging with it.[16] And second, it presumes that risk factors such as poverty and minority race and ethnicity are fixed and unmodifiable. This retains the focus firmly on obesity and away from broader social agendas of addressing the structural inequalities that are inextricable from negative health outcomes (see Chapter 8 for further discussion of this issue). Obesity functions here as a master status to which other axes of oppression can be subordinated,[17] placing responsibility firmly at the feet of the fat individual not only for their own health, but also for the survival of the NHS. As the policy paper notes: 'We owe it to the NHS to move towards a healthier weight.'

The wielding of 'big, round and highly contestable numbers' both compounds the urgency of these demands and amplifies the force of the weight loss imperative. The 2020 policy paper cites Scarborough and colleagues' 2011 paper but elevates their £5.1 billion estimate to £6.1 billion, noting that the original figure of £5.1 billion has been 'uplifted to account for inflation'. This can be understood as an example of what Gard calls 'the alchemy' of the obesity epidemic, transforming 'speculative afterthought into scientific fact'.[18] Details of the calculations to arrive at the conveniently round additional £1 billion are not given, but they are also unnecessary, since the claim's primary function is rhetorical rather than actuarial, cultivating authoritative urgency around the threat posed by fatness to the NHS.

The litany

The third trope mobilised by Lambert in the extract from *The Daily Telegraph* is what I came to call 'the litany' – the *ad nauseam* listing of the presumed consequences of obesity, and by implication sugar, as a means of ratcheting up the sense of urgency. In such litanies, obesity emerges variously as a cause of disease, as a visible marker of a diseased body and as a disease in itself, always without recognition of the slippage between the categories. This slippage illustrates what US sociologist and fat studies scholar Natalie Boero calls obesity's 'diagnostic fluidity'.[19] For example, an article in *The Guardian* in October 2015 offered a familiarly linear account of sugar's effects on the body: 'How is sugar intake linked to ill-health? Consuming too much sugar through your diet is closely associated with being overweight. That in turn increases the risk of some of Britain's biggest killers: heart disease, type 2 diabetes, stroke and certain cancers.'[20] In this scenario, sugar causes fatness, which in turn causes disease. This aligns with the logics of empty-calories accounts of sugar, resisting claims of sugar as uniquely toxic, but instead holding it responsible for fatness, which then wreaks its own bodily havoc. The concluding list of 'some of Britain's biggest killers' fosters urgency and shores up the mutual culpability of both sugar and fatness.

Alternatively, in a feature on David Gillespie in *The Times* in October 2013, journalist Rachel Carlyle warns that sugar 'not only makes us fat, but it's linked to type 2 diabetes, high blood pressure, bowel cancer, lower cognitive function, ageing skin, a depressed immune system and liver and kidney disease'.[21] In line with Gillespie's sugar-as-toxic stance, sugar is figured here as directly 'linked to' an array of health problems, and even though the article shies away from claims of direct causation, the piling up of conditions leaves little room for doubt about sugar's culpability. In contrast to the previous example, obesity here serves as a precursor to the litany of diseases rather than a cause of them. It is a taken-for-granted undesirable consequence of sugar consumption which forewarns of the less immediately visible consequences of consuming sugar to follow.

For others, fatness joins the litany as a sugar-related disease in itself. For example, in February 2014, an article in *The Daily Telegraph* argued that 'it is virtually certain that deriving more than 10 per cent of your calorie intake from added sugars increases the risk of obesity, diabetes and heart disease – as well as self-loathing'.[22] Obesity here joins the ranks of other chronic diseases, although the afterthought addition of 'self-loathing', like the inclusion of 'ageing skin' in the previous extract, signals the ways in which concerns about obesity are never fully medicalised and are inseparable from moral and aesthetic judgements about fat bodies.

These moral and aesthetic concerns seep through the data in a slow and steady trickle. In some cases, they are overtly and deliberately fatshaming, but more commonly, these concerns manifest themselves as warnings dressed as well-meaning worry about parents too busy to cook healthy food, incontinent consumption (of food, of public resources), reduced productivity and low self-esteem, which under neoliberal imperatives of self-entrepreneurship is as unforgivable as fatness itself.[23] This is exemplified by PHE's chief nutritionist, Alison Tedstone, who issued this litanical warning in *The Guardian* in November 2015: 'Being obese can have a devastating impact on a child's life. They are more likely to experience bullying, low self-esteem, be absent from school and have a higher risk of developing type 2 diabetes and heart disease in later life.'[24] The alignment of being bullied and having low self-esteem with developing type 2 diabetes positions both as equally treatable by weight loss, placing responsibility for the damaging experience of being bullied firmly onto the victim and those responsible for them rather than the perpetrators (or the social norms that make fatness a target in the first place). This highlights the ways in which the primary intent of these litanies is to establish fatness as an irredeemably abject state whose only possible escape is weight loss.

Lustig illustrates this abjection in his case study of Kay, who underwent weight loss surgery (a lap-band procedure) at the age of seven to stem her weight gain. He tells us that she lost thirty pounds within six months post-surgery, noting triumphantly that 'her face was now separate from her neck'. He continues: 'All her labs improved. Her mother was ecstatic, in no small part because Kay could now wipe her own behind.'[25] Lustig's evaluation of the procedure runs together biometric quantifications of health with aesthetic and practical evaluations, gratuitously focusing on the child's personal care to drive home the unacceptability of the fat body. His assessment echoes the 2001 National Audit Office policy paper *Tackling Obesity in England*, whose own litany of 'diseases associated with obesity' includes 'humiliation arising from practical problems' as both a consequence of fatness and an incentive for weight loss.[26] The ableism of the claim that assistance with personal care is humiliating is bypassed by the assumption that it can be prevented by weight loss. In this way, fear of both sugar and fatness are framed by the rhetorics of health but are always only partially medicalised.

Boero argues that the tensions between the incomplete medicalisation of obesity and the unshakeable certainty that obesity is a threat to health can coexist because of 'invisible but powerful scientific black boxes'.[27] These place limits on critical thought and position the wrongness of the fat body as no longer open for debate. This enables 'scientific facts' to be reproduced, particularly via the media, as simple truths that align comfortably with common-sense knowledge about the problem of fatness (and of fat people). This uncritical appeal to common-sense knowledges is evidenced by the striking absence across the data gathered for this study not only of self-doubt in declarations of obesity's wrongness, but also of other critical voices.

The primary challenges to the certainties and practices of the war on obesity have come from fat activism and the intersecting field of fat studies.[28] Their critical focus includes the moral dimensions of obesity science;[29] the shaming, stigmatisation and deviant categorisation of fat bodies;[30] the historical contingency and diagnostic limitations of key technologies of weight management such as body mass index (BMI);[31] the inefficacy and harms of weight loss interventions;[32] the misplaced use of weight as a proxy for health;[33] and the gender, race and class dimensions of an institutionalised attack on fat bodies.[34] But in spite of the burgeoning fat studies scholarship, alongside a long and vociferous history of fat activism that precedes the current war on obesity by decades,[35] these voices are conspicuously absent from popular representations of the intersecting problems of sugar and fatness, only ever appearing as a straw man to be knocked down. Lustig, for example, seats 'The Fat

Activists' at his imagined 'table of blame', arguing that 'it's my job as a paediatrician to protect these kids from such misguided thinking'.[36] The voices of those who are fat are also largely absent, except in narratives of repentance, conversion and transformation through weight loss, and as discussed in Chapter 6, even the manufacturers of sugary food and drinks don't refute the problem of obesity or that sugar plays a role in it (although the precise nature of that role is a point of dispute).

In the end, the lack of consensus over precisely what kind of problem the fat body constitutes does nothing to disrupt the absolute certainty of its wrongness. As shown above, obesity can be seen as a disease in its own right, a marker of other diseases or the cause of those diseases; it can be a cause of economic ruin; it can signal moral failure; and it can be the result of a positive energy (im)balance or of the metabolic disruptions created by the sugar. But as American sociologist Abigail Saguy argues in her landmark book *What's Wrong With Fat?*, rumbling debates about the specific nature of the problem of obesity only serve to reinforce it as a problem. This resonates strongly with the case of sugar, where the common-sense knowledge that sugar is a problem quietly smooths over questions about the nature of the problem itself. In this way, sugar and obesity operate as mutually animating problems, each giving certainty to the other.

Addiction

The second discourse through which this hanging together of sugar's competing explanations is achieved is that of addiction. In January 2014, the campaigning organisation Action on Sugar launched itself into the public eye with the declaration by clinical epidemiologist Simon Capewell that 'sugar is the new tobacco'.[37] The claim quickly entered the anti-sugar lexicon, speaking directly to intensifying concerns about sugar, particularly in the context of a war on obesity. The analogy between sugar and tobacco has several valences which will become relevant as the book progresses. First, it references the ways in which the tobacco industry aggressively marketed its products, including extensive efforts to deny the now widely accepted relationship between smoking and harm to health. As discussed further in Chapter 6, many see the sugar and tobacco industries as sharing a playbook in this regard. Second, tobacco exemplifies the transition of a consumer product from wide social acceptability to tight regulation and legal circumscription in ways that are seen by many as a model for sugar regulation. And finally, the 'new tobacco' claim endorses the proliferating attempts to categorise sugar as addictive.

This section explores the ways in which discourses of addiction, like those of obesity, help to hold together competing understandings of the problem of sugar. First, I look at the ways in which the category of addiction shares the uncertainties and multiplicities that we have also seen in relation to both sugar and obesity. Second, I explore sugar's discursive alignment with other substances readily understood as addictive. Third, I consider the contested positioning of sugar within a hierarchy of drugs. And finally I discuss the role of addiction attributions in the cultivation of urgency.

The conceptual chaos of addiction

To claim sugar is addictive is to mobilise a term riven with long-standing definitional uncertainties. The histories of substances commonly understood as addictive, such as illicit drugs, alcohol and tobacco, demonstrate the shifting and uneven regulatory and conceptual foundations of both addiction and its associated substances.[38] In an echo of obesity's diagnostic fluidity, Australian sociologist Helen Keane describes addiction as existing in a state of conceptual chaos, ranging across chronic disease, visceral drives, acquired tastes, habits and irrational attachments.[39] These definitional uncertainties are reflected in successive iterations of the *Diagnostic and Statistical Manual of Mental Disorders* (*DSM*), with the fifth (and most recent) version (*DSM*-V) maintaining the previous edition's rejection of addiction as a diagnostic category. Instead, it opts for the umbrella term 'substance use disorder' (SUD) – a decision intended to circumvent addiction's stigmatising potential and problems of definition.[40]

The specific diagnostic content of SUD is less important here than the title of the *DSM*-V chapter where it is discussed: 'Substance-related and addictive disorders'. This is significant because despite addiction's exclusion as a distinct diagnostic category, its qualified reintroduction opens up the possibility of non-substance and behavioural addictions in which sugar can potentially be included. This reflects the expanding attribution of addiction to include process addictions such as gambling or eating.[41] While gambling disorder is the only example included in the *DSM*-V, the manual's publication was preceded by extensive debate about whether obesity and/or food could be meaningfully described in terms of addiction.[42] This conceptual shift has been facilitated by the rise of neuroscientific accounts of addiction, which see addiction as a disease of the brain marked by the 'hijacking' of the brain's reward systems. Neuroscientific models of addiction gained momentum (and funding) in the context of President Richard Nixon's 'war on drugs', which was launched in 1971, and these molecular models of drug addiction were solidified by the late twentieth-century development of neuro-imaging technologies through which people were able to 'see' the effects of drugs on the brain.[43] However, it is important not to overstate the scientific consensus around these models, and in 2014, a letter co-signed by ninety-five scientists and researchers was published in *Nature* protesting the journal's characterisation of addiction as 'a brain malfunction', arguing that 'substance abuse cannot be divorced from its social, psychological, cultural, political, legal and environmental contexts'.[44]

Both the expansion to include non-substance and behavioural addictions and the (contested) rise of neuroscientific accounts of addiction are foundational to claims that sugar is addictive. Unlike dietary fat, which is widely (but reductively) understood as manifesting itself on parts of the body in visible ways as fat, particularly where sugar is seen as toxic, it is conceptualised as flowing invisibly through and around the body's structures and systems, including the brain, wreaking unseen havoc as it goes. It is also strongly associated with pleasure, and the familiar experience of craving more of something sweet gives common-sense purchase to the discourse of addiction as a disruption to the brain's hedonic pathways.[45]

But this alone cannot explain the recent proliferation of discourses of sugar addiction, and just as the war on drugs enabled the neuroscience of addiction to gain ground, the war on obesity provides vital context for the attribution of sugar addiction. Every war needs an enemy, and as discussed in the previous section, without the war on obesity, there would not need to be an attack on sugar, whose primary sin is its presumed role in weight gain. The past failures of the war on obesity create spaces for its own reinvention into which sugar addiction fits neatly, particularly when located within a newly elevated neuroscientific frame. This provides both an alibi for past shortfalls and a manifesto for future research and intervention, bolstered by the added urgency that the attribution of addiction brings.

A drug like any other

In newspaper reports and popular self-help books, sugar addiction is constituted through two key discursive strategies: first, by setting sugar alongside other substances widely understood as addictive; and second, by establishing (contested) hierarchies among those substances to calibrate the seriousness of the problem of sugar. In both cases, sugar addiction is realised by association with other substances whose addictiveness is treated as beyond dispute, as demonstrated in this extract from an article in *The Sun* in August 2017: 'Tobacco. Alcohol. Drugs. Sugar. A devilish quartet crooking their boney fingers at us, promising all sorts of fun. Then kidnapping and force feeding us to a standstill.'[46] The substances – or what the article in a typically tabloid flourish calls 'the four horsemen of the addiction apocalypse' – form a collective whole through which sugar, as addiction's latest arrival, can be known. The running together of sugar with these other more recognisable substances of abuse amplifies the risk, which is brought to life through the language of bodily force. This generalisation across substances and bodies erases the differences in social acceptability, legality, modes of consumption and embodied effects and pathways between substances.[47] This sameness across substances is further consolidated in newspaper, lifestyle and scientific texts through the lexicon of drug addiction: sugar is 'pure, white and deadly'; it is 'the white stuff'; consumers are 'hooked' and 'tripping out'; they have to be 'weaned off' sugar or go 'cold turkey'; purveyors of sugary foods are 'pushers' and street-corner 'dealers' who 'spike' and 'lace' everyday foods with sugar.

These affinities are solidified in the newspaper reporting by reference to two scientific articles that have become viral touchstones for the claim that sugar is addictive. Neither of these papers was reported widely in the newspapers when it was published, but they became go-to sources as anxiety around sugar began to rise. Reporting follows familiar patterns of newspaper coverage of scientific research, adhering closely to the abstracted conclusions rather than engaging critically with the material, avoiding discussions of methodology, treating science as authoritative, generalising attributions ('some scientists') and overstating findings, especially when they reaffirm social values.[48]

The first of these is a 2007 paper by French research scientist Magalie Lenoir and colleagues, which describes an experiment where rats, by pulling on levers, could choose between intravenously administered cocaine and water sweetened with saccharin.[49] The sweetened water proved by far the most common choice, even for rats considered to be 'addicted' to cocaine. The subsequent conclusions are reproduced as fact, as in this extract from *The Daily Telegraph* in April 2013:

> French scientists in Bordeaux reported that in animal trials, rats chose sugar over cocaine (even when they were addicted to cocaine) and speculated that no mammals' sweet receptors are naturally adapted to the high concentrations of sweet tastes on offer in modern times. They worried [...] that the intense stimulation of these receptors by our typical 21st century sugar-rich diets must generate a supra-normal reward signal in the brain with the potential to override self-control mechanisms and thus lead to addiction.[50]

In her discussion of neuroscientific accounts of food addiction and obesity, Australian sociologist Suzanne Fraser argues that discourses of hijacked hedonic pathways rely on what John Law calls 'collateral realities'.[51] These are 'truths' that are reproduced incidentally in ways that position them as conceptually stable and beyond dispute.[52] Lenoir and colleagues' conclusions are built upon a number of collateral realities, which are reproduced repeatedly in the subsequent newspaper and popular self-help accounts. First, the paper opens with the claim that 'overconsumption of diets rich in sugars contributes together with other factors to drive the current obesity epidemic'.[53] As discussed in the previous section, this opening gambit endows the problem of obesity, and sugar's role in it, with a knowable certainty, erasing the need for any discussion of how that conclusion has been reached and any uncertainties surrounding it. In this way, the possibility of challenge to this foundational premise is foreclosed.

Three further intersecting collateral realities follow. First, the paper assumes that the taste of sweetness can be meaningfully compared with the effects of an intravenously injected substance; and second, it assumes that for a taste sensation to be preferred over the effects of intravenous cocaine, that sensation too must signify addictive potential. These assumptions are held in place even though the authors also note that cocaine activates brain stress pathways in rats and that in choosing the sweetened water, they may be trying to avoid negative side effects rather than seeking something even more compelling.[54] This points to the final collateral reality – that the findings from animal models are readily transferable to humans. This is achieved through generalisations about evolved sensitivities to sweetness across 'most mammals, including rats and humans',[55] concluding that more research is needed on animals raised in sugar-rich environments 'to better approximate the modern human condition'.[56] Such slippage between animals and humans is also evident in the *Daily Telegraph* extract above, which moves seamlessly from the rats' choices to mammalian evolution to 'our typical 21st century sugar-rich diets'. As American medical historian Nicole Nelson observes in her ethnography of an animal behaviour genetics laboratory, 'using mice as stand-ins for humans in scientific experiments has today become so commonplace that news articles [...] can effortlessly slide back and forth between the animal and the human with only a hint of a caveat'.[57]

The claim that rats prefer sweetness over cocaine is frequently paired with a second study, conducted by research neuroscientist Nicole Avena and colleagues in 2008, which claims that under certain circumstances, rats can become addicted to sugar.[58] The study deprived rats of food daily for twelve hours, then gave them twelve-hour access to a sugar solution and regular chow. When the sugar solution became available, the rats would consume it heavily. This was followed by what were interpreted as symptoms of withdrawal, including anxiety, depression and cravings. The paper looks to neuroscience to cement the affinities between sugar and drugs that are already widely recognised as addictive, arguing that sugar activates the same neurochemical changes as addictive drugs, rendering sugar addiction 'plausible'. They conclude, 'the rise in obesity, coupled with the emergence of scientific findings of parallels between drugs of abuse and palatable foods has given credibility to this idea'.[59] Resting on assumptions about obesity rates in which sugar is confidently implicated, the drawing of parallels with substances already widely understood as addictive and articulated through the authoritative voice of neuroscience makes sugar's addictive qualities real.

A hierarchy of drugs

These two claims – that rats prefer sweetness over cocaine, and that sugar is addictive for rats – can be combined to solidify the much more potent claim that sugar is more addictive than cocaine. Cardiovascular research scientist James DiNicolantonio made this claim explicitly in *The Guardian* in a 2017 piece debating the findings of his recently released review article, which made the case for sugar as addictive.[60] Referencing studies showing rodent preferences for sweetness over cocaine, he argues in the newspaper article, 'in animals, it is actually more addictive than even cocaine, so sugar is pretty much probably the most consumed addictive substance around the world and is wreaking havoc on our health'.[61] This marks a different understanding of addiction from the undifferentiated merging of substances of abuse, and instead enacts a hierarchy of addictions, with sugar at its peak.

But the precise order of the hierarchy is uncertain, as signalled by DiNicolantonio's qualification that sugar is *'pretty much probably* the most consumed addictive substance' (my italic). For example, in December 2013, Lustig argued in *The Sunday Times* that 'sugar is addictive – not as addictive as tobacco or alcohol, but if it's everywhere, you can't get rid of it'.[62] However, in an earlier article in *The Guardian*, he is reported as claiming that sugar is not only the most addictive foodstuff but also the most toxic, implicated in 'all the diseases associated with "metabolic syndrome"'.[63] Together, these invoke a hierarchy of addictive drugs, a sub-hierarchy of addictive foodstuffs and a hierarchy of toxicity, whereby addiction *per se* is rendered less important than the inherent harms of sugar, which are seen as amplified by addiction-driven over-consumption enabled by easy availability.

Even direct contestation of addiction claims leaves this unify-ing conclusion intact. For example, the *Guardian* article discussing DiNicolantonio's claim includes strong rebuttals from psychiatrists Hisham Ziauddeen and Maggie Westwater, whose 2016 review of the issue, co-authored with Paul Fletcher, concluded that there was little evidence to support the claim for sugar addiction in humans.[64] In the newspaper article, Ziauddeen resists the idea that sugar is 'this terrific demon by itself because of some innate properties in it'. But this still does not let sugar off the hook: 'Where the problem lies is that there are huge amounts of sugar that are put into various foods that substantially boost the calorie content of those foods.'[65] The recourse to energy balance opens up the gulf between the empty-calories and sugar-as-toxic discourses, but at the same time reinforces sugar as a problem characterised by overconsumption, whether driven by the excess calories of a sugar-rich environment or the compul-sions of addiction. Addiction, then, operates as a proxy for overcon-sumption, pushing the conceptual chaos of addiction quietly into the background.

Cultivating urgency

Urgent demands that something must be done are a hallmark of anti-obesity discourse and practice,[66] and this urgency, bolstered by attributions of addiction, has transferred itself easily onto sugar as the newly elevated enemy in the war on obesity. This fuels the demand for new anti-sugar interventions in a context where action is prioritised over the demonstrable efficacy of those interventions. For example, an article in *The Observer* in August 2013 about proposals to introduce a tax on sugary drinks included a brief interview with pharmacologist David Colquhoun, who is known for vigorously debunking what he calls 'dubious and dishonest science' in his popular blog, 'DC's improbable science'.[67] Asked in the article whether he endorses the view that fizzy drinks are actively harmful, he is reported as replying: 'Bugger all is known with certainty about the effects of diet and health […] Nevertheless, the best current guess is that sugar is a much bigger problem than fat. And it's addictive, which is why manufacturers do it (I'll happily eat a whole bag of jelly babies). That can't be good – so yes, I'd say let's tax it.'[68] The comment is deliberately offhand, but the inability to stop eating a bag of sweets is enough for Colquhoun to confirm sugar's addictive potential, which then confirms the need for taxation – an intervention whose efficacy is also assumed (see Chapter 6). Against the background of his well-established scepticism about diet and health claims, his anecdotal claim to sugar's addictive potential makes sense only in the wider context of the urgency surrounding obesity.

Appeals to sugar addiction, therefore, are not only stabilised by urgency, but also function discursively to cultivate that same urgency. In this context, the precise content of the category of addiction is less important than its rhetorical weight; addiction doesn't need to be 'real' to be mobilised as a motivator for change. This rhetorical function was made explicit by the chair of Action on Sugar, Graham MacGregor, in an article in *The Times* in January 2014:

> I agree that sugar is not like tobacco. It's not as addictive, but it's a major source of hidden calories and if you get it down it will help with obesity. It's an overstatement. Sometimes to get your point across you need to make it stronger. [But] sugar is addictive, particularly in young children, and the food industry uses it as a weapon to sell rubbish food to young children.[69]

Even after hedging the claim that sugar is like tobacco, he reinstates the seriousness of the threat relative to tobacco by attaching the risks of sugar to young children, particularly in relation to obesity. Regardless of the confessed overstatement, the urgency invoked by the discourse of addiction, the logics of energy balance and the calls for regulation that characterise Action on Sugar's campaigns remain in place.

In this way, we can see that the contested and expansive problems of sugar, obesity and addiction constitute a mutually endorsing triumvirate, each propping up the others to give solidity and singularity to multiplicity and uncertainty. This in turn shores up the imperative to act. In the case of sugar, discourses of both obesity and addiction grant a sense of urgency that centralises the (over)consumption of sugar, rendering sugar reduction the only possible response. Sugar reduction is then able to operate as a lowest common denominator, enabling different articulations of the problem of sugar to hang together with the appearance of singularity. This purposeful limiting of anti-sugar's field of vision (for example, to exclude other social determinants of health) constitutes the boundedness that is necessary to prevent the fracturing of the problem of sugar under the weight of the contestation on which it is founded. Simultaneously, the expansiveness of the problem of sugar facilitates its construction something that affects 'everyone everywhere'.[70] This makes possible generalised claims that 'we are eating too much sugar and it is bad for our health', creating space for competing understandings of the mechanisms and consequences of that (over)consumption without disturbing the claim itself.

Nostalgia

The final unifying discourse is that of nostalgia. A commonly repeated claim across the different articulations of the problem of sugar is that our bodies are out of step with our sugar-rich environments, which have changed so rapidly that we have been unable to adapt effectively to them. This results in a potent nostalgia for a time before things went awry alongside the implied possibility of a return or restoration. There are two temporal scales to this nostalgia: first, nostalgia for an imagined post-war, mid-twentieth-century past of home-cooked food, physical activity through labour and play and limited access to sugar; and second, nostalgia for a pre-modern, hunter-gatherer past in which the human body was in concert with its 'natural' food environment.

'Back then, we weren't fat'

Nostalgia for a lost recent dietary past is a feature common in newspaper reporting, invoking better, simpler days. For example, in *The Daily Telegraph* in October 2015, journalist Judith Woods recalled fondly: 'In the seventies […] there were no "treat cupboards" or giant piping candy, chocolate bars or buckets of Haribo. Sure, the hairstyles were awful, we nearly died from boredom on Sundays and there was a half-day closing midweek which has left me with a vestigial sense of gloom every Wednesday. But back then, we weren't fat.'[71] In a similarly nostalgic vein, in September 2014, Ian Birrell – a journalist and former speechwriter for Prime Minister David Cameron – recalled in the *Daily Mail* how his father, an executive at the sugar company Tate & Lyle, would bring home their latest sugary innovations for 'testing'. The potential harms of these treats were offset by a blissful childhood of hand-prepared food and running around: 'Back in the Sixties and early Seventies, of course, most of the rest of my diet was prepared by my mother or school dinner ladies and, like other children, I spent long hours running around parks and playing fields.'[72] In *Fat Chance*, Lustig makes a similar claim, citing an interview with Swiss molecular scientist Markus Stoffel, who recalled an idyllic childhood with equally nostalgic fondness:

> He recounted his childhood. He ate lunch at noon, would get out of school at three, and then rush straight to the playground. For three hours, he and his classmates would play their hearts out and drink water from the school fountain. At 6.00 pm, they'd return to their homes famished. 'That six-hour interval of no food, only water, and vigorous activity was absolutely essential … to keep our livers happy, refreshed and insulin sensitive, so the next day we could go at it all over again.'[73]

These memories of a lost past begin from the conviction that, as Woods observes, 'back then, we weren't fat'. This past-without-fatness is then connected causally to a nostalgic vision of home-cooked meals, an abundance of physical play and the absence of over-sized packages of confectionery. While obesity rates have undoubtedly risen since this fondly remembered, if ill-defined, time-before-fatness, the denial of past fatness is in tension with explicit concerns about fat bodies in circulation at the same time. For example, the widespread problematisation of fatness is illustrated by both the post-war boom of the slimming industry and the consumer demand for artificial, low-calorie sweeteners,[74] as well as by the rise of fat activism, which has its roots in the 1960s civil rights movements.[75]

This also sits alongside another nostalgic recollection – that of the good old days when fat people could be bullied into submission without fear of censure. For example, writing in *The Daily Telegraph* in August 2015, journalist Philip Johnston recalls: 'Back when I was at school, I can hardly remember any fat pupils [...] Anyone who was marginally overweight was mercilessly pilloried. It would be called bullying – or fatshaming – nowadays, but stigma once played a key role in determining social mores ... [...] Since no-one is allowed to be censorious any more, we must reap the consequences.'[76] In this recollection, fat people are both present (and therefore liable to bullying) and absent – a tension that matters less than the construction of a present gone awry. Just as warnings of a crisis of obesity encompass everyone, everywhere, the imagined time before is painted with a broad brush, operating rhetorically rather than literally to signal that something important has been lost.

There are three key dimensions to the summoning of this nostalgia for an idealised post-war time before ubiquitous sugar-fuelled obesity. First, it is located firmly in childhood memories, with the innocence of childhood eliding smoothly with an innocent dietary past, and with heaving shelves and oversized packages of sweets replaced by physical play punctuated by regular hand-prepared meals. Woods' resentments from the 1970s are equally childish, focusing on the boredom of closed shops and lost chances to socialise.

Second, they are profoundly gendered, recalling a simple playful child-hood world without any consideration of the labour involved behind the scenes – a permissible oversight for a child, perhaps, but not for an adult. For example, apart from the occasional treat from his father, Birrell's meals were prepared by women – his 'mother or school dinner ladies' – and although there is no mention of who prepared Stoffel's meals, which appear magically at the appointed hour, this too was probably the unseen food work of women.[77] This reflects a nostalgia not only for a dietary 'time before', but also implicitly for one where women stayed home and cooked.[78] As food sociologist Christine Knight observes in relation to nutritional nostalgia in low-carbohydrate dietary discourse, 'home baking, from-scratch cooking and ever-ready hot food and drink are all very well when all one has to do is turn up and be served'.[79] As discussed in Chapter 8, this lost idealised past of home-cooked (woman-cooked) food also positions women as responsible for perceived dietary failures in the present.

An exception to the invisibility of women in these accounts is the frequent summoning of the figure of the grandmother, whose imagined food knowledges and practices serve as a touchstone for the lost past. For example, Sarah Wilson, the creator of the *I Quit Sugar* franchise of recipe books and sugar reduction programmes, told *The Guardian* in June 2017: 'A good adage is: if your grandmother can't identify what's on the plate, avoid it.'[80] She advises readers 'to go back to how our grandparents lived and ate', adding, 'Britain was at its healthiest during wartime ration-ing'. Appeals to wartime austerity are addressed more fully in Chapter 7 below, but the key point here is that the figure of 'your grandmother' serves as an icon of a recoverable lost past that rests on women's invisible labour.

A third key theme for these nostalgic reminiscences is the emphasis on sustained physical activity. This speaks directly to an energy bal-ance model, with burning off energy by running around outdoors working in tandem with a home-cooked, snack-free diet to balance energy intake with output. This model stands in direct contrast to contemporary panics surrounding indoor, screen-based leisure and the perils of sedentariness, particularly in relation to children. It reproduces the problems inherent in the energy balance model, and Gard and Wright cite multiple studies that dispute the assumptions that physical activity in children is declining, that childhood physical activity can be mapped cleanly onto health and that hours spent watching TV or gaming are a reliable predictor of weight.[81] In line with the logics of sugar as toxic, Markus Stoffel takes this a step further, seeing the long, snack-free interval between lunch and dinner as beneficial not simply in terms of energy balance but also as producing positive metabolic effects in its own right. As discussed below, this speaks to a nostalgia on a very different timeframe, looking back to an imagined time of prehistoric feast and famine for which we are 'designed' and which is reflected in the contemporary dietary trend of 'intermittent fasting', which is a common companion of low-carbohydrate eating. The simplicity of a childhood uncontaminated by technology – in the form of either highly processed food or screen-based play – and full of energetic play serves as idealised, albeit chronologically vague, past that allows competing perspectives to coalesce around the longing for a return to that lost past.

Setting aside the question of whether we really are less active, and how this might be connected to fatness, the nostalgia for these childhood days filled with physical play also betrays unspoken privileges of gender and (dis)ability. For example, wistful recollections of hours spent running around ignore the ways in which disabled children, both then and now, may not be able to play in those normatively celebrated ways because of the lack of appropriately adapted and inclusive play spaces and facilities.[82] Furthermore, lack of entitlement to space and gendered social norms of behaviour, movement and dress can limit girls' access to physical play. When I read these accounts of blissful childhoods of racing around outdoors for hours, I recalled my own primary school days in the 1970s, where playtime was strictly segregated. Girls were sent to play on a small playground the size of a single netball court, while the boys occupied an area of three five-a-side football pitches. The expectations of who would (and should or shouldn't) run around were clear. Furthermore, beyond the school grounds, nostalgic recollections of unfettered outdoor play presume a safe living and home environment that were no more universally available then than they are now. As with the claim that 'we are all eating too much sugar', who constitutes the 'we' of 'we weren't fat' and whose experience is excluded from these nostalgic reminiscences is left unspoken.

Paleo-nostalgia

As suggested by Stoffel's childhood memories, for sugar-as-toxic advocates, this idealised recent past is not simply about energy balance (no snacking, plenty of filling, home-made (woman-made) food, energetic play), but is also about systemic regulation. At first glance, this is at odds with the model of metabolic disruption that is a key marker of distinction between those who see the problem of sugar as toxicity rather than one of emptiness (as discussed in the previous chapter). If food is not processed by bodies in universally predictable ways (energy in, energy out), and if, instead, metabolic systems are formed in heritable ways through what bodies ingest, then there can be no pure, originary body to which our bodies can be returned, especially by relinquishing a single nutrient. As Landecker observes, '[...] the layers of human intervention go all the way down'.[83]

However, the claims that sugar is uniquely toxic and that we are living in a time of unprecedented exposure to it together (partially) ameliorate this tension. Where the onslaught of sugar on metabolic function is understood as an exceptional crisis, then it is still possible to hold in place a healthful and well-regulated 'before' to which we might meaningfully return. But for the sugar-as-toxic advocates, this 'before' lies not only in an idealised post-war past, but also in a much more distant hunter-gatherer past that preceded the rise of agriculture and a grain-based diet. For many, and in line with the logics of low-carbohydrate diets more broadly, this transition marks the beginnings of the deviation from the 'diet that nature intended'[84] and constitutes 'the first catastrophe to befall the human diet'.[85]

At the beginning of *Pure, White and Deadly*, Yudkin maps out 'the origins of the human diet', arguing that 'for at least two million years our ancestors were largely meat eating', resulting in a diet that was 'rich in protein, moderately rich in fat and usually poor in carbohydrate', with dietary carbohydrates coming primarily from seasonal fruits.[86] As Lustig explains: 'for our ancestors, fruit was readily available for one month per year, called "harvest time". Then came four months of winter and no food at all. We needed to stock up – to increase our adiposity in preparation for four months of famine. In other words, in the doses that were available to our forebears, sugar was evolutionarily adaptive.[87] Shifting easily from humans to animals, Lustig illustrates this point with the observation that Indonesian orangutan binge on fruit in times of plenty, causing cyclical adiposity. For Lustig, the fact that sugar is now ubiquitously and continuously available means that this cyclicality has been lost and the bodily processes of energy storage have become maladaptive in the face of an abundance of food, and particularly carbohydrates. Yudkin locates this transformation of dietary composition and the loss of cyclicality 10,000 years in the past, with the rise of agriculture, including animal domestication and the cultivation of grains and cereals, leading to a diet rich in carbohydrates and poor in protein and fat.[88] This was followed, according to Yudkin, by a second food revolution over the last few decades, when food, storage and transportation technologies increased food supply and choice in ways designed to appeal to palatability rather than satiety.

This narrative is reproduced in other early anti-sugar texts,[89] which, Christine Knight argues, provide a clear lineage for contemporary low-carb diets, which rest heavily on a nostalgia for lost distant past and an investment in an unchanged genome outpaced by a rapidly changing food world.[90] As Loren Cordain, author of *The Paleo Diet*, explains: 'we are Stone Agers living in the Space age; our dietary needs are the same as theirs. Our genes are well-adapted to a world in which all the food eaten daily had to be hunted, fished or gathered from the natural environment – a world that no longer exists.'[91]

There are a number of reasons to approach these accounts of what Knight calls 'nutritional primitivism'[92] with caution. First, they rely on an unchanging consonance between human diet and Paleolithic 'design' across large and ill-defined tracts of time, with our geographically scattered ancestors imagined as a singular kind across time and location. As evolutionary biologist Marlene Zuk argues, these 'paleo fantasies' misunderstand the evolutionary process, which is continuous and in interaction with specific environments, never reaching a point of perfect adaptation. This means that 'we do not have genes plunked wholesale into one environment or another, whether Paleolithic, medieval or industrial; we have genes that respond to that environment and to each other'.[93] There is no untouched genetic, hormonal or metabolic past to which we can meaningfully return.

The second challenge to the paleo-nostalgia of sugar-as-toxic advocacy (and low-carb evangelists more generally) is that they rely on what Gard and Wright call 'just-so stories' – that is, 'rather than being based on evidence, it is a story wheeled in "after the fact" to support an existing hypothesis; a hypothesis about a hypothesis as it were'.[94] These just-so stories are exemplified by a paper published in 2000 by Loren Cordain and colleagues, who set out an analysis of the eating habits of 229 modern hunter-gatherer communities based on ethnographic data published in 1967. They argue that between 45% and 65% of dietary energy came from animal foods, concluding that these findings 'might provide insight into potentially therapeutic dietary recommendations for contemporary populations'.[95] The account reflects the same performance of nutritional precision that we saw in the fine-grained attempts to quantify sugar reduction and is premised on the convictions that we can know with any accuracy how people ate and that this provides a model for how we should eat now.[96] In the same special issue as the paper by Cordain and colleagues, dietary ecologist Katharine Milton argues that the original data is flawed because the ethnographers spent most of their time with men in the studied communities, rendering women's food work invisible. She also notes that plant food does not leave the same obvious traces as animal foods, further exacerbating its invisibility and distorting the presumed macronutrient ratios.[97] Lustig amplifies this erasure, arguing that 'In the beginning there were the hunters. Most hunters killed their food, while some fished. They ate fat and protein, went long stretches between kills and had to live off their fat stores.'[98] The gathering of fruits and plants that is associated with women is completely absent from this originary just-so story, focusing instead on a diet of animal protein in a rhythm of feast and famine. This resonates with Stoffel's account of (albeit modest) fasting as enabling the body to restore and regulate itself.

I return to these paleo fantasies in Chapter 8 with a particular focus on their mobilisation of a colonialised and racialised gaze. But for now, I want to argue that this nostalgic yearning for a world that no longer exists serves as the third unifying discourse (along with obesity and addiction). Even though two widely different timescales are at work here (the post-war and Paleolithic periods), they find unity in their claim that our contemporary foodscape is out of step with our bodies' capacities to navigate it, defusing their differences. In the end, inconsistencies in the just-so stories of the lost 'before' are unimportant because their primary function is to shore up agreement about a catastrophically sugar-filled present (and menacing future) that is out of step with the needs and capacities of the well-tuned body of the imagined past.

Conclusion

Although there are multiple, and sometimes competing, accounts of what kind of problem sugar is, this chapter has shown how these are able to hang together. This hanging together rests, first, on the expansiveness of the attack on sugar; that is, it offers a sufficiently capacious lowest-common-denominator platform to accommodate multiple understandings of the problem at hand. And second, it rests on the boundedness of the attack on sugar; it is only about sugar. This allows for a simplified solution – eat less sugar – without the intrusion of the wider social context and its attendant inequalities. In this chapter, I have argued that this hanging together is achieved via three key discourses, all equally expansive and bounded: the obesity epidemic, addiction and nostalgia.

These provide the foundations for a strategic consensus around the problem of sugar; if nothing else, they insist, we can all agree that we are eating too much sugar and it's bad for our health.

Although 'What's wrong with sugar?' is a good starting point, especially for a book about sugar, it may be the wrong question if we want to understand sugar's social life. The problem of how sugar interacts with the body is foreclosed by appeals to consensus, and the focus instead is shifted away from the nature of sugar's effects on the body and onto how it gets into the body. While conflicting ideas about what's wrong with sugar drift in and out of the foreground from time to time, the wrongness of sugar remains a confident, solidified and simplified certainty, and the focus inevitably moves to the question of resolution: if 'we are eating too much sugar and it's bad for our health', then the answer is to eat less sugar. This lies at the heart of the social life of sugar. Consequently, while the book circles repeatedly back to differing accounts of the ways in which sugar impacts on the body, the imperative to reduce sugar consumption is the primary focus of the remaining chapters.

3

Hidden

In January 2019, Change4Life launched its new year 'Sugar Swaps' campaign with the release of an animated film.[1] In the film, angry cubes of sugar emerge from everyday food packaging, grumbling menacingly and running amok in the family kitchen to a horror soundtrack. Two children take cover from the onslaught behind their father, who desperately tries to fend off the attacking cubes with a frying pan, until the day is saved by the appearance of their mother triumphantly brandishing two bags of shopping. A child's voice tells us: 'Now Mum's got an easy way to cut back on sugar with lower sugar swaps on the things we eat every day.' Empowered by her 'smart swaps', the mother whistles to the rampaging cubes, who run obediently out of the back door. 'Make a swap when you next shop', urges an adult female voiceover at the end of the film.

Although the film sets the scene with a familiar warning that eating too much sugar causes type 2 diabetes and heart disease, the problem of sugar requires no substantive explanation. Instead, the film addresses the problem of how it gets into our diets, beginning from a core feature of sugar's contemporary demonisation: that it is not only hidden, but also that it actively hides. It is an enemy that seeps unseen through the porous boundaries of the home, wreaking havoc as it goes. Consequently, the problem of sugar cannot be resolved simply by choosing to stop consuming it; you must be able to find it first. The work of giving up sugar, then, is also the work of rooting it out of hiding in our everyday diets. This is a process that requires instruction.

We are surrounded by information about how to eat, live, sleep and exercise in the name of health, and these 'life lessons'[2] are not confined to the classroom or the clinic, but circulate across social, cultural, economic, political and public health domains. These are never purely informational, but instead aim to cultivate the good citizen; or, more accurately, the good bio-citizen – that is, a citizen whose primary obligation is to take responsibility for their own physical wellbeing and make the 'right' choices informed by health expertise.[3] As such, they not only constitute lessons in what to eat or how much to exercise, but are also run through with 'virtue discourses' which establish certain behaviours and qualities as worthy and desirable and which distinguish the good bio-citizen from the failed one.[4] The 'Sugar Swaps' campaign, then, not only offers information about how to reduce a family's sugar consumption but is also heavily laden with the expectation that they should change their behaviour accordingly (or at least, that mothers should).

Focusing on the common theme of sugar as hidden (and hiding), this chapter explores the ways in which sugar's secretive entry into our everyday diets is constructed and the implicit and explicit expectations of individual behaviour change that this produces. For this chapter, I look most closely at the newspaper data, in recognition of the ways the mass media constitutes a privileged (but by no means exclusive) site from which people acquire health information. However, this is also considered in the wider context which renders news coverage plausible. The chapter begins with the phenomenon of the 'hidden-sugar shock' story – a common device which uses staged exposés to simultaneously demonstrate the problem of hidden sugar and instruct readers in rooting it out. I argue that there are two key strands to warnings about sugar as hidden. These each targets a different kind of food, manifesting itself in two different kinds of hidden-sugar shock stories. The first targets obviously sugary foods such as cakes and biscuits and expresses the problem of hidden sugar in terms of excess and unpredictable variation; and the second strand targets foods that are easily coded as healthy such as smoothies or cereal bars, with the problem framed in terms of accumulation and deception. Both unite around the imperative to become a 'sugar detective'[5] and to maintain a constant state of vigilance in the face of the hidden threat posed by sugar. The final section of the chapter discusses the limitations to these incitements to constant sugar surveillance, highlighting the ways in which efforts to contain and simplify the problem of hidden sugar are disrupted by the irrepressible sociality of food, the uncontainable leakage between healthy/unhealthy food binaries and the clash with other forms of health advice.

Hidden-sugar shock stories

In the previous chapters, I discussed the ways in which sugar is seen as operating unseen in the body, wreaking quiet health devastation that may not become apparent until it is too late. The common representation of sugar as hidden (and hiding) in everyday foods shores up this framing of sugar as a sneaky foe against which constant vigilance is needed. One of the characteristics of sugar as a foodstuff is that it is rarely consumed on its own and is more commonly combined with other foods. Home consumption of store-cupboard granulated sugar – for example, for baking or to sweeten hot drinks – receives relatively little attention from anti-sugar campaigns. Instead, the primary focus of the attack on sugar is processed foods in which added sugar is integral but not self-evidently visible, leading potentially to unintended (over) consumption. The 'hidden-sugar shock' story is a staged exposé of this unseen sugar lurking in our everyday food, and it is designed not simply to tell readers where sugar might be hidden but, more importantly, to jolt readers into embracing the work of sugar reduction.

The campaigning organisation Action on Sugar is a key instigator of these stories, which can be endlessly resurrected by moving from foodstuff to foodstuff, providing a steady stream of media content. It begins with a survey of multiple iterations of a genre of food (e.g. cakes, biscuits, cereals, shakes), the findings of which are released to the press with attention-grabbing displays of shock and horror, expert declarations of frustration and calls for changes in both the regulation of sugar and in the behaviour of consumers. For example, in February 2016,

Action on Sugar released news of a survey of the sugar content of flavoured hot drinks sold in high-street coffee shops. The headline to the
press release announced dramatically: 'Up to 25 teaspoons of sugar per
serving: equivalent to ≈ 3 cans of Coca Cola.' This was followed immediately by the claim that '98% of hot flavoured drinks would receive a
"red" (high) label for excessive levels of sugars per serving – with 35%
containing the same amount or more sugar than a can of Coca Cola.' In
a pattern typical of the genre, the press release then names its headline-
ready worst offender: 'Starbuck's Hot Mulled Fruit – Grape with Chai,
Orange and Cinnamon Venti is the worst offender, containing a whopping **25 teaspoons** of sugar – more than **THREE** times the maximum
ADULT daily intake of free sugars (7 tsp/d).'[6] This is a deliberate shock
tactic designed to attract media and public attention. The fact was recognised explicitly by Action on Sugar chair, Graham MacGregor, in an
interview in *The Sunday Times* in 2016 about the sugar tax. Reflecting
on the flavoured hot drinks campaign, he explained the organisation's
strategy: 'We grab the headlines with horror stories and then come in
with the facts [...].'[7]

Writing of mass media coverage of obesity, sociologist Marc
Lafrance and colleagues argue that the dominant obesity discourse
relies on three mutually constituting techniques: moralism, sensationalism and scientism.[8] All three elements are present here in relation to
sugar. First, the wrongness of such high sugar content is run through
with moral judgements about both the creators of these drinks and
their consumers, who are seen as having slipped far below acceptable
standards of responsible sweetness. The sensationalism is also obvious in the emphatic capitalisations, the vocabulary choice ('whopping')
and the powerful image of the twenty-five teaspoons. This is an extension of the familiar use of spectacular bodies in obesity reporting,[9]
instead using heaped-up sugar to perform the same function. These
piles of sugar, like the 'headless fatties' that litter obesity reporting,[10]
are designed to sensationalise the story and generate disgust-filled reactions. And finally, the story is run through with scientism, where 'facts'
are credited as such and granted authority because a scientist (or other

expert) states they are so.[11] According to MacGregor in his explanation of Action on Sugar's hidden sugar shock strategy: 'We have the right science behind us and that's essential.'[12]

The press release strategy worked and the hot drinks story was picked up by several newspapers. With a typically tabloid flourish, *The Sun* led with the headline 'Fatty latte',[13] while *The Guardian* used the '25 teaspoons' statistic to grab the readers' attention: 'The cafes serving drinks with 25 teaspoons of sugar per cup'.[14] The *Guardian* coverage of the story provides a model for the structure and content of hidden-sugar shock news stories, following the headlining teaspoons statistic with a sensationally dire warning in its opening paragraph that 'Millions of Britons are putting their health at risk by ordering hot chocolate and other trendy chai drinks that contain staggering amounts of sugar – up to 25 teaspoons – in just one serving.' The article then repeats almost verbatim Action on Sugar's warning that 98% of the drinks would warrant a red warning label, before describing the Venti Hot Mulled Fruit drink that the press release had singled out, discursively positioning the worst case as a representative of the whole.

Although the original press release makes no specific mention of the sugar as hidden, it is implied in calls for clearer labelling so that consumers can be informed about the unseen sugar content of their drinks. But the *Guardian* article makes it explicit: 'It is thought that up to 20% of the population visit a coffee shop on a daily basis, but many will be unaware how much hidden sugar they are consuming in flavoured drinks.' The claim inadvertently exposes one of the key flaws in the hidden-sugar shock stories – their inability to account for patterns of consumption. In this case, the high numbers of customers visiting high-street coffee shops are elided with high consumption levels of their most sugary products. This is exemplified by warnings common to the genre against the mundane consumption of high-sugar foods and the failure to treat them as exceptional treats. The same article in *The Guardian*, for example, reports the advice of Action on Sugar's Kawther Hashem that 'said these hot flavoured drinks had to become an occasional treat, rather than an everyday purchase'. Hashem's warning is premised on the unevidenced assumption that consumers incontinently consume the largest and highest-sugar drinks daily, despite the considerable cost of the large-sized drink targeted in the press release.

The story also relies on the assumption that people are unaware that the drinks contain a lot of sugar. A dismissive challenge to this assumption was made by *The Daily Telegraph* in a derisive comment piece that reflects both the paper's commitment to individual choice over regulation and a classed disregard for modes of consumption that defy middle-class tastes: 'Of course Starbucks' drinks are full of sugar. Go to a proper coffee shop instead.'[15] But looking beyond this haughty dismissal, the assumption that people are consuming the drinks every day out of ignorance rests on the conviction that food and drink choice is (or should be) determined primarily by nutritional content and that if only consumers knew about the sugar content, they would make better choices. This, after all, is the *raison d'être* of the hidden-sugar shock story and of information-based health interventions more generally.

One effect of this single-nutrient focus is the dislocation of consumption from its context to the exclusion of the social, cultural and gustatory comforts and pleasures that may be involved in the decision to consume a sugary hot drink or snack – even one that has found itself at the top of a survey hit list. In her book *How the Other Half Eats*, sociologist Priya Fielding-Singh tells the story of Nyah, a cash-strapped single mother who spent $10 on two coffee-caramel milkshakes topped with whipped cream for her and her fourteen-year-old daughter, even though she barely had the money to keep her car on the road or the home stocked with staples. It's the kind of story that easily attracts the accusations of nutritional and financial fecklessness heard in everyday discourse about 'the poor' and their irresponsible consumption habits (see Chapter 7). But that's not the story. Instead, the treat was a chance for Nyah to give herself and her daughter a moment of shared happiness together amid their difficult life and, for once, to be the mother that she wanted to be and to be able to say 'yes' to her daughter rather than the usual 'no'.[16] Similarly, in their study of anti-obesity interventions in a poor Australia suburb, sociologists Megan

Warin and Tanya Zivkovic found that outside efforts to encourage sugar reduction were thwarted by their failure to consider the ways in which sugar served as a form of care, both for the self and others, especially when constrained circumstances limited the opportunities for gratification and comfort. Sugar, they observe, 'may be empty calories, but it is not an empty category'.[17]

Telling the hidden-sugar shock story

Within the genre of the hidden-sugar shock story, two categories of food are addressed, each of which requires a differently structured story: first, obviously sugary foods; and second, 'health halo' foods where you might not expect to find sugar. While the formulaic presentations of these two strands are similar, they focus on two related, but distinct, elements of the problem of how hidden sugar gets into our diets, looking at absolute quantities of sugar and cumulative quantities respectively. These are addressed in turn in this section, beginning with coverage of obviously sugary foods.

The unsurprising presence of sugar

In the period covered in this research, hidden-sugar shock stories, primarily instigated by Action on Sugar surveys, covered an array of obviously sugary foods, including fizzy drinks, energy drinks, coffee-shop cakes, chocolate nut spreads, confectionery price promotions, muffins, milkshakes, waffles and festive hot drinks. At first glance, these may seem unlikely targets for stories about hidden sugar, but nevertheless, they dominate the hidden-sugar shock genre. This can be explained, first, by the shock value of the stories, as in the examples in the previous section. This shock comes not from the presence of sugar *per se*, but from its unexpected quantity, making for impactful headlines. As a spokesperson for the Obesity Health Alliance observed in a report in *The Guardian* about a survey of supermarket fizzy drinks: 'It will be no surprise to most people that soft drinks contain a lot of sugar, but it's the sheer amount of sugar that will come as a shock for many [...].'[18] And second, this primary shock is used strategically to draw attention to the unpredictable variation of sugar content within food categories. For Action on Sugar, these examples provide the basis for calls for reformulation – a key plank of its campaigning platform – with lower-sugar versions taken as evidence that even a self-evidently sweetened product could contain less sugar if the manufacturers were sufficiently motivated.

The food survey is a powerful instrument for communicating a crisis of quantity. For example, in 2018, Action on Sugar conducted a survey that reviewed the nutritional information on the packaging for 381 cakes and 481 biscuits sold in nine UK supermarket chains. The survey was published in the open-access journal *British Medical Journal Open*,[19] granting it a gloss of scientific authority. In line with the hidden-sugar shock convention of selecting one product as a worst-case example, the survey (and subsequent press coverage) settled on Battenberg cake – a familiar tea-time confection of chequered pink and yellow sponge squares, held together with jam and wrapped in a layer of marzipan. Among the cakes, Battenberg had the highest levels of sugar (an average of 56.4 g per 100 g), although when evaluated by recommended serving size, it was only seventh highest in terms of sugar content (an average of 19.7 g per serving) and ranked twenty-second when judged by calories per serving.

One of the challenges faced by campaigners and reporters when communicating sugar content is the task of making it legible and impactful for the reader, especially when attempting to give significance to relatively fine-grained differences. For example, the Battenberg cakes in the study included a range of sugar content from 46 g to 62 g (per 100 g of cake) – a difference that would be barely tangible in hand-held weight or even visually as mounds of sugar on a plate. In response to this problem, commentators and campaigners hop between units and scales in search of the most impactful soundbites. For example, in *The Guardian*, nutritionist and Action on Sugar researcher Kawther Hashem observed that a 50 g serving of Battenberg could contain as much as 30 g of sugar.[20] In making this claim, she increased the recommended 30 g serving size cited in the study, elevating the quantity of sugar to match the daily allowance of sugar for an adult. This makes for a more attention-grabbing and legible claim. Elsewhere, the sugar content is presented as a percentage, based on the per 100 g figure. For example, *The Sunday Times* reported Hashem's observation that '[...] some Battenberg cake had 62% sugar but others 46%'.[21]

An alternative strategy is to convert the weight-based figures into teaspoons or sugar cubes – a familiar way to make the quantities more tangible. For example, the *Daily Mail* reported that 'The cakes have up to 15 teaspoons of sugar content per 100g cake portion',[22] tripling the serving size used in the study by treating the 100 g measure (used to standardise across products in the study in the interests of comparison) as a single portion for dramatic effect. This confusing movement between units and scales in the search of legibility recalls anthropologist Emily Yates-Doerr's study of obesity and health in Guatemala, with nutritionists in the weight-loss clinic switching seamlessly between pounds, kilos and body mass index (BMI), leaving patients confused about the significance of the figures.[23]

Where traditional weights and measures, teaspoons and sugar cubes create too much uncertainty or are unable to generate sufficient levels of shock, other foods can be used as comparators. The most common food unit is the can of Coca-Cola – an anti-sugar touchstone which has become emblematic of nutritionally empty, high sugar consumption:

'Natural' food has more sugar than Coca Cola.[24]

More than one third of the drinks tested were found to contain the same – or higher – levels of sugar as a can of Cola.[25]

A sweet and sour chicken meal sold by Marks and Spencer, contained 60 g of sugar – a single can of Coca Cola has 35 g, equivalent to nine teaspoons.[26]

The can of Coca-Cola operates here as a unit of sugar, reflecting the journalistic trick of using something familiar to explain the size of something new. Environmental campaigner Elaine Graham-Leigh cites the examples of describing an oil slick as the size of Wales or using double-decker buses to illustrate the height of a dinosaur.[27] The can of Coca-Cola is the Wales or double-decker bus of the world of anti-sugar, providing a tangible measure of excess that not only quantifies the sugar content in the comparator product but also marks it as equally empty and unnecessary.

The utility of the can of Coke as a point of reference is amplified by the fact that its sugar content marginally exceeds the revised daily allowance of added sugar for adults. As the *Daily Mail* explained in July 2015: 'The new guidelines from the Scientific Advisory Committee on Nutrition mean that men and women should consume no more than seven teaspoons of added sugar a day – equal to less than a single can of Coke.'[28] The comparison provides both a benchmark and a warning that is more legible than grams, percentages or even teaspoons. But the can of Coke is not alone and popular sugary breakfast cereals and chocolate bars provide additional benchmarks against which products containing hidden sugars can be measured:

'Healthy' breakfast biscuits contain more sugar than a bowl of Kellogg's Coco Pops.[29]

[...] some of these quick-and-easy oats breakfasts have more sugar per recommended serving than a bowl of Frosties [...][30]

A 500 g jar of Dolmio original bolognese sauce contains more than 6 cubes of sugar – the same as a Mars Bar.[31]

Chocolate fingers are another popular comparator, with their relatively small individual size allowing for attention-grabbing cumulative totals. For example, in October 2017, following an Action on Sugar survey of meal deals, *The Guardian* reported that two of the surveyed meals contained thirty teaspoons of sugar – 'the same as in 79 chocolate fingers'.[32]

The hidden-sugar shock story, then, mingles units of measurement to produce the desired level of shock, with reports hopping between grams, calories, percentages, spoons, cubes, cans of Coke, doughnuts, bowls of cereal and pieces of confectionery to drive home their message. This runs counter to the presumed precision of nutritional science, and the careful denomination of sugar quantities down to fractions of a gram in the surveys. By discounting the specifics, this imprecision operates rhetorically to communicate the message that the sugar content is both a lot more than you thought and in unhealthy excess. These lessons in sugar literacy and translation, then, are not simply informational, but also carry moral weight, delineating simultaneously what a responsible individual should or shouldn't eat and what they should know to make the right choices.

From the perspective of the hidden-sugar shock stories, it is not only the quantity of sugar that is hidden, but also the variation in sugar content across similar categories of foods. The stories expose this variation to raise awareness of the possibility of lower-sugar choices, even in high-sugar products. But more importantly, it reinforces the campaigning message of the possibility and desirability of product reformulation to bring all similar products in line with the lower-sugar versions. For example, after the cakes and biscuits survey, Action on Sugar's Kawther Hashem wrote a blog post asking, 'Is Battenberg a health risk?'[33] The post responded to criticism that the press coverage of the cakes and biscuits survey had overstated the health risks of the cakes in general, and of Battenberg in particular – a charge which is dismissed and redirected: 'We send our surveys to hundreds of journalists and yes, sometimes the headlines they choose are misguided but unfortunately, that is out of our hands. However, informing consumers that they can find a Battenberg with less sugar and that manufacturing companies should be pressed to make healthier varieties of all foods is not scaremongering.'[34] The dismissal of alarmist reporting is somewhat disingenuous given that the survey's launch on the Action on Sugar website includes a series of quotes warning of the health risks of sugar consumption, including the claim from Katherine Hale of the World Cancer Research Fund that excess sugar consumption 'is a cause of 12 different types of cancer'.[35] The objection that Action on Sugar is scaremongering is quickly set aside to focus on the core messages of the survey: enabling consumers to make lower sugar choices and pressing manufacturers towards reformulation.

Elsewhere in her blog post, Hashem enacts a similar redirection, this time in response to objections about the obvious sugariness of cakes and biscuits:

> Of course, you know a Battenberg contains sugar, you know it is calorific, and you know you should not eat the whole log. However, what you may not know is manufacturers use different recipes. Manufacturing companies are perfectly able to make Battenberg with less sugar or energy (calories) and although lower-sugar and lower-calorie versions are available, companies need to be pressed to produce more varieties that are 'healthier' (but not necessarily healthy).[36]

This claim is repeated in the press release, which uses the example of the Victoria sponges from the survey, which contained sugar ranging from 23.4 g to 59.2 g per 100 g. Hashem cites this as evidence of the possibility of reformulation, arguing that 'if some manufacturers can produce a similar cake with far less sugar or calories so can others'. This possibility was pounced on by *The Guardian*, whose reporting of the story of the 'dangerously sugary' Battenberg included a recipe for a low-sugar version using medjool dates, strawberry coulis or an apricot jam sweetened using only the naturally occurring sugars in the fruit.[37] It is an expensive alternative, the article concedes, 'but remember you are no longer buying Mr Kipling and this homemade Battenberg will be exceedingly better for you'.

The problems with the framing of varying sugar content as evidence of the possibility (and, therefore, necessity) of reformulation are twofold. First, they assume that people don't already distinguish between products within categories. Purchasing is governed not only by cost, but also by preference and occasion – a rich, thickly iced (and more expensive) sponge cake might be selected for a celebratory occasion, while others might be selected for a more mundane treat. This is not to suggest that price and sugar content can be mapped predictably against each other, but rather that in making these choices (where resources allow for choices to be made), consumers already know that those two products are not the same and are balancing multiple factors (taste, cost, richness, sweetness, texture, provenance) accordingly. To argue, therefore, that variety in sugar content across a given category is evidence of the possibility of reformulation is to ignore the fact that those products are more than their sugar content. This not only applies to their material constitution, but also highlights the second problem with the framing of sugar content variety across similar products as evidence of scope for reformulation: their varying social significance.

When the cake and biscuit survey hit the newspapers, the stories were liberally illustrated with pictures of Battenberg cake, prompting in me a powerful taste-memory from childhood, of having tea at my grandmother's house. She would buy 'posh' cakes as a treat, with Battenberg cake (always Mr Kipling's) being an absolute favourite. I always took a deconstructive approach to mine, peeling away the thick strip of marzipan from around the edge to save for last, and then breaking apart the chequered squares and eating them one by one. I rarely had it at any other time and haven't eaten it for decades, but in my memory, it is inextricable from the memories of a loving grandmother, delicious treats and happy days. This signals what is lost when food is evaluated, first, by the presence of a single nutrient, and second, as an assemblage of nutrients. This nutricentric approach erases the irretrievably social nature of food and eating; the meanings that it bears can never be entirely contained in the nutritional information label.

Hiding behind a 'health halo'

Alongside these stories of spectacular quantities of sugar and the unpredictable variability across products, a second strand of hidden-sugar shock stories focuses on less obviously sugary products, with particular attention to products that are either are savoury, and therefore where sugar might not be expected (e.g. soups, ready meals, pasta sauces, salad dressings) or are coded as healthy but which still contain sugar (e.g. baby food, cereals, breakfast biscuits, instant porridge pots, juices and smoothies, and processed fruit snacks). In isolation, these products generally lack the high levels of sugar in a cake or syrupy hot drink and therefore have limited capacity to shock in terms of individual quantities.

As a result, these stories are less newsworthy, which makes it harder for them to be mobilised in the same way. So while the first strand of stories cultivate shock in the quantity of sugar and the variety in sugar content across similar products, these stories focus on the twin shocks of deception and accumulation.

A key target for deception stories is foods that enjoy a 'health halo' that masks sugar content. Fruit-based products such as juices, smoothies, processed fruit snacks and cereal bars, all of which are easily marketed as healthy, are prime targets for hidden-sugar shock deception exposés. For example, in September 2020, Action on Sugar launched a survey of processed fruit snacks.[38] The survey follows the familiar pattern of opening with 'shock' facts, announcing that '65% of the products had the equivalent of 2 teaspoons of sugars or more in just one single portion – just the same as eating an iced doughnut.' However, the sugar content of these products is relatively unspectacular, and two teaspoons, while perhaps unexpected, lacks the headline-grabbing impact of a twenty-five-teaspoon coffee-shop drink. So instead, deception is placed at the heart of the story; as the press release notes, the snacks are 'loaded with sugar and misleading claims'. Katharine Jenner, Action on Sugar's campaign director, elaborates on this theme in the release saying: '[…] manufacturers are hiding behind 'health halos' of messages such as "*with real fruit*" and "*no added sugar*" [sic] to obscure the fact that processed fruit-based snacks are as unhealthy as sweets and sugary drinks'.[39]

Here, the deception of hidden sugar is framed explicitly as an act of bad faith, not only with sugar sneaked into foods under the cover of health claims, but also with nutritional information hidden away on the back-of-pack labels. For example, Marie Farmer, founder of the Mini Meals app for monitoring children's nutrition, voices this sense of betrayal in the press release:

> Claims like *no added sugar, all natural ingredients, this is high in fibre etc* [sic] are all parents have time to focus on before they make a decision to buy those products. When this is brought to their attention, most parents are shocked and feel some brands have abused the trust they've given them and many vow to change their shopping habits.[40]

The accusation of underhandedness and abuse of trust makes for a much better story than the relatively small amounts of sugar involved, with manufacturers positioned as the primary targets of this anti-sugar ire. For example, a 2013 article in *The Sunday Times* described sugar as being 'sneaked into savoury foods including bread, pasta sauces and even bacon by manufacturers to make them tastier'.[41] The same paper in January 2014, in the first of a series of articles on how to give up sugar, cites popular anti-sugar author Robert Lustig as charging the food industry with having 'contaminated the food supply with added sugar', noting that '[of] the 600,000 food items in American grocery stores, 80% have been spiked with sugar'.[42]

In these accounts, sugar is never just 'added', but is sneaked underhandedly into food; sugar is not simply invisible but is actively hidden in bad faith. The use of 'contamination' locates the addition of sugar within a long history of nefarious food adulteration for profit,[43] and the verb 'spiked' directly invokes not only illicit drugs but also their non-consenting consumption. In the 'health halo' stories, then, sugar is not so much in excess as entirely out of place, doing double damage by adding to accumulating dietary sugar and doing so dishonestly. As journalist Louise Carpenter remarks in a 2014 article in *The Observer* about her attempts to reduce her family's sugar consumption: 'I'm working out that I resent hidden sugars more than the obvious sugars. In other words, yoghurts, sauces and cereals are worse than biscuits for me because I consciously choose to allow the biscuits in moderation.'[44]

Not being duped requires a consumer to become a sugar detective who is able scour out hidden sugar, even when it is hiding in plain sight. For example, long lists of different names for sugar are a regular feature of the newspaper reporting, with readers urged to commit them to memory so as not to be fooled by sugar in disguise:

> Even though it is a long list, it is important that you educate yourself with the vocabulary, much of which is made to sound healthy, organic and pure. The most common terms are: barley malt syrup, beet sugar, brown rice syrup, cane crystals, coconut sugar, corn sweetener, corn syrup, crystalline fructose, dextrin, evaporated cane juice, fruit juice concentrate, fruit purée, fruit

pulp, agave, molasses, organic evaporated cane juice, palm sugar, raw sugar, saccharose, sorghum, treacle, turbinado sugar and xylose.[45]

These lists serve as a warning not only against sugar that might not be recognised as such, but also against the potential manipulation of labelling conventions to disguise the total sugar in each product: 'the industry hides the sugar well. There are 56 different names for sugar: by choosing different sugars on the fifth, sixth, seventh and eighth ingredients, sugar can rapidly add up to being the dominant ingredient.'[46] The nefarious practices of the food industry are framed here as actively obstructing the work of making informed food choices, requiring constant consumer vigilance.

But the manufacturers are not the only culprits here, and the nefariousness of this deceptive sweetening is also attributed to sugar itself, which is transformed into a malevolent actor. For example, in 2015, *The Guardian*'s Sam Wollaston warned that 'sugar gets inside us, deviously, stealthily'.[47] Sugar is portrayed not simply as being added or sneaked into everyday foods by manufacturers, but as stealthily creeping. It is a 'dietary villain'[48] and 'a bastard';[49] it is the 'Lex Luther' of the dietary story.[50] Like testosterone in Jordan-Young and Karkazis' research, it is a 'wilful character' that is 'at once a specific molecule and mercurial cultural figure'.[51]

The anthropomorphising of sugar is nothing new. For example, in 1949, Tate & Lyle created the popular mascot Mr Cube as part of their campaign against Labour plans to nationalise the sugar industry, placing him on sugar packaging, ration cards and delivery trucks.[52] Mr Cube also made an appearance at the Ideal Home Exhibition in 1950 in animatronic form, answering visitors' questions. Tate & Lyle 'sugar girl' Ethel Alleyne recalled watching a staged encounter between a fifteen-year-old factory employee, Daphne Tarsey (selected for the role from the factory's amateur dramatics society), and Mr Cube, who assured her that 'in moderation sugar can actually aid slimming'.[53] The demonisation of sugar would make such a figure impossible in the current moment, and the work of marketing sugary products, and most notably breakfast cereals, is left to cartoon animals such as Sugar Puffs' Tony the Tiger and the Coco Pops monkey, both of whom are firmly in the anti-sugar-regulatory firing line. Instead, like the marauding sugar cubes in the Change4Life animation, it takes treacherous form.

Where sugar is seen as both hidden and hiding, food itself is rendered dishonest. As in the press release about the fruit snacks, it is made up of both sugar and misleading claims. This shores up the moral as well as the physiological perils of sugar; it simply cannot be trusted. Celebrity chef Jamie Oliver made this explicit in a 2018 article in *The Guardian* about his food campaigning:

> People want to get it wrong – I do too – I want to eat cake, they want to have a burger but in a way, Coke and burgers are the most honest food you've had in the last 40 years; they've never lied to you. But when you go down the cereal aisle and it should really be called the cake aisle, that's what has changed in the last 40 years.[54]

Oliver's acknowledgement of the shared desire to eat food commonly coded as unhealthy shores up his 'man of the people' brand while simultaneously reminding readers that 'getting it wrong' is understandable … but still wrong. He nods nostalgically to an arbitrarily designated better time when food was honest, whereas now, even staples like cereal cannot be trusted; it is the foods themselves that perpetrate the lie. He also locates himself firmly within the domain not only of nutritionism, whereby food is the sum of its nutritional parts, but also of mono-nutritionism, evaluating food entirely on the basis of sugar content. It makes sense to categorise cereal as cake only if the only point of comparison is a single shared ingredient: sugar.

Deception is only one part of this second strand of hidden-sugar shock stories. As has already been mentioned, however unexpected sugar may be in foods sheltering under a 'health halo', the individual quantities are relatively small. As a result, they lack the shock value that attaches more easily to obviously sugar-laden foods like cakes. So instead, this second strand of stories focuses on the shock of accumulated dietary sugar – the hazards of a little bit here and a little bit there throughout the day, leading to an unseen accumulation. Surveys of single foods are unable to communicate the threat of accumulation effectively, and therefore a different device is required to get the message across: the food diary, or in its most common form, the 'mortified mother' narrative. These stories constitute another newspaper staple, particularly in the tabloid press, which tends towards stories about individuals and their behaviours alongside lists of everyday foods as a means of connecting with readers.[55] These stories focus not on specific foods, but rather on patterns of consumption, usually in a heteronormative nuclear familial setting involving both adults and children. Like the survey stories, they follow a predictable format: a family member (usually the mother) records the food consumption of individual family members – sometimes just the children, sometimes adults and children – and this is then evaluated by a nutritionist or dietician, who brings expertise to bear on their efforts and provides corrective advice.

The shock of the stories lies in the accumulated sugar totals, usually despite the mothers' best intentions. For example, in 2015, journalist Antonia Hoyle calculated her family's sugar consumption for an article in *The Mail on Sunday*, leading to the shock-filled headline: 'My "healthy" family are eating the equivalent of 215 Krispy Kreme doughnuts every WEEK!'[56] Hoyle enters into the diary project with confidence that there wouldn't be much cause for concern, noting, 'we aren't big on junk food and the children are young enough that we are able to limit their intake'. But nutritionist and low-carb advocate Zoë Harcombe quickly sets about dislodging the 'healthy halo' of the family's everyday foods, including the children's snacks of dried fruit ('raisins have more sugar than a Kitkat') and Hoyle's use of ready-made sauces ('avoid things with labels altogether'). She finally zeroes in on the children's yoghurt and fruit purée snack pots, declaring uncompromisingly: 'This snacking nonsense should stop. I have a saying – unless you are a cow, or want to be the size of one, stop grazing.'[57]

But despite this fat-shaming outburst, and while these mortified mother stories are designed to cultivate maternal guilt and shame to drive behaviour change, this is very different from the familiar right-wing tabloid shaming of abjected Others such as migrants or (so-called) benefit cheats (see Chapter 7). Instead, the mortified mothers are a cautionary tale; they are sympathetic everywomen who have naively fallen into the hidden-sugar trap despite their best intentions. For example, when Change4Life launched its 'Sugar Smart' campaign in 2016, singer and TV presenter Jamelia was recruited as the campaign's public face, bringing the glamour of celebrity along with a down-to-earth maternal concern about sugar. In a short film introducing the new Sugar Smart app, she tells the viewers that 'as a mum myself, I'm worried and would like to learn more', before being talked by nutritionist Amanda Ursell through an array of everyday foods, each with a small stack of sugar cubes next to it marking out the hidden sugar. She picks up a split-pot yoghurt and uses the app to scan its barcode; a graphic of five and half sugar cubes appears on the screen and she gasps in surprise.[58] In an article by Ursell in *The Sun* a month after the campaign was launched, Jamelia described using the app to calculate her children's sugar consumption after her ten-year-old daughter had to have a dental filling. In the spirit of the mortified mother story, her shame at her children's high sugar intake is absolved by a commitment to root out sugar that was 'lurking in the most unlikely places', swapping sweetened yoghurt for plain and soda for fizzy water with sugar-free squash. But she adds quickly that she's not trying to make people feel bad by getting involved with the campaign: 'I know it's not easy. I'm saying, "Hands up. I got it wrong" – even though I thought I was on the right track.'[59] It is an understandable error, and once corrected, a forgivable one given the sneakiness of hidden sugar.

Alongside the guilt and shame, the stories are run through with disappointment and betrayal at the deception perpetrated against them. For example, a 2017 article in *The Sun* evaluated the weekly family food diary of a mother of three, Donna, who prides herself on feeding her family a healthy diet, with lots of fruit and vegetables.[60] She batch-cooks meals 'such as casseroles using jarred sauces' to freeze, and the family sometimes has 'old-fashioned fruity puds like crumble from the supermarket freezer section'. However, nutritional therapist Claudia Le Feuvre soon disillusions her, and Donna articulates a keen sense of betrayal in the thwarting of her efforts to feed her family well:

> I had no idea there was so much hidden sugar in jars of vegetable sauces or cereals. I also feel duped that the cereal bars, which are aimed at kids and plastered with labels about being full of nutrients, are secretly loaded with sugar too. For years I've trusted big brand names without realising the potential harm they're doing to the people I love most.[61]

Her sense of betrayal echoes Jamie's Oliver's nostalgia for a more innocent time when both food and food providers could be trusted. The 'old-fashioned' style of her family's weekend pudding or the nutrient-filled boasts of the sauces and cereal bars offer no protection from the harms of the 'big brand names', who are no longer deserving of her misplaced trust.

This recalibration of the relationship with familiar brands from one of trust to suspicion is central to the project of becoming of what Change4Life calls being 'Sugar Smart'. In a 2017 feature in *The Guardian* about the sugar content of breakfast cereals, Robert Lustig expressed this imperative with an uncompromising invocation of personal (parental) responsibility, insisting: 'Don't let your child be a loser by succumbing to corporate interests. Make sure they eat a real breakfast of champions.'[62] The loss here is not simply the inadvertent consumption of potentially health-damaging sugar – what Lustig refers to in the article as 'the alcohol of the child' – but also being duped into it. Just as Antonia Hoyle is described as having fallen for the 'healthy snacks trap', being fooled is seen as a failure in itself. Good bio-citizenship is not only about eating a low-sugar diet, but also about never lowering your guard and being tricked.

Guardian journalist Louise Carpenter is similarly emphatic in the conclusion of her article about her experimental sugar-free month: 'I don't believe that the levels of sugar my children eat compromise their health. They are fit and slim. But I'm not prepared to be hoodwinked by products stuffed with hidden sugars.'[63] She uses a virtue discourse of successful parenting to distance herself from the failed, nutritionally irresponsible Other, but regardless of her apparent success in raising 'fit and slim' children, being 'hoodwinked' remains incompatible with responsible motherhood. This understanding leads her to privilege being 'sugar-aware' – a vigilant condition of constant watchfulness – over being sugar-free in the article's conclusion. In Lustig's terms, only losers fall for industry smoke and mirrors, and the consequences are simultaneously impaired health, prospect-damaging gullibility and the loss of competitive edge in a world where we make our own luck (and that of our children).

Clashing advice

It is easy to think of these life lessons around sugar as both ubiquitous and relentless. Reaching far beyond the most obvious pedagogical settings of the school and the clinic, the requirement to manage sugar consumption and the tools for doing so are widely dispersed across multiple informational and practical sites; demands to root out sugar, and particularly sugar in its morally perilous hidden form, seem both everywhere and incontestable. But a closer look exposes the cracks in the constructed certainties and simplicities of tracking down hidden sugar. In particular, this section addresses the points of fracture that occur when advice about sugar clashes with other mainstream health advice, disrupting its taken-for-grantedness. I illustrate this point using two examples: firstly, clashes between different strands of food advice; and secondly, the tension between advice focusing specifically on sugar and wider pedagogies of health and family life.

One of the unacknowledged assumptions about dietary sugar is that while it might be tricky to root out, we know what sugar is and the problems that it causes. However, as discussed in the opening chapters of this book, there is very little consensus about what we are looking for when we go hunting for hidden sugar. The most common target is 'added sugar' or 'free sugars' – what the Scientific Advisory Committee on Nutrition (SACN), following the definition given by the World Health Organization (WHO), described as sugars 'added to foods and beverages by the manufacturer, cook or consumer, and sugars naturally present in honey, syrups, fruit juices and fruit juice concentrates'.[64] Intrinsic sugars – that is, those commonly found in fruits and vegetables – are excluded from regulation. However, fruit has experienced dramatically changing fortunes in the rush to target sugar and emerges as a point of confusion and contestation. For example, the fruit smoothie – a product which has conventionally enjoyed a 'health halo' – is a frequently mentioned site of hidden sugar, and in a 2014 survey of children's juices and smoothies, Action on Sugar declared that many smoothies have at least as much sugar per equivalent serving as a can of Coca-Cola.[65]

But the advice on fruit is unclear and inconsistent. For example, popular anti-sugar advocate David Gillespie was cited in *The Sunday Times* in 2014 as recommending 'kiwis, apples, grapefruit, blackberries, pears, strawberries, blueberries, raspberries and lemons', but not 'bananas, watermelon, pineapple, mangoes, papaya and grapes'.[66] Conversely, in *The Times* in 2015, Robert Lustig advised people to 'Eat all the fruit you want', before adding the proviso that grapes should be avoided as they are 'just little bags of sugar'.[67] In her 2014 article about reducing her family's sugar consumption, Louise Carpenter expresses her frustration at being unable to get a straight answer about fruit from multiple experts. In the end, she compromises and removes fruit from her own diet but continues to give it to her children, reasoning that 'the children are small and I'm not prepared to experiment with them in the way I can myself'.[68] In a similar family experiment, journalist Anna Maxted also decides to continue giving her children fruit, on the grounds that 'they're not waddling 55 year olds, but growing kids'.[69] This struggle constitutes a clash of food advice, with prohibitions against sugar running up against the familiar injunction to eat five portions of fruit and vegetables a day, which is too entrenched for the women to relinquish.

This confusion also extends to carbohydrates more generally, reflecting the rise of the low-carbohydrate diet trend. For example, Zöe Harcombe warns Antonia Hoyle that not all vegetables are equal, arguing that 'the starchy ones such as carrots, parsnips and beetroot are much higher in sugar' and therefore should be eaten more judiciously.[70] In the same vein, in May 2017, the *Daily Mail* ran a hidden-sugar shock survey story under the headline '"Healthy" vegetable crisps contain the equivalent of EIGHT teaspoons of sugar – more than in six chocolate digestives.'[71] The article explains how they are 'packed with beetroot, carrots, parsnips and sweet potato', which are 'rich in natural sugars'. Vegetables, generally seen as sitting outside sugar's risk categories, are now introduced as problematic, further muddying the waters and pushing against the aspired-for simplicity of the sugar reduction message.

These category confusions recall the struggles documented by Emily Yates-Doerr in her ethnography of obesity interventions in Guatemala. She describes the work of instructors who try to teach local women to organise foods according to category: healthy, middle, unhealthy. The exercise encourages the women to evaluate the foods only in terms of health as bestowed by nutrients, but the foods resist easy placement.[72] Where, for example, should a food low in fat but high in sugar be located? Similarly, while fruit was categorised as 'good' by the instructors, the women refused the blanket approval, pointing out that fruit bought from street stalls might be contaminated with exhaust fumes or chopped with an unclean knife, while they could be confident that the sealed bags of crisps they could buy from the same stalls would pacify their children's hunger without making them sick. For others, when a food categorised by instructors as unhealthy had been prepared lovingly by someone else, refusing it was inconceivable. Yates-Doerr argues that the black box of the nutrient erases the complexities that lie behind the certainties of nutritional knowledge, which are treated as stable and universal. However, for all the attempts to keep nutritional messages simple, those nutrients transform across contexts, and complexity intervenes regardless. In this way, we can see that the confident certainties of rooting out hidden sugar cannot contain either complexity of nutrition or the irrepressible sociality of food.

A second point of tension can be seen in relation to two competing injunctions: that we should constantly monitor and regulate our sugar consumption, and that we shouldn't become obsessed and inflexible about food. The fine line between ordered and disordered eating, especially for women, has been well documented in the feminist literature,[73] but this takes on particular salience in relation to children, opening up new avenues for mother-blaming. For example, in her experiments with sugar reduction, journalist Anna Maxted, frustrated at the confusing messages she was receiving about sugar and fruit, expostulated: 'I refuse to dissuade [my children] from eating bananas. Even sugar is healthier than neuroticism around food.'[74] This tension is made explicit in another of the mortified mother stories, billed as an opportunity for 'Three mums to find out how [sugar] savvy they are' and examining the food diaries of three families.[75] Earlier in this chapter, we met one of the mums, Donna, who expressed her disillusionment at the treachery of trusted brands selling traditionally styled food. The final case in the article focuses on a mother of two and family therapist, Zariya. Unusually, nutritional therapist Claudia can barely find fault with the family's diet, which is packed with fresh fruit and vegetables, and includes hardly any added sugar or processed foods. However, Zariya's successes have revealed new opportunities for maternal failure, and Claudia warns: 'It's worth remembering that we do need sugar for energy, so we shouldn't cut it out completely [...] The other thing Zariya should be aware of is being too strict or food-focused, as it can make some kids rebel or lead to eating disorders.'[76] Zariya takes the warning to heart, conceding: 'While I'm aware we eat very healthily, I think Claudia might have a point about being too strict in case it makes my children crave things. I'd hate for it to become an issue, so I'll make sure they still get the odd sweet treat every now and then.'[77] This highlights the tension that runs through dietary advice in general and advice about sugar in particular: that we should meet the moral requirement to maintain rigorous and detailed scrutiny over our sugar consumption while avoiding being 'too strict' and creating collateral problems of health and wellbeing. The tension is created by the centralising of (hidden) sugar as the primary problem to be solved, and as in relation to so many food-related questions, the circle is squared by maternal labour. It is Zariya who absorbs the intense moral and practical demands of sugar reduction in order to create a 'balanced' environment for others.

Conclusion

Against the background of the cultivated certainty that sugar is a bad thing, this chapter has explored the ways in which sugar is represented not simply as a dietary enemy, but also as a dangerously elusive one, lurking in everyday foods and trapping the unwary into inadvertent (over)consumption. It is an animated foe, actively creeping into the food supply and abetted by a food industry that has betrayed consumer trust. Journalistic devices such as the hidden-sugar shock story, the food diary and its sub-genre, the mortified mother story, communicate life lessons that not only share techniques for spotting hidden sugar but also reproduce the moral imperative to do so. The hidden-sugar shock story, then, is a virtue discourse *par excellence*, providing a means of demarcating the good citizen from the failed one. The sympathetic reception given to the mortified mothers in the stories reminds us that being tricked in the first instance is not the site of failure, especially given sugar's deviousness; instead, failure lies in not remedying the situation once the nefariousness of hidden sugar has been made clear. But this also raises new tensions as categories of food clash and the healthy/unhealthy binary divisions fracture under the shifting realities of everyday consumption, the sociality of food and the need to walk the fine line between vigilance and giving way to dangerous obsession and inflexibility. The navigation of these tensions is taken up in the next chapter, which looks at book-length self-help manuals which establish the work of giving up sugar not simply as a normative investment in health but also as an act of self-making.

4

Giving up sugar

This will not be fun at first. But starting is half the battle. Hold the line. There is no moderation. You have stopped poisoning yourself. If you can just get past the next few weeks of danger, you will enjoy the health sugar has sucked from your life to date. Then, all of a sudden, your desire for sugar will vanish. I know it will sound strange, but it just goes. Bang![1]

In the previous chapter, I explored sugar's designation as hidden and the ways in which the hidden-sugar shock news story functions as a tool for establishing not only the skills for rooting out hidden sugar but also the moral obligations to do so. But these news stories are just a beginning. They are a powerful source of attention-grabbing headlines designed to shock readers into awareness and action, providing a bridge between detailed accounts of the problem of sugar (as in the first two chapters) and what the implications might be for individual consumers. But the necessary brevity of the medium prevents the more detailed elaboration of the process of giving up sugar and the work that it entails. A burgeoning genre of self-help texts steps into this breach, offering to guide readers expertly through the why and the how of relinquishing sugar. As in the extract above from David Gillespie's *The Sweet Poison Quit Plan*, they promise an alluring prize for those prepared to 'hold the line': not simply a health-giving sugar-free diet, but also the spectacular and transformative end of the desire for sugar ('Bang!'). The readiness to do the work of giving up sugar (or in the lexicon of the self-help genre, to liberate yourself from it) becomes a marker of the disciplined individual who is willing and able to take control of their life and body and who can't be seduced by false pleasures. Giving up sugar, then, is never only a form of dietary change, but also becomes of means of establishing who we are.

This chapter explores this by focusing on nine self-help texts, which were all either cited in the news coverage, among the most popular and reviewed texts in online bookstores or prominently displayed on the shelves of large bookshops. As such, they should be seen as exemplars from a crowded field rather than a definitive account of the genre. To contain the sample, I have focused on texts that both set out a rationale for the sugar-free lifestyle they are advocating and offer advice on how to achieve that dietary change. While most of the texts selected include recipes, they are not primarily recipe books, which I chose to exclude in order to keep the focus on the ways in which sugar (and giving it up) is explained. At the same time, the texts addressed here are different from those discussed in Chapter 1, which articulate in detail the problems of sugar and why it should be relinquished but without any sustained attention to the how. And finally, I have excluded dietary self-help books where giving up sugar is incidental to a broader 'healthy eating' regimen.

The analysis looks at the sugar talk that makes up the texts, exploring how authors represent sugar consumption and their advice for giving it up, and asking what those texts can tell us about the wider social world in which they come to make sense. As a result, what follows in this chapter cannot speak to the ways in which these books are received or used by readers, since, as with all health and wellness advice, we can never know in advance how those representations are worked out on the ground. For example, sociologist Paul Lichterman warns that content-based studies of the self-help genre risk assuming a passive audience whose behaviours are governed by the ideologies of individual responsibility that characterise the texts. Instead, his study of readers of self-help psychology texts showed that they interacted 'thinly' with the material, engaging sporadically and without retaining enduring insights.[2] Other studies have shown that readers piece together useful insights from multiple texts rather than investing loyally in a single one.[3] Consequently, I cannot know how the books examined here are used by their readers, and just as people accumulate recipe books into which they dip rather than working through them systematically, it is plausible that these texts too are appropriated thinly. This is a project for another day. But for now, I begin from the understanding the books reflect and reproduce the ideologies and assumptions of the wider social world in which they make sense as a genre. Thus while they may not determine behaviour, they allow us to see the socially approved pathways to the 'good' body and, by extension, the possibilities for failure, which readers then must navigate.

After a brief introduction to the nine books under discussion, the chapter introduces one of the most common claims across the genre: that what they are advocating is categorically not a diet. The next section explores the ways in which giving up sugar is portrayed as an act of liberation that simultaneously frees the individual from the grip of sugar and restores them to an imagined clean slate that is left when the tide of sugar recedes. Focusing on the familiar self-help device of 'the challenge', this section explores the work of relinquishing sugar, including both practical steps to create and maintain a sugar-free environment and the ongoing work on the self that is required to execute those changes successfully and sustainably. The final section considers how the everyday work of going sugar-free is cast as effortless and pleasurable in ways which discount both the ongoing burdens of additional labour that the process generates and the uneven distribution of that labour. The chapter concludes that the 'giving up sugar' self-help genre rests upon a fantasy of the ideal neoliberal subject, who, free from social, economic and cultural constraints, rises to a challenge, takes control of their appetite and body, postpones pleasure and takes responsibility for their own health and wellbeing.

Giving up sugar in the world of self-help

All the texts address here take sugar as their core focus (they all have 'sugar' in the title or subtitle) and are primarily oriented to facilitating its removal from readers' diets. However, they cover a range of styles, formats and focus. Elsa Jones' *Goodbye Sugar* and Sarah Wilson's *I Quit Sugar* are both beautifully presented, glossy texts in soft colours, including carefully lit, aspirational photographs of the authors on their covers, and in Wilson's case, throughout the book.[4] Both books fall within the feminised 'wellness' genre, advocating 'a kind of luminous good health and preternatural vitality'.[5] The subtitle to Jones' book, for example, promises 'weight loss, great skin, more energy and improved mood'. Dan DeFigio's *Beating Sugar Addiction for Dummies* is equally invested in the rhetorics of wellness ('clean', 'mindful'), but in contrast to the softly and glossily styled books by Jones and Wilson, it follows the style and format of the *For Dummies* brand, with a bold black and yellow cover and a text composed of short, punchy paragraphs interspersed with inset boxes, tick lists and thematised icons ('warning', 'remember', 'tip').[6] DeFigio's book is the least sugar-focused of all the books, and his advice about giving up sugar is heavily embedded in more generic diet, exercise and lifestyle advice.

Paul McKenna's *Get Control of Sugar Now!* and Allen Carr's *Good Sugar, Bad Sugar* both offer a systematic programme for giving up sugar, insisting that the books are read from cover to cover without skipping any sections or exercises.[7] For each author, the focus on sugar is one among many problems to which their system has been applied. Carr, for example, is best known for his trademarked 'Easyway' method of smoking cessation, which he has also applied to alcohol, gambling, drugs, technology, debt, caffeine, vaping, fear of flying and weight loss,[8] while McKenna has applied his hypnotherapeutic approach to a variety of aspirational goals, including charisma, wealth, weight loss, confidence, happiness, intelligence, mending a broken heart and even an improved golf game.[9] The two books maintain a steady focus on techniques for giving up sugar and unlike most dietary self-help books, do not provide recipes. As such, they are not offering a dietary system or regimen (although Carr makes unelaborated calls for an ill-specified diet of fruit, vegetables and nuts and seeds), but rather a 'closed system' for self-management and control that is seen as complete in itself.[10]

Both David Gillespie's *The Sweet Poison Quit Plan* and *Sugarproof* by Michael Goran and Emily Ventura offer more textually dense accounts than the previous books, presenting detailed explanations of the risks posed by sugar and the process of quitting.[11] For Gillespie, this is done through the lens of addiction, while Goran and Ventura focus on children, whom they describe as 'uniquely vulnerable' to the dangers of sugar.[12] The authors locate themselves firmly as scientifically literate experts – Gillespie as an autodidact lawyer and seeker of scientific truths (as we saw in Chapter 1 in relation to his first book, *Sweet Poison*) and Goran and Ventura as a paediatrician and expert in nutrition education respectively. While all the books addressed here articulate the problem of sugar to some extent, these two do so most substantially and in the greatest detail. For example, the first 136 pages of *Sugarproof* are dedicated to demonstrating the harms of sugar on children. For Gillespie, the first forty-two pages of his book are dedicated to explaining sugar addiction and its health consequences, which he sees as a motivating precursor to quitting, promising: 'Once I've convinced you that sugar will make you fat, give you diabetes, clog your arteries and give you Alzheimer's disease (to name just a few of its delights), I will show you exactly how to break your addiction.'[13] In these books, the catastrophic potential of continuing to eat sugar is a far stronger motivator than the pleasures to be derived from stopping that dominate more wellness- oriented texts.

The final pair of texts – Nicole Mowbray's *Sweet Nothing* and Eve Schaub's *Year of No Sugar* – are both first-person narratives of experimental sugar abstention.[14] These exemplify the 'my year of …' memoir genre, and the authors light-heartedly document the motivations, struggles and triumphs of their abstentions to entertaining, but always didactic, effect. The texts include sugar-free recipes, shopping tips and lifestyle strategies, and conclude by passing along the lessons learned from the period of experimentation, which the reader is intended to use to inform their own transition to sugar-free living. This instructive mission is made evident in the subtitle to Mowbray's book – *Why I Gave Up Sugar and How You Can Too* – locating the books firmly within the self-help genre, even as memoirs. They are not alone in drawing on personal experience, and both Wilson and Gillespie feature their own stories of initial experimentation (followed by revelation and conversion) in their books, giving first-person authenticity to their claims through the confessional modes common to the self-help genre.[15] However, for Wilson and Gillespie, these confessions provide a jumping-off point for the instructional substance, while for both Mowbray and Schaub, the experimental narrative is the instructional substance. Furthermore, they not only position themselves outside conventional scientific authority (as journalists, as women) but actively take pride in it, making only passing efforts to grasp, translate or align themselves with nutritional science. Instead, their authority comes from their everywoman status and their accumulated experiential knowledge. For example, Mowbray describes herself in *Sweet Nothing* as 'a normal woman in my early thirties',[16] concluding the book with the final evangelical sentence: 'If I can do this, anyone can.'[17]

'This is not a diet'

One of the most consistent claims across the texts is the insistence that 'this is not a diet'. For example, in relation to their seven-day sugar-free challenge, Goran and Ventura declare: 'This is not a diet, it's a nutritional challenge …';[18] and Gillespie describes *The Sweet Poison Quit Plan* as an 'anti-diet book'. This rejection of dieting should not be confused with rejection of weight loss as a goal or practice, and the books are still firmly embedded in the wrongness of the fat body as a site of sugar-fuelled ill-health, systemic dysregulation, mortification and unfulfilled potential. For example, Mowbray 'hates diets' but still promises a way 'to quickly and easily make yourself look younger and slimmer',[19] and McKenna warns that 'diets are a con' and 'a recipe for disaster' while still railing against 'the global obesity epidemic'.[20] His disgust at fatness reveals itself in his encouragement to readers to boost their defences against advertising by imagining the characters of fast foods ads as obese, explaining with undisguised contempt for the fat body: 'The picture always lies: beautiful, thin people don't eat garbage.'[21]

For others, fat bodies serve as figures of pity and as the cautionary tales of anti-sugar evangelism. Schaub, for example, describes an encounter in a hospital cafeteria, where a 'heavy set' couple were sharing a meal of salad, bread sticks, diet drinks and pie. She recalled, 'I idly wondered if perhaps one of them suffered from one of the many variants of metabolic syndrome, and if so, if anyone would ever offer the suggestion that they might be healthier forgoing the salad with dressing in favour of the pot roast and mashed potatoes.'[22] Schaub confirms the observation by Australian sociologist Sam Murray that 'we read a fat body on the street and believe we "know" its "truth"',[23] confidently speculating on the health status of the couple and their motivations for their food choices. She longs to intervene to correct what she presumes to be their ignorance about the sugar that 'was freakin' *everywhere* [sic] on their tray'. This betrays a knowing sense of superiority that the books actively cultivate. For example, in a section on having 'the right attitude', Gillespie argues that rather than feeling deprived without sugar, readers should 'take pity on the poor, hopeless addicts who are all around you ingesting poison'.[24] McKenna offers an even more triumphalist account, congratulating those who have got to the end of the journal exercise that structures his programme and noting: 'Sadly, there will be a few people who did not make it [...] You did! This is what separates you from the rest. You are a winner.'[25] This reflects a wider textual separation between the 'we' of those who are compliant with the programmes – a club into which the readers are invited – and the non-compliant, failed Other whose fatness and out-of-control appetites will always give them away.

The claim that 'this is not a diet', then, is never a rejection of weight loss itself or an acceptance of fatness, and even though they are intended to mark a radical departure from the mainstream weight loss industry, these declarations end up being its perfect echo. For example, the Slimming World website invites potential customers to 'discover a world of weight loss without dieting'.[26] Instead, the insistence that 'this is not a diet' distances the authors from a style of weight management that is characterised by unsustainable restrictions driven by oppressive and superficial aesthetic ideals. The tired format of 'the diet', we are told, has failed, and in its place the books offer up a prescription that sits at the heart of neoliberal consumer culture: that people (and particularly women) should simultaneously exercise bodily discipline and restraint and engage in (expert-informed) consumption.[27] This claim that the books offer a positive alternative to dieting rests on two key discourses: (1) keeping it simple; and (2) doing it for health.

Keeping it simple

The unsustainable complexity of conventional diets is a common point of reference, with authors boasting of programmes 'without gimmicks or special 'diets'';[28] of not having 'to count points or calories';[29] and of incorporating 'no shakes, no pills, no off-limits food groups'.[30] Gillespie, for example, claims that *The Sweet Poison Quit Plan* 'is not a diet book with simple presumptions and complex rules; it is an anti-diet book with detailed evidence but simple rules'.[31] The simplicity of the task is encapsulated in his single 'super rule': 'Don't eat sugar.'[32] Mowbray offers a similarly simple solution for tackling obesity through sugar reduction: 'It's actually very easy. We just stop buying products with sugar in them.'[33] This appeal to simplicity is shored up with bullet-pointed and numbered lists of rules or steps which simultaneously invoke obedience and autonomous choice. In an echo of the twelve steps of recovery programmes like Alcoholics Anonymous, and in line with his heavily structured self-management system, Carr's plan consists of twelve key instructions, the first of which is to 'follow all the instructions'. A further three of the twelve take up this theme, admonishing readers to ignore any advice that goes against the book's instructions, advice from anyone claiming to have quit by willpower and any advice that conflicts with the system being offered in his book.[34]

In many cases, the rules or steps are difficult to distinguish from the generic dietary advice that they emphatically distance themselves from. For example, Jones offers 'five golden rules' in support of her '10-Day Sugar Challenge':

1. Stick to the foods listed on the plan.
2. Include a portion of protein with every meal and snack.
3. Get the balance right at mealtimes.
4. Eat every two or three hours.
5. Limit stimulants and alcohol.[35]

Similarly generic advice runs throughout the books, including only eating when hungry, getting enough sleep, drinking lots of water, exercise, eating 'real' food and avoiding simple carbohydrates. Most lists also include some form of attitudinal or emotional management instruction. For example, Gillespie's first rule is 'Have the right attitude';[36] DeFigio instructs readers to 'Stay mindful' and 'Avoid boredom';[37] and Carr insists that readers 'Keep an open mind' and 'Never doubt your decision to quit.'[38] While the lists vary in tone and detail, the substance across them shares considerable common ground, not only within the genre but also in the wider world of body (and especially weight) management. This is evident in the appeals to simplicity that are a mainstay of the mainstream weight loss industry; the Slimming World website, for example, boasts a programme that includes 'no weighing no measuring and no counting calories'.[39] This reflects the nature of self-help books more generally, which position themselves as offering a uniquely effective path to problem resolution or self-transformation while relying on repetitively and unimaginatively similar advice that fails to generate new ways of talking or thinking about the problem at hand.[40]

This enticing simplicity is deceptive and begins to fall apart even with the definition of sugar itself, which always requires explanation. In some cases, what counts as sugar is deliberately loosely defined through an appeal to common-sense understandings of what constitutes 'healthy eating'. For example, in the introduction to *Beating Sugar Addiction for Dummies*, DeFigio asks 'the chemistry geeks to forgive me as I use the word *sugar* [sic] in more conventional terms, referring to junk food and processed sweeteners'.[41] For Goran and Ventura, added sugar is the focus of their abstention challenge, including any sugar or sweeteners added to home cooking or packaged foods, as well as artificial sweeteners and fruit juices; for Jones, it is foods with a high glycaemic index; and for Gillespie, the exclusionary focus is specifically on fructose. The books also struggle to draw boundaries around hard-to-categorise foods such as fruit (as discussed in the previous chapter), or alcohol, which frequently figures as a forgivable 'in moderation' exception to the no-sugar rule. For example, Goran and Ventura propose that 'a drink or two' during their sugar-free challenge week are not a problem even though 'alcohol adds empty calories to your diet and can also contribute sugar',[42] while Mowbray gives the nutricentric justification that 'a dry red wine is not particularly high in sugar and contains lots of anti-oxidants, namely polyphenols and resveratrol, which are contained in grapes'.[43]

Highlighting these is not intended as a 'gotcha' move to discredit the authors by identifying incidental inconsistencies, since to do so would wrongly suggest that dietary purity is ever possible.[44] Instead, I want to highlight that the seemingly simple instruction – 'Don't eat sugar' – always requires further explanation to navigate the necessary arbitrariness of dietary boundaries. Recognition of this is central to the experimental memoirs by Mowbray and Schaub, for whom the struggle to delineate what 'counts' as sugar and what might be a legitimate exception is fundamental to the narrative arc of struggle and resolution that structures the books. But across the genre in general, the fact that a book-length account is needed at all suggests that claims to simplicity are rhetorical rather than literal. Instead, their primary function is to market the proposed regimen as something new; a fresh departure from the tarnished practice of dieting.

Doing it for health

A second key feature of the rejection of dieting is the need to grant seriousness to the endeavour of giving up sugar: it is about health, not something as trivial and discredited as dieting. What constitutes health in these claims is rarely articulated directly, appearing instead as an indisputable good that needs no explanation and that is there for the taking for those willing to do the work of self-care. For some, health is the absence of illness. For example, as suggested by the title of their book, *Sugarproof*, Goran and Ventura focus on protecting children from the health-harms of the sugar-drenched environment, warning: 'If you want to help protect your children's brains from a devastating disorder later in life, begin now by reducing their sugar and sweetener intake.'[45] In *Beating Sugar Addiction for Dummies*, which has 'getting off sugar and living a healthier lifestyle' as its introductory goal, DeFigio also positions chronic disease prevention as the motivational bottom line, speculating: 'if obesity, diabetes, fatigue, metabolic syndrome, osteoporosis and inflammatory diseases aren't enough reason to change your eating habits, perhaps my next book should be Wheelchairs for Dummies'.[46] The casual ableism of DeFigio's quip demonstrates the assumption of insufficiency that underpins the self-help genre (and which is encapsulated in the *For Dummies* brand name).[47] This exposes the moralism of his vision of health, whereby illness and disability represent the refusal to act in the face of risk. He can only wash his hands of those who fail to get on board and make the necessary changes.

For others, health is a more expansive category that extends far beyond the absence of illness. Mowbray, for example, describes her transformation after quitting sugar in glowing terms: 'Within days I looked and felt healthier. Within weeks I was slimmer, with better skin and better sleep. Finally free from cravings, I felt in control of my life for the first time in a long while.'[48] Weight loss is just one among many collateral benefits, holding the claim that 'this is not a diet', or at least that it is more than a diet, in place. In a similar vein, Jones urges readers not to weigh themselves during her ten-day sugar challenge because 'a boost in energy and mood and a reduction in craving are actually better indicators of progress'.[49] Health in these promissory lists is a positive mode of wellness rather than the absence of disease, where glowing skin, high-quality sleep, improved mood, high energy and appetite control combine to signify the self-made healthy body. Whether as wellness or absence of disease, health is good thing, determinedly detached from the complexities of political and social life, that is there for the taking for those willing to make the effort.

The primary effect of this claim to health, however ill-defined, is to create a moral distance between the urgent seriousness of the endeavour of giving up sugar and the trivial over-investment in appearance that is attributed to dieting. It thus pre-empts accusations of over-investment in superficial concerns about appearance to which women are especially vulnerable. For example, Mowbray notes how she carefully managed her explanation to others of her year without sugar, avoiding the word 'diet' because 'I saw what I was doing as a holistic change for my health rather than just for my waistline.'[50] This caution establishes the seriousness of the endeavour of giving up sugar, but it also reflects the competing pressures on women to be happy with themselves while always working on themselves. Mowbray exemplifies this in her rejection of dieting: 'I've always felt uncomfortable about admitting to being "on a diet". Perhaps it's because I feel it shows that you're unhappy with yourself in some way, that you want to change yourself. Although I wanted to slim down and get healthy, I didn't want people to think I was "unhappy" with myself.'[51] The use of health as a motivation attempts to square this circle, with weight loss positioned as a reward for investing in health without the appearance of being duped into punitively restrictive eating by body image pressures.[52] As discussed in the previous section, this is not a rejection of weight loss itself, which instead is promised as a happy by-product of the laudable work of investing in health; in a world where health and fatness can never be imagined as co-existing, becoming healthy must inevitably bring weight loss along with it.

But even in the name of health, control over food and the body must never be taken to excess. For example, at the end of her sugar-free year, Schaub lays claim to being a 'Sugar Avoider' rather than a 'Sugar Nazi' or 'Sugar-phobe',[53] and in her introduction to *Sugarproof*, Ventura reassures readers: 'we don't want you or your children to see sugar as a villain, but we also don't want to sugarcoat it'.[54] It is a disappearingly fine line to walk in a book where sugar is described as having 'destructive and possibly lasting effects on learning, memory, addictive tendencies, taste preference, appetite regulation, impulse control and metabolism'.[55] Similarly, DeFigio warns readers to avoid 'being obsessive or neurotic about food'[56] but also advises readers to keep a detailed food journal ('if you bite it you write it'),[57] and to squeeze extra activity into every moment, including marching on the spot while watching TV or brushing their teeth.[58] Like Zariya, discussed in the previous chapter of this book, who is warned that being too strict about healthy eating might give her children an unhealthy relationship with food, those seeking the sugar-free life must be vigilant but not fanatical, balancing the abjection of 'letting yourself go' and the fantasy of absolute control. Appeals to health offer the promise of achieving this balance, with the bonus of weight loss as a collateral reward.

Setting yourself free

So how, then, is this state of wellness and balance to be achieved? In the case of these books, the answer lies in a liberating reset that will break sugar's hold over the body and its appetites to allow people to consume according to their 'natural' needs. Once this has been achieved, readers are promised, the unsustainable control that dieting demands through the exercise of willpower will no longer be necessary. As Gillespie promises in the epigraph to this chapter: 'your desire for sugar will vanish'. The first step in the process of becoming sugar-free, then, is to break free from sugar's grip, or as Carr describes, to 'free yourself from slavery to your present tastes and eating habits'.[59] It is a cruel analogy given the sugar industry's long history of exploiting enslaved and indentured labour and the casual implication that slavery is something from which enslaved people could choose to free themselves. But the premise, however tastelessly expressed, reproduces the central pillar of the anti-sugar self-help domain: that the work of liberation from sugar falls to the individual and that (ill-)health is a personal choice. As Wilson observes in relation to her own decision to quit sugar: 'These things are always a matter of choosing. And committing.'[60]

Fundamental to these exhortations to individual choice and responsibility is the conviction that below the chaos of sugar's metabolic disruptions there is a 'real' self whose appetites are naturally oriented towards healthful, sugar-free consumption. Readers are urged to reclaim this true self by undertaking time-limited sugar-free challenges that will 'wipe the slate clean'[61] and 'establish a clean canvas'.[62] These are intended to 'reset your fullness signal',[63] give the body chance to 'recalibrate',[64] give your body a 'fresh start',[65] restore the body's 'natural homeostasis'[66] and enable the reader to follow their 'natural instinct'.[67] These exhortations presume the latent presence of an authentically pristine body, uncontaminated by modernity, that is robustly healthy and whose imagined appetites and dietary needs are universal and predictable. Echoing the paleo-nostalgia discussed in Chapter 2, this imagined clean slate relies upon an understanding of the body as metabolically disrupted by sugar alone; the authentic self lies just below the surface, waiting for the tide of sugar to recede.

The 'challenge' as a pathway to the clean slate is the primary site of struggle in the books, where simply accepting the challenge already marks the individual out positively as someone willing and ready to make a change. This is the stage at which willpower is needed to break the desire and drive to consume sugar, and the language of addiction ('withdrawal', 'detox') runs through descriptions of this initial phase, with readers promised short-term pain for long-term gain. Wilson, for example, advises readers that they will 'feel crap', but should think of it as a strengthening process: 'every day that we flex our "I'm not eating sugar muscle", the stronger we get'.[68] The need for willpower is commonly associated with the dieting behaviours which the self-help books determinedly distance themselves from, so this potentially contradicts their repeated claims that 'this is not a diet'. But the discourse of the clean slate resolves this tension with the promise of restoration to 'natural' appetite control, making the need for willpower only temporary. Carr is an exception here, arguing that the positive choice to remove 'bad sugar' from your life makes willpower immediately irrelevant, insisting: 'You only need willpower if you have a conflict of will.'[69] But more commonly, willpower plays a starting role, with the reader needing to hold out just long enough for the body to reset.

The initial rewards come in the form of appetite control:

[...] your body simply won't crave sugar or fast release carbohydrates the way it used to.[70]

Once you are sugar free, you really can eat anything you like as long as it doesn't contain sugar. Your body will moderate your consumption and keep you on the straight and narrow.[71]

The body here is separated from the self, guiding food decisions, removing the need for willpower and offering up the tantalising dietary fantasy of being able to eat whatever you want because you will only ever want 'good' food. As Gillespie promises, 'Once your sugar addiction is broken, a triple-layer chocolate cake sitting next to your cuppa will not be the remotest bit tempting.'[72] It is a model that ensures the erasure of social, economic or cultural influences on food choice, which are all sublimated to the 'natural' biological drives.

But even so, the classed presumptions underpinning these discourses of restoration to an authentic dietary self seep through. For example, Schaub describes her experience of eating a cookie or some chocolate once her year of no sugar was over: 'I realised that after a moment my mouth felt … *funny* [sic]: cloying and overly sweet, like I just drank a whole glass of maple syrup. A few minutes would pass, and I'd feel a small headache-y feeling creeping around the base of my brain, followed by a weird energised feeling, a sugar "buzz" if you will.'[73] Sugar-heavy foods figure here not as without taste, but as having a blunt excess of taste. In this way, the anticipated changes in taste after quitting sugar also mark a transition to their becoming tasteful, exposing the classed foundations of the sugar-free life. For example, after her no-sugar year, Schaub explains her enjoyment of 'things with a much subtler sweetness', declaring proudly that 'sodas, ice cream sundaes, carnival cotton candy all now strike me as slightly gross'.[74] For Gillespie, this transformation in taste renders him a connoisseur, and he boasts excitedly that 'I could really tell the difference between cabernet sauvignon and shiraz! (Before it had all tasted like red wine).'[75] The consumption of sugary, heavily processed foods, then, is in poor taste, becoming a marker of uncontained, thoughtless eating, with crude, excessive, effortless sweetness signalling a lack of refinement and an impatience for pleasure. Conversely, the sugar-free consumer is discerning, in search of subtle and exotic taste experiences to be enjoyed slowly and from quality foods.[76] This classed transformation exemplifies the argument I made at the beginning of the chapter that giving up sugar makes a positive claim about who you are: in this case, a responsible and tasteful middle-class subject who is reaping the just rewards of their bodily control.

In line with the expansive promises of the self-help genre more generally,[77] these transformations in appetite control and tasteful moderation are just the beginning of the promised freedoms and pleasures of the sugar-free life. Set against a Wonder Woman cartoon figure, Jones claims that by the end of her ten-day sugar-free challenge, 'you'll feel clean, empowered and in control',[78] and DeFigio argues that a 'simple sugar detox' can 'improve your mental clarity and lead you to a more empowered and fulfilled life'.[79] The content of the category of empowerment is unspecified in these claims, signalling a generalised self-efficacy that is presumed to carry over to all aspects of life. DeFigio, for example, sees giving up sugar as a step towards 'creating or improving other positive things in your life – relationships, exercise, career issues, time management and self care'.[80] Carr, whose vision of life under the thrall of sugar is especially bleak and friendless, also imagines a sun-lit sugar-free future where 'situations that you have come to regard as unstimulating or even irritating become enjoyable again: things like spending time with your loved ones, going for walks, seeing friends'.[81] The sugar-free life is also a hyper-productive one. McKenna promises a reduction in 'idle thoughts',[82] and for Carr, 'work will become more enjoyable and you'll become better at what you do'.[83] Free from sugar, you can make your own luck and the world is your oyster. Bang!

The belaboured self

However tantalising they may be, a tension lies at the heart of these promised transformations. On the one hand, claims to simplicity allow for their presentation as verging on the miraculous, with just a few days or weeks of struggle resolving into a blissful state of tasteful appetite control. But on the other hand, the privileged reader is one who is prepared to take responsibility for their health and body by putting in the requisite work. One way in which this is resolved is through the representation of the effort of transformation as effortless; it is not that there is no work involved, but that it doesn't feel like work. As cultural sociologist Micki McGee describes it, it is 'effortless effort, passive activity and endless work imagined as effortless exertion'.[84] In this way, the self of the self-help genre is endlessly, if invisibly, belaboured. As McGee observes, 'The belabored self presents itself as overworked both as the subject and as the object of its own efforts at self-improvement.'[85] This next section explores the effortless effort of giving up sugar by looking not only at the practical food preparation tasks assigned to readers but also at the rigorous monitoring of food and mood through quizzes, journaling and reflective exercises. The final part of the section considers the gendering of this work.

'Set yourself up for success'

The books all include some form of practical preparatory task to 'set yourself up for success' by making over the kitchen as a precursor to making over the self. Jones urges readers to 'go through all your food cabinets, fridge and freezer, and if possible, give away or else throw out foods that are not on your food plan and/or foods that are personally tempting for you'.[86] While DeFigio recommends taking any unwanted food to a foodbank or soup kitchen,[87] for most, the priority is simply to get it out of the house. As Jones notes: 'Don't feel guilty about throwing out unhealthy food. It's going to be wasted one way or the other, either in the rubbish bin or in your body, where it will get stored as fat'.[88] The fat body is synonymous with the rubbish bin here, and food coded as unhealthy has no place in either the healthy body or what DeFigio calls the 'organised nutritional sanctuary' of a well-stocked kitchen.[89] The kitchen clear-out serves the dual function of removing temptation and making space for sugar-free supplies. As with the hidden-sugar shock and mortified mother stories discussed in Chapter 3, readers are urged to become sugar detectives as they clear out and then restock their kitchens, scouring labels in both cupboards and supermarkets for signs of hidden sugar. The list of sugar synonyms discussed in Chapter 3 is also a ubiquitous feature, with readers instructed in the art of 'sugar spotting'.[90] Once the shelves and cupboards are appropriately stocked, readers are urged to cook in large batches and freeze leftovers ready for busy days; to have a steady supply of sugar-free snacks to hand; to plan their menus for the week; and to be adventurous, expanding their food vocabularies to maintain variety. For example, Mowbray urges her readers to 'go wild in the aisles and discover new things', describing encounters with 'buckwheat groats', 'cocoa nibs' and 'emerald green, rich-buttery tasting queen olives the size of walnuts that will set your taste buds aquiver'.[91] In a section on how to 'replenish your cupboards', she recommends some 'hero products' that will 'bring a touch of glamour to your larder', including coconut oil, nut butters, quinoa flakes, avocado and smoked salmon.[92]

The labour of creating a 'Sugar Smart' kitchen, then, reveals an inescapably privileged world view, with advice structured around middle-class tastes and food opportunities. This reflects the way middle-class food experiences have been rendered normative, with food adventurism, spicy food, and global ingredients and dishes all encouraged as markers of being open-minded and tasteful.[93] The waste that accompanies food experimentation – for example, where children refuse to try something new or the taste is unpalatable – is never even considered, and there is also little attention to cost. Instead, the books' implicitly middle-class readers are urged to shop at farmers' markets for locally sourced food, organic produce and grass-fed meats, with no consideration of expense or whether people even live somewhere within reach of those food opportunities. Unusually, Mowbray remarks on the expense of re-stocking her kitchen, complaining that 'my bank balance was groaning under the strain of all the fresh produce I was loading up on',[94] but this is a demonstration of her whole-hearted embrace of the sugar-free project rather than a complaint. In a modest nod to the possibility that this may exceed some people's means, she concedes: 'If you can't afford organic meat, buy free range. If you can't afford free range, buy what you can afford.'[95] The privileged economies of shifting from organic to free range overlook the lived realities of food insecurity and instead render a healthy diet a simple product of household economy. Social geographer Bethan Evans and colleagues note the same assertion at work in the UK's

Change4Life campaign, which refutes the notion that cost is a barrier to healthy eating with the claim that 'You just need to be clever about it.'[96] By embedding dietary change in the rhetorics of smartness (sugar smart, smart swaps), socioeconomic complexity and inequality are flattened out, rendering healthy eating a matter of choice, not privilege.

'What kind of sweet freak are you?'

The second dimension to the belaboured self of the giving-up-sugar genre is the work of cultivating self-knowledge in the form of short quizzes, journals and reflective exercises. The quizzes are situated early in the books, providing opportunities for readers to identify their own deficiencies and therefore as needing the advice which follows, drawing them into the book and into an imagined community of readers facing the same challenge. For example, DeFigio offers a series of quizzes under the heading 'What kind of sweet freak are you?',[97] while Jones asks, 'Are your sugar cravings out of control?', 'Are you an emotional eater?' and 'Are you ready and willing to change?'[98] The quiz options lead readers quickly to the 'right' answer, affirming their need to keep reading. For example, answering 'yes' to even just one of Jones' quiz questions about sugar cravings means that 'you are likely to benefit from reading this book'.[99] And although the questions in the emotional eating quiz are heavily weighted towards a 'yes', even those whose eating cannot be categorised as emotional according to the quiz need to keep reading to 'get a better understanding of what influences your eating behaviour so you can gain more control over your eating habits'.[100]

These diagnostic tests give way to further extra-textual work that reaches beyond the initial challenge period and aims to equip the reader with the skills to continue their self-invention after finishing the book.[101] The miraculous vanishing of the desire for sweetness, it turns out, is always precarious, and self-knowledge is positioned as the only way to avoid repeating mistakes and falling back into old habits and behaviours. In this way, the 'real me' to which the sugar-abstainer is presumed to return is also a 'new me' that requires new skills and insights to fend off the temptations of sugar.[102] For example, Jones concludes each chapter with a reflective exercise under the heading 'What are you thinking?', which aims to pre-empt any negative thoughts that might be interfering with the transformation process. For example, the 'negative, unhelpful thought' that 'I don't want to make changes to my schedule. I'm busy enough as it is' is recast as 'I am willing to do what it takes to succeed, even if it requires an initial sacrifice. Being slim and healthy is worth it to me.'[103] Concerns about time and capacity are quickly discredited, reducing success to a matter of motivated choice and careful strategizing.

Another core prescribed activity is journaling. The act of journaling serves multiple purposes and is a staple of the self-help genre. Jones recommends keeping a 'Food and Mood' journal to identify eating triggers, while for DeFigio, a food journal not only 'Makes you think more about what you choose and how much you eat' but is also a 'lie detector'.[104] Introducing 'the power of journalling' early in his book, McKenna interrupts the text by instructing readers to 'grab a pen and turn to page 153 now' to record their sugar consumption for that day as the first journal entry before returning to pick up where they had left off.[105] Subsequent daily entries ask the reader to document whether they had a healthy (sugar-free) breakfast, what 'cravings or random sugar thoughts' they experienced, which of his prescribed techniques they used that day, what positive changes they have noticed and whether they have listened to the 'Mind-Programming CD' that accompanies the book.

These journaling tasks expose the limits of the books, which present themselves as the answer to the problem, while at the same time insisting that readers will need to look beyond the texts if they are to succeed. The texts appear self-sufficient, but are ultimately insufficient, and the reader ends up being both the problem and the solution. McGee argues that this work of authoring the self is a trap whereby the newly emerging, authentic self must be constantly at work on itself and that the journals that the readers keep are not a simple memoir of their experiences, but rather are a form of ongoing labour.[106] They are never designed to be read by others as finished products, but rather are part of a process without end. Furthermore, it is never enough simply to recognise their own failings in their journals, for readers must also take recuperative action: negative thoughts must be replaced with positive ones; 'bad' eating habits have to be reformed; and constraints in time and money have to be circumvented through smart self-management. These unimaginative and unforgiving prescriptions highlight the ways in which the writing tasks are not designed to foster the invention of a new sort of self, but rather offer a prescribed language to ensure that readers remain within the bounds of the good neoliberal dietary citizenship on which the books are premised.

'It won't seem like an effort at all'

The previous section explored the preparatory and ongoing work of giving up sugar, but in the texts, there is no discussion about who performs this labour of label-reading, planning, shopping and cooking, which is inescapably coded as the work of women even amid the disingenuous gender-neutrality of the books. One way in which this is achieved is through the recasting of domestic labour as leisure. As McKenna observes:

> In the end, as the old saying goes, there is no such thing as a free lunch. As you move away from sugar you will find at first that you spend a bit more time finding foods without sugar. You may start cooking differently or cooking more often. You may spend an extra minute or two peeling fruit and having to wash your hands afterwards instead of just opening a carton of juice. Of course, when you have established your new routines and found better food to buy or cook, it won't seem like an effort at all. You may discover you enjoy it more.[107]

The reduction of the labour of going sugar-free to a few minutes of fruit peeling and hand washing wilfully obscures the extensive time and effort involved. Instead, McKenna articulates a patriarchal fantasy of (primarily) women's unpaid labour as too pleasurable for it even to be classed as work while stopping well short of suggesting the redistribution of that labour or that it has brought new joy to his own life.

Gillespie offers a similarly rose-tinted view of the labour of going sugar-free, offering a lengthy section on how to navigate the supermarket to avoid the aisles containing sugary and processed foods, including aisle-by-aisle recommendations and warnings. At the end of the section, he concedes, 'I know this feels like a complex analysis of the weekly shop, and it is, the first time you do it.' However, familiarity saves the day, and he promises that 'after a few weeks, you will become used to restocking from the same relatively limited sections. Your shopping time will decrease. Your shopping bill will decrease (all that packaged food costs a fortune). And your sugar-free kitchen will be preserved automatically, simply because you will be in the habit of shopping this way.'[108] Just as the promise of pleasure erases the labour of sugar-free living for Carr, habit does so for Gillespie, and the categorisation of the labour of stocking a sugar-free kitchen as automatic means that it can be disregarded as work. As McGee observes of the belaboured self of the self-help genre: 'Work is reimagined, not as a deprivation for which one ought to be compensated but as a means of expressing oneself, as a source of identity and personal fulfilment.'[109]

Mobilising the same logics that see smart money management as a means of getting around financial limitations, time, or the lack of it, is equally a matter of careful economies and micro-efficiencies that require no structural or fundamental change in the organisation of everyday life. Jones, for example, urges readers to 'create time to succeed' by 'decreasing or eliminating some activities, delegating tasks and practising smart time management'.[110] She presents the case of Susan, who divides up her daily tasks into 'essential' and 'desirable' to help her prioritise. Her essential tasks include paid work, 'mother duties', essential housework, food shopping, meal preparation and managing the household finances, while desirable tasks include checking social media, reading a book, visiting her mother and taking her daughter, Amy, to parties and activities. Susan, we are told, creates time for her new, sugar-free eating plan with 'some clever problem-solving and delegating'. She starts getting up ten minutes earlier to make a healthy packed lunch and then 'asked her husband to take over Amy's bedtime routine on weeknights, which meant she had an extra 15 minutes every evening to plan meals for the next day and make her food shopping list'.[111] The micro-economies of finding time mirror those of sugar reduction, where savings are parsed by the teaspoon and gram by mortified mothers. By finding ten minutes here and fifteen minutes there, she squeezes her new eating plan into her packed day, but this is not creating time. Instead, the labour of sugar-free food preparation eats into her sleep time, and while the bedtime routine is passed to her husband, the work of delegation still lies with Susan and the transfer of the task simply opens a narrow window for yet more labour. The work of introducing and maintaining a sugar-free life appears effortless and simple only because it is the work of women and is therefore easily disregarded as work. The work of giving up sugar, then, is not only without end but also unevenly distributed in ways that allow for its categorisation as not-work and its dislocation from the uneven social relations and structures that frame our everyday food work. I revisit this issue in Chapter 8 in relation to the gendering of sugar-free family life.

Conclusion

The rise of sugar as the dietary enemy *du jour* has created a space for a burgeoning genre of self-help texts like the ones discussed here. They are founded on the expectation that the management of food, health and the body are the responsibility of the individual and that we make our own luck with the choices that we make and how 'smartly' we navigate our busy day and household budgets. The books brook no excuses; armed with the necessary information, the winners rise to the challenge, while the losers fall by the wayside. The act of giving up sugar in the self-help domain, then, is an act of self-making; it is testimony to the willingness of the individual to take responsibility, exercise control over the body, defer pleasure, act on expert advice rather than impulse and consume tastefully. In doing so, readers can distance themselves from the feckless overconsuming Other whose abjection hangs quietly, and sometimes not so quietly, in the air, surrounding every exhortation to transform both the diet and, by extension, the self. In this chapter, I have focused on a shift in scale from punchy, shock-filled reporting of hidden sugar of Chapter 3 to the more carefully paced, book-length manuals for becoming the good, sugar-free citizen. In the next chapter, I continue to widen the perspective of my analysis, this time to consider documentary films, whose more expansive scope and scale make it both possible and narratively necessary to place sugar consumption in a wider context, bringing both the good citizen and its failed Other into sharp relief.

5

Entertaining sugar

In one of the earliest scenes of the TV documentary *Jamie's Sugar Rush*, celebrity chef Jamie Oliver is filmed visiting St George's Hospital in London, where six-year-old Mario, a small Black boy clutching a soft toy, is being anaesthetised to have six teeth removed.[1] We are told that he brushes his teeth every day, but that he has a weakness for sugary drinks, which have irreparably rotted his teeth. Dressed in surgical scrubs and passing looks of wide-eyed horror at the camera, Oliver watches as the boy's teeth are pulled out one by one. It is an inescapably physical process, and along with Oliver, we watch the surgeon levering out tooth after tiny tooth and dropping them into a small glass dish of water, now stained pink with blood. Oliver is visibly distressed by the encounter, observing that it is 'absolutely brutal – the only way to get the teeth out is to yank 'em out'. It is, warns Oliver, 'a tough watch but it's important to see'.

Oliver is an inescapable figure in the attack on sugar in the UK, and in the newspaper data collected for this study, he is the most-mentioned individual. In a study of UK newspaper coverage of the sugar tax, for which Oliver was an avid campaigner, public health nutritionist Christina Buckton and colleagues describe Oliver as having a presence 'larger than any of the soft drink manufacturers or political stakeholders',[2] and he is widely credited, not least by himself, as having been a key factor in securing the introduction of the tax. For example, in 2018, the campaigning organisation Sustain published *How the Sugary Drinks Tax Was Won*, offering '10 lessons for committed campaigners'. Lesson 7 – 'Work with the (right) big name' – claims that 'it was the exceptional profile, passion and expertise of campaigning chef Jamie Oliver and his team that made all the difference' and that his involvement 'took the case to the next level'.[3] I will return to these claims of impact and influence later in the chapter, but the key point here is that in the years leading up to the sugar tax, Oliver was a ubiquitous figure.

Jamie's Sugar Rush was a key factor in Oliver's prominence, airing on Channel 4 in September 2015. In the film, Oliver sets out to understand the problem of sugar as the first step in fighting his 'biggest battle ever' against it. The setting-out of the anti-sugar case through a prime-time documentary combines pedagogic purpose with entertainment, grabbing and holding the viewers' attention to make its lesson palatable enough to consume for entertainment but discomforting enough to persuade. But even though the film, and Oliver himself, have become inextricably associated with the sugar tax, it is a mistake to frame its influence purely in relation to the tax or other attempts to regulate sugar consumption. Instead, we should see this and other anti-sugar entertainment as prime examples of 'governing at a distance'; that is, where power is not exercised in a top-down way (for example, by the state banning a particular product, restricting access to it or levying taxes against it), but rather operates in dispersed ways that exhort individuals to manage their own health and behaviours under the guidance of distant experts in order to become responsible citizens.[4] In this way, the use of documentary film shares common ground with the self-help books of the previous chapter in their commitment to the cultivation of individual responsibility for health via sugar reduction. But at the same time, it uses the visual punch of a swiftly paced narrative arc composed of carefully calibrated graphic images, dramatic set pieces, constantly shifting locations and 'talking head' experts to widen its appeal and invite the reader to confront the realities for sugar for themselves. *It's important to see.*

This chapter explores this by drawing on two anti-sugar documentaries: *Jamie's Sugar Rush* and the 2014 feature-length documentary *That Sugar Film* made by Australian TV and film actor Damon Gameau.[5]

I explore the ways in which the films are constructed to simultaneously communicate their anti-sugar lessons and cultivate good neoliberal citizen-consumers, arguing that the documentaries rely on easy stereotypes and over-simplifications for dramatic effect, flattening out social, economic and environmental inequalities in their rush to do something about sugar. In doing so, the male protagonists, Oliver and Gameau, position themselves simultaneously as ordinary and extraordinary, and as non-expert experts, operating as 'moral entrepreneurs'[6] for whom the solution to the problem of sugar lies in the self-entrepreneurship that they model for the viewers. In doing so, they expose their inattention to history, poverty and class in the constitution of the problems they seek to address in ways that align comfortably with the prevailing values of neoliberal citizenship. I start with a brief description of the two films, followed by an examination of their use of spectacle as a way of simplifying the problem of sugar. I then explore the ways in which they adopt the role of social explorers, visiting socially, economically and geographically distant Others as a means of illuminating their own journey of discovery, and the final section considers the ways in which both Oliver and Gameau position themselves as trustworthy authorities and men of influence and action in the fight against sugar.

Documenting sugar

Of the two films being discussed here, perhaps not surprisingly given the UK context, Oliver's film received considerably more coverage in the UK press than Gameau's. However, the two films are connected by their release in the middle of coinciding national debates about sugar, particularly in relation to taxation. It was in this context that immediately after the 2016 budget announcement of plans to introduce the sugar tax in the UK, an article in *The Guardian* reported Oliver as urging the Australian government to 'pull your finger out' on the tax issue,[7] and on the front jacket of the *That Sugar Film* DVD, Oliver endorses the film as 'a definite must-see'. I could have added other films to the selection that hit the screens around the same time. For example, the 2014 documentary,

Fed Up focused on sugar's role in childhood obesity,[8] and in 2015, *Sugar Coated* drew parallels with the tobacco industry to argue that the sugar industry is hijacking science for profit.[9] The films feature many of the same experts and commentators and cultivate the same urgency of action. However, these differ from both *Jamie's Sugar Rush* and *That Sugar Film* in that their narratives do not hinge on a central character. Instead, my interest here is the ways in which Oliver and Gameau each mediate the anti-sugar message as an extraordinary everyman who conducts the work of normalising self-governance in the face of sugar.

Jamie's Sugar Rush is staged as a journey of discovery, with the problem of sugar explained to the audience via Oliver's own process of 'getting his head around it' as he visits hospitals, schools and shops, interspersed with expert interviews. A trip to Mexico inserts a travelogue element of colonial exoticism to the programme, with the final segments of the programme showing Oliver, fully fired up after his information gathering, launching into campaigning mode. The documentary builds on his already high levels of public recognition as a celebrity chef, cookbook author and school meals campaigner, positioning him as a voice to be reckoned with specifically in relation to the food crisis of the day: sugar. The film was accompanied by the publication of *Jamie's Sugar Manifesto*, which declared the introduction of the sugar tax as its 'big aim', alongside calls to give legislative force to the Responsibility Deal (see Chapter 6), ban junk food marketing before 9 pm, make traffic-light labelling mandatory for front-of-pack packaging and show the sugar content of sweetened drinks in teaspoons for easy legibility.[10] The film also marked the launch of an online petition calling for a sugar tax that viewers of the show were encouraged to sign. He subsequently appeared in his capacity as a high-profile anti-sugar campaigner as a witness before Health Select Committee hearings on childhood obesity, first in 2015, and then again before the renamed Health and Social Care Select Committee as a double-act with celebrity chef Hugh Fearnley-Whittingstall in 2018.

Like Oliver in *Jamie's Sugar Rush*, the protagonist in Damon Gameau's *That Sugar Film* is the filmmaker himself, supported by a cast of experts as well as celebrities, including actors Stephen Fry and

Hugh Jackman. But while Oliver takes on the role of the naive observer inspired by the revelations of his journey of discovery, *That Sugar Film* uses the narrative device of self-experimentation, with Gameau committing to eating forty teaspoons of sugar a day for sixty days, but only by eating processed foods coded as healthy rather than obviously sugary foods such as chocolate, biscuits or soda. The film echoes Morgan Spurlock's *Super Size Me*, where Spurlock ate only from McDonald's for thirty days while documenting the impacts on his health.[11] This connection is recognised in an endorsement on the DVD cover, where Spurlock urges viewers to 'binge on That Sugar Film and transform your life'. The format is the mirror image of the experimental abstention narratives ('My Year of ...') that are a staple of the popular anti-sugar domain, and the narrative arc of the film rests on the drama of his health decline, which is resolved at the end of the film by his swift restoration to sugar-free health. Alongside the self-experimentation, like Oliver, Gameau engages in a journey of discovery about sugar through pedagogic encounters with experts and by travelling to bear witness to excess sugar consumption in contexts of exoticised poverty. The film exploits self-deprecating humour, bright colours, playful sets, music and animations to get its message across, punctuating this hyper-stimulating, sugar-filled aesthetic with invitations into the calmer space of Gameau's home, where we meet his pregnant partner, Zoe, and are drawn into a relationship with him that invites trust and sympathy. The film is accompanied by a book – *That Sugar Book*[12] – as well as the *That Sugar Movement* website, which offers a programme (for a one-off payment of $79) to 'Kick Sugar In 30 Days'.[13]

Spectacular simplicity

In *That Sugar Film*, Gameau offers us a dentistry scene whose shock value far outdoes Oliver's London hospital encounter with Mario. Larry, a white seventeen-year-old living in a poor rural Appalachian town, is preparing to have all his teeth removed by dentist Edwin Smith, who provides mobile dental care to those without access to it from an adapted motorhome that is funded by PepsiCo. The drinks giant makes the highly caffeinated and sugary drink Mountain Dew, which dominates sales in the area and which Larry drinks constantly, bathing his teeth relentlessly in it to devastating effect. All attempts to inject local anaesthetic prior to the extraction fail because his teeth and gums are so infected, and in the end, poor Larry can take no more and he leaves with a promise to return the following day. The scene is drawn out and, for this squeamish dentophobe, almost unwatchable. The dentist tells Gameau that the high rates of tooth decay in the area are the result of poverty, but this line of thought is never pursued in the film. Back at his hotel room, Gameau talks to Zoe in a video call, telling her that PepsiCo paid for the motorhome but that what the local people really needed was education. I couldn't help but think that a more pressing concern was the affordable healthcare or insurance that would have enabled Larry to undergo the horrific procedure under a general anaesthetic.

The spectacle of the cases of both Mario and Larry packs a powerful punch. Their goal is to grab the attention of the viewer, who is forced to confront the disfiguring and painful predations of sugar. *It's important to see*. But the prominence given to dental problems in the films is not reflected either in the newspaper coverage or in the anti-sugar self-help books discussed in the previous chapter, which largely treat sugar-related tooth decay as a footnote to the problem of obesity that remains the headlining concern. There are some exceptions to this in the newspaper reporting. For example, in March 2017, the Faculty of Dental Surgery at the Royal College of Surgeons (RCS) reported that hospital tooth extractions in children aged up to four had risen by 24% in the previous decade, totalling 9,206 procedures in 2015/16[14] – a figure that was widely reported for its shock value. This is not to argue that it is not a shocking statistic, but rather to suggest that when dental stories appear, they are mobilised explicitly to be shocking, ratcheting up the heat on the attack on sugar. For example, a *Daily Telegraph* headline following the release of the RCS report declared, 'Rise in removals of rotting milk teeth fuelled by children's sugary diet',[15] and in April 2016, following the release of a report by the Local Government Association on rising rates of tooth extraction in children to the cost of £35 million per year, the *Daily Mail* led with 'Sugar-addict children who need every tooth removed'.[16]

Larry's devastated mouth, with teeth too badly rotted down to blackened stumps to be pulled without excruciating pain, serves as the extreme case that is at once attention-grabbing (an entertainment requirement), cautionary (above all things, we should not be like Larry) and silencing of the critical questioning that might add complexity to the sugar narrative. The brutal scene leaves no space for thinking about how his poverty might relate to his poor dental health, or why he can't be fully anaesthetised. Nor can the arresting headlines about children having all their teeth removed explain why, as the RCS report notes, 42% of children didn't see a National Health Service (NHS) dentist in the previous year, with calls for increased dental education distracting from the growing difficulty people face in accessing NHS dentistry because of service cuts.[17] But these are more complex, structural questions for which no space is left by the visual and discursive spectacle of 'yanking' out children's teeth because they drank too much sugar. Spectacle, then, simplifies the problem (drinking too much sugar) while intensifying the urgency of action.

The use of graphic dentistry constitutes a spectacle that is observed and then curated for dramatic purposes, but the two films also make use of a series of staged set pieces designed to shock. In common with anti-sugar pedagogies more generally, a common spectacle-generating device is the 'sugar reveal', whereby the sugar hidden in everyday foods is exposed. For example, in *Jamie's Sugar Rush*, we see Oliver in his kitchen with 'my mate Lucy' (dietician Lucy Jones) preparing a breakfast of a large bowl of cereal with milk, topped with low-fat yoghurt and some berries along with a glass of orange juice. Oliver expresses his shock at the revelation that at fourteen teaspoons, the breakfast is already double his daily sugar allowance. The exercise is repeated for a lunch of tinned tomato soup and bread, an afternoon snack of a cereal bar and fruit drink and a dinner of stir-fry made with a ready-to-use sauce. The day of 'healthy' eating – 'no chocolate bars here' – totals thirty-six teaspoons of sugar. Oliver meets each revelation with wide-eyed horror, although his naivety – a documentary and reality TV staple[18] – stretches credulity. The point is driven home with the ubiquitous visual device of the pyramid of sugar cubes. Jones warns emphatically: 'whenever you buy something that's in a packet, or in a bottle, read the label'. The stack of sugar cubes stands as a reminder that the self-regulation of sugar requires constant vigilance through label-reading, with the expert advice of Lucy mediated by Oliver, who simultaneously occupies the position of food expert and self-educating naive consumer. This enables him to act as a knowledge intermediary, or what cultural geographer Christine Barnes calls a 'talking label',[19] with the domestic setting of his kitchen creating a sense of intimacy for the viewers that enables him to translate the shock of sugar accumulation into the take-home lesson to 'read the label'.

Gameau takes the set piece stunt one step further by declaring Day 14 of his experiment 'Sugar Comparison Day', adding actual cubes or spoons of white granulated sugar to otherwise unsweetened foods to reflect the quantities of sugar in the sweetened versions. We see him heaping spoons of sugar into a glass of water, piling it into plain yoghurt, spooning it onto a piece of roasted chicken in lieu of a teriyaki sauce and crunching into a layer of sugar cubes sandwiched between two plain crackers as the sugar equivalent of a 'healthy' cereal bar. As he heaps the sugar onto some plain sugar-free wheat biscuits and takes his first bite, he points to a bowl of his usual sweetened cereal left out for comparison, declaring: 'This now equals that.' The rhetorical point of the set piece is that we wouldn't eat forty teaspoons of actual sugar, so why would we eat it hidden in our everyday foods? But this reduces food not only to the sum of its nutritional content, but also to a specific nutrient. The two breakfasts are equal only if the only point of comparison is sugar content. The shock tactic, therefore, demands the radical decontextualisation of sugar. Furthermore, the stunt exposes the inflammatory premise of the experiment itself, which is based on the claim that Australians eat an average of forty teaspoons of sugar a day. In a Deakin University press release, health scientist Tim Crowe notes that this figure includes intrinsic sugars in milk and fruit and that added sugar would total only approximately sixteen teaspoons – a point that is wilfully lost as Gameau heaps on cubes and teaspoons of white table sugar.[20]

This is not to argue in defence of sugar or to align with the 'everything in moderation' argument that is the mainstay of food industry defences of sugary products. Instead, I want to highlight the ways in which spectacle is used to narrow the field of vision and, by extension, the terms of the debate. These films, therefore, use spectacle to teach the viewers to sharpen their focus on sugar by bringing it into the foreground. This is something that Oliver does literally in the concluding shots of the film's opening montage, where a pyramid of sugar sits in the foreground before being shattered from behind by Oliver, who fires the cubes towards the viewer. This foregrounding of sugar, both rhetorically and literally, exemplifies what medical anthropologist Harris Solomon describes in his study of metabolic disease in India as the 'aperture effects' of chronic disease discourse.[21] In photography, a wide lens aperture decreases the depth of field, resulting in a hyper-focus on the subject of the image against a blurred background. The result in the case of discourses of metabolic disease, he argues, is that 'any number of risk factors float in the background, but the consuming subject stands at the fore'.[22] The visual spectacle of sugar works to similar effect; like the opening montage of *Jamie's Sugar Rush*, it flings sugar in our faces. It is a lesson not only in the importance of seeing, but also in what and how to see (and what to ignore).

'I have never been to a more foreign land …'

In teaching us how to see and recognise sugar, the films also adopt an Othering gaze that is unmistakably colonial in tone. This is demonstrated in the travelogue segments of both films, where the protagonists take on the role of social explorer to extract narrative value. We could view Gameau's Appalachian trip in this light, with Larry and his devastated mouth as his exoticised anthropological subject, but this is eclipsed by a trip much closer to home to the Aboriginal community of Amata. The background to the trip is the memory of a visit in 2002 to the town of

Ramingining, where he recalled with horror the high levels of Coca-Cola consumption. In *That Sugar Book*, he relives his shock at the encounter: 'To this day, I have never been to a more foreign land – and I was in my own country.'[23] This instant erasure of the colonial history of the violent dispossession inflicted on Aboriginal people ('my own country') secures the foreignness of the encounter, giving the viewer licence to stare aghast at the primitive Other who is helpless in the face of sugar. Speaking in the film of the same 2002 visit, Gameau observes that 'like so many indigenous cultures introduced to a Western diet, their relationship with sugar seemed particularly destructive'. In this account, Gameau not only reduces the violent oppressions of colonialism to a well-mannered introduction, but he also reproduces the idea of racialised Others as especially ill-equipped to resist the lure of sugar.

As part of his sugar experiment, Gameau decides to 'return to an Aboriginal community [...] to find out if the situation had improved'.[24] Happily treating all Aboriginal communities as interchangeable, he heads off to Amata, which is noteworthy for a public health intervention – Mai Wiru – which combined educational initiatives with removing Coca-Cola and deep-fat fryers from the local store and providing water fountains. Sugar consumption fell dramatically, but the subsequent withdrawal of funding made the changes unsustainable, and the people of the town continue to suffer devastatingly high rates of diabetes, kidney disease and other chronic health problems.

The segment is punctuated with grainy historical documentary footage of naked Aboriginal people hunting and foraging, with a clipped, British-accented voiceover observing that they eat almost no sugar. We see Gameau in conversation with local Aboriginal activist John Tregenza, who is locally nicknamed 'the Chainsaw' because 'he cuts through the bullshit'. From Tregenza, we learn that only forty years ago, local people were still living off the land, but the community became reliant on the local store (and its shelf-stable sugary offerings) after the introduction of foreign grasses which drove out native plants and animals. Aboriginal artist Inawinytji Williamson, who has produced art documenting her own experience of kidney disease,[25] is more explicit about the colonial dimensions of the situation in Amata. She explains to camera that her grandparents ate bushtucker and were healthy, but 'then the white fella came into Australia. He bring all the sweet things like lollies, biscuits, everything.'[26] The arrival of the 'white fella' and its implications are erased by Gameau in order to keep the focus on sugar consumption and the need to educate the community of Amata into healthier behaviours. He shows little interest in learning about the diet and everyday lives of earlier generations; knowledge can travel only from Western experts to the community.

Towards the end of the segment, we see him walking through the majestic landscape, musing that 'what is happening to my body is perhaps a concentrated version of what is happening here and in many other indigenous communities'. In this, he allows his body to stand unthinkingly for all bodies, extracting value from the Aboriginal case for what it can say about him and his experiment, while pushing into the background the cross-generational psychological, physical and structural disadvantages inflicted by colonisation. He ends with a warning that if the positive changes initiated by Mai Wiru are not restored, 'then the oldest living culture on Earth is in great danger of disappearing' – a determined refusal of the devastation and loss that already mark the history and present of Aboriginal experience at the hands of colonisers.

Oliver's social exploration takes him to Mexico, where heavy sugary drink consumption, high rates of obesity and diabetes and the recent introduction of a sugar tax make it simultaneously the perfect cautionary tale of sugar run amok and a role model for fiscal intervention (see Chapter 6). Oliver travels to the Chiapas region of southern Mexico, an area with a rich indigenous culture, a troubled history of colonisation and armed conflict and high levels of poverty and inadequate investment in public services and infrastructure. In recent times, the region has become infamous for its high Coca-Cola consumption, including the incorporation of the drink into local ceremonies and spiritual practices, making an appealing journalistic spectacle for a Western audience.[27] At the beginning of the segment, he meets local activist Alejandro Calvillo, who takes him out to some of the region's rural villages, and here Oliver, from the flat-bed of a pick-up truck, bears witness to the blanket Coca-Cola branding on sign-boards, trucks and store fronts, before joining a family gathering involving a ceremony at an altar to his host's father-in-law. The ceremony includes offerings of Coca-Cola and other soft drinks, and in conversation with his host, who is never named in the film, Oliver comments that 'Coke has been embraced as a spiritual, authentic part of the experience', describing it awkwardly as 'the modern holy water'. His obvious disapproval at the incorporation of the drink into the ceremony implies a corrupted purity of tradition, overlooking the ways in which the ceremonial traditions are never 'pure', not least because they already incorporate elements of the Catholicism of the region's colonisers.

The implied inauthenticity of Coca-Cola in the ceremony is contrasted with the meal prepared afterwards. Oliver observes the preparations approvingly – 'this is my idea of heaven' – commenting that 'this absolutely beautiful traditional dish seems completely at odds with the drink it's being served up with'. This search for exotic authenticity is an ongoing theme for Oliver. In the 2005 TV show *Jamie's Italian Escape*, he goes in search of authentic Italian cuisine, but ends up disappointed when he gives a creative twist to a traditional lamb dish and the meal is criticised as failing to respect local traditions. He leaves disillusioned at the conservatism of his hosts. Conversely, in his Mexican adventure, he is disappointed by what he sees as the failure to respect traditional cooking by drinking Coke with the 'beautiful traditional dish'. These exotic strangers become the bearers of an authenticity that is evaluated by Oliver's own standards as either too authentic or not authentic enough, reaffirming the social hierarchy in his favour.[28] Tradition and authenticity, both in Italy and now in Mexico, become a means for Oliver to mark out his own distinction and authority.

Oliver's Mexican adventure cultivates governance at a distance in multiple ways. First, as discussed in the previous section, it relies on spectacle to narrow the viewers' field of vision, sharpening the focus on (over)consumption and blurring the wider context into the background. This is achieved most powerfully via images of babies being fed Coke. This is a repetitive trope in the film, including the opening montage, where a clip from the Mexico segment shows a young toddler being fed sips from a glass Coke bottle. In the film, Oliver gestures to a child on its mother's lap, happily being helped to a mouthful of Coke, and observes that he saw the same woman breastfeeding the baby earlier. He asks his host the morally loaded question: 'Do most mothers feed their babies Coke and breastfeed at the same time?' The juxtaposition of breastmilk and Coke is deliberately arresting for the viewer, leaving little space for critical questioning and intensifying the urgency of the problem of sugar. The image works to silencing effect, issuing an unspoken demand for consensus: you can ask questions about how much sugar is too much or the role of the state in controlling it, but can't we all agree that babies shouldn't be drinking soda?

Medical journalist Mary Otto provides a striking counterpoint to this act of discursive closure in her book *Teeth*. She describes an encounter with dentist Edwin Allgair, whose practice serves a Native Alaskan community beset by crushing poverty and its accompanying health problems, including poor dental health. Allgair describes the familiar scenario of mothers and grandmothers putting soda in babies' bottles, noting that rather than judging, it was important to 'keep asking why'. He recounts a meeting with a mother who told him that the soda was to keep the baby quiet. When asked why she had to quiet the baby, she explained: 'Because if he cries when his uncles come in, they'll beat him.' Reflecting on the encounter afterwards, Allgair observes that 'being quiet has a higher survival value than having perfect teeth'.[29] Oliver shows us the babies sipping soda but he never asks why.

Even with some possible explanations right in front of him, Oliver clings to the host family's presumed lack of knowledge about the risks that soda poses. For example, he bemoans the fact that he 'hasn't seen one kid drink a glass of water' during the family meal, but he seems to have forgotten his earlier conversation with Calvillo, who explained that the scarcity of potable water in the region is a key factor in the rise in soda consumption. Oliver ignores this structural constraint, even though the shortage is widely attributed not only to low levels of infrastructural investment, but also to the region's Coca-Cola bottling plants, which rely on the low-cost extraction of local resources, including water.[30] Instead, knowledge deficit, compounded by vulnerability to the lure of advertising, remains the only possible explanation. For example, in the same segment, during a visit to a local hospital, we see a group of older women in traditional dress awaiting diabetes treatment. The camera lingers pointedly on the women's bare feet as Oliver discusses the region's high amputation rates with Calvillo: 'Do the people know about the scale of the [health] complexities and amputations?' The question is rhetorical, and he moves on without waiting for an answer because the only imaginable explanation is a knowledge deficit: if only they knew, they would surely change their behaviour. It is a discursive move that naturalises expectations that, under the guidance of distant experts, people will manage their own health appropriately.

The second way we can understand the travelogue segments of the film as governing at a distance is the ways in which it reinforces a white, middle-class viewing position that is sympathetic with its exoticised subjects, while rendering them categorically 'not me'. Oliver is not ashamed of this privileged viewing position, noting in an interview in *The Guardian* in April 2018 that disadvantaged communities view the world through a completely different lens from that of the middle classes, 'who have got a clear view'.[31] In the midst of the family meal with his Mexican hosts, Oliver firmly distinguishes himself from the scene he is witnessing, offering commentary and knowing looks to camera in an exercise of voyeuristic power into which the viewer is also drawn. The unnamed family can only be known rather than knowers, allowing the viewers to feel normal and sedimenting their place in the social hierarchy.[32] The lingering shot of the baby sipping Coke from its mother's bottle invites viewers to agree that they, like Oliver, know better.

In doing so, the segment simultaneously takes the viewer into entertainingly exotic spaces while connecting them to the situation at home. For example, both Gameau and Oliver punctuate their films extensively with montages of fat bodies, and especially what fat activist Charlotte Cooper calls 'headless fatties',[33] tucking into junk food or walking past fast food advertisements and outlets. The bodies are coded as working class through their clothing and their proximity to fast food, which social scientist Julie Guthman argues signifies 'common tastes, mass production and massive bodies'.[34] Similarly composed shots from both their home locations and their exotically Othered destinations (Aboriginal communities in Australia, Chiapas in Mexico) flatten out the differences between them, enabling the two protagonists to foreground discourses of ill-informed overconsumption for which education is the primary solution ('Do the people know ... ?'). This is achieved by erasing the histories of those spaces and contexts via a universalising colonial narrative where the white, middle-class body can stand for all bodies. In this way, the engagement of both Gameau and Oliver with the exotic Other is primarily extractive, with the travelogue segments simultaneously reassuring audiences of their own place in the social hierarchy and serving up a cautionary tale. This enables both men to return to their familiar surroundings fired up with renewed enthusiasm and campaigning zeal.

Men who get things done

In both *Jamie's Sugar Rush* and *That Sugar Film*, Oliver and Gameau are not simply narrators of a story about sugar; they are themselves the story. They function as role models not only in specific relation to sugar consumption, but also of a way of being in the world that aligns with neoliberal values of self-efficacy, self-discipline and entrepreneurialism. Above all else, they are men who get things done. This is achieved through two key aspects of their self-narratives: (1) their moral entrepreneurship; and (2) their reconstitution of expertise.

'I'd put him in charge of the country'

When *Jamie's Sugar Rush* aired in September 2015, journalist Sam Wollaston wrote an enthusiastic review in *The Guardian* hailing Oliver as 'brilliant' and as 'a man who people listen to and who gets things done', concluding, 'I'd put him in charge of the country.'[35] This echoes the tongue-in-cheek recommendation in the medical journal *The Lancet* in 2005, which, in the wake of Oliver's school meals campaign, proclaimed 'Jamie Oliver for Chief Medical Officer'.[36] The editor praises Oliver for 'not doing this for political gain', for being 'a rebel chef who genuinely cares about food and nutritional standards' and for getting out into the community 'where the real action is'. These endorsements reiterate Oliver's standing as a man who does something, making him the perfect answer to a crisis about which, above all else, something must be done. In an article in *The Guardian* in April 2018 (shortly after the implementation of the sugar tax), he uses this commitment to action as a marker of distinction, observing, 'as time has gone on and we've got some stuff done, you realise that getting stuff done isn't that common'.[37] While, as discussed later in this chapter, the 'stuff' that gets done is not always clear, being seen to take action where others in power have failed to do so lies at the heart of his, and also Gameau's, campaigning brand. In this way, they establish their credentials as moral entrepreneurs; as people who, regardless of risk, are willing to take the initiative to address the problem of sugar and its consequences while others continue to dither and obfuscate. They see what needs to be done, and they step up and do it.

The refusal to defer action is at the heart of the brands cultivated by both Oliver and Gameau. For example, on returning from Mexico, Oliver wonders whether the UK government will impose a sugar tax, before declaring: 'I don't know, but I'm definitely not going to wait to find out.' Waiting is not an option, and action is always better than inaction. For Gameau too, the refusal to wait is made into a virtue, especially when coupled with a drive to 'find out'. In a foreword to *That Sugar Book*, David Gillespie commends Gameau to the reader: 'What you have in your hands is the story of a man who wanted to answer a question for himself, fully aware that it would help others. Damon stepped up. He couldn't help himself.'[38] As a vociferous anti-sugar campaigner and moral entrepreneur in his own right, Gillespie finds a like mind in what he sees as Gameau's unstoppable drive for information. Gameau, in turn, recognises a kindred spirit in Gillespie, whom he dubs 'The Crusader' in the film. This congratulatory shared drive to know and understand the problem of sugar doesn't simply teach viewers about sugar, but also communicates the kind of person they should be. By being seen to act, both Oliver and Gameau model neoliberal imperatives to take responsibility for health by gathering, sifting and acting on information without procrastination.

A second dimension to this moral entrepreneurism is the readiness to take risks to get the job done. While the business entrepreneur is willing to take risks for financial gain, the anti-sugar moral entrepreneur is framed as doing it for others. For example, Gillespie proclaims: 'Damon took a risk for all of us. He did it for you, your kids, those you hold dear. And, like most curious people, he did not think of the consequences.'[39] In Gameau's case, the risks lie primarily in the threat to his health of his sudden change to a high-sugar diet, adding a note of suspense that typifies what cultural studies scholar Laurie Ouellette describes as 'do-good' programming.[40] The film returns repeatedly to this theme, with Gameau insisting that the only way to really understand the harms of sugar and to resolve any confusion about its health impacts once and for all is through his own body. The camera lingers on the expressions of concern on the faces of his team of advisers, and during a preliminary meeting staged in a sweet shop, Gillespie says he is glad to know that Gameau will be under medical supervision 'because I think you're going to need it'.

For Oliver, the risks relate not to his physical wellbeing but to becoming the target of push-back from industry and government in the form of personal and reputational attacks. In an interview in *The Guardian* in October 2015 about his sugar tax campaign, he declared: 'I know I'm going to get a bashing.'[41] Giving evidence at the Health Select Committee hearing on the childhood obesity strategy in that same month, he set out his heroic stall, citing risk to amplify his commitment to the cause: 'I don't want business being put before child health. End of story. Over my dead body. So I don't care that I'm uncomfortable. I don't care that I'm going to get a rattling from industry.'[42] His determination in the face of opposition echoes the anti-sugar voices discussed in Chapter 1, who make a virtue of going against the dietary grain as a mark of independent thinking.

In *Jamie's Sugar Rush*, this willingness to take risks because 'doing nothing is unforgiveable' is exemplified in his set-piece decision to introduce a self-imposed tax of 10p on sugary drinks sold in his 'Jamie's Italian' chain of restaurants. He announces this to a staged gathering of food industry representatives set against the backdrop of a tower of plastic lower limbs to illustrate the ravages of sugar-induced type 2 diabetes. The representatives shift uncomfortably in their seats as he encourages them to send a signal to government by doing the same. A later evaluation of the intervention in his restaurants found that it was associated with an 11% decrease in the number of sugary drinks sold in the first twelve weeks, and a 9% decrease at six months (but only in restaurants with medium to high baseline sales). It concludes that fiscal measures can cause a reduction in sales, which is assumed to lead to health benefits, but argues that other factors may also be playing a role in the fall in sales. These include Oliver's donation of the money raised to the Children's Health Fund, a redesign of the menu, widespread media coverage and the association of the Jamie Oliver brand with food campaigning.[43] But for Oliver, the precise efficacy of the measure is less significant than its rhetorical impacts, and towards the end of the film, he reflects: 'My biggest worry is the urgency, the urgency in which change is needed. And I know personally that I hate doing nothing. So definitely a rocket up the arse of the government is a really positive thing.' This highlights the ways in which the specific forms that doing something might take are less significant than attention-grabbing visibility of any action which can stir a response. As an article in *The Times* in July 2015 observed: 'you have to hand it to Oliver: he may have all the subtlety of an overgrown puppy with a new chew toy, but he knows how to attract the public's attention'.[44]

This approval highlights the ways in which the approach of diving in is never only about risk, but also brings significant gains to the two protagonists, shoring up their moral entrepreneurship and enhancing the value of their brand. For example, the documentation of Gameau's bodily changes draws on tropes familiar to reality and make-over TV genres, where the spectacle of dramatic transformation is critical to the narrative arc of the show. As the blood tests begin to show negative changes in the health of his liver, Gameau recalls his producer's delight that 'we actually had a story'.[45] But in creating a story, both the physical risks of overconsuming sugar in the experiment and the moral hazards of weight gain are in fact superficial for Gameau. For example, his post-experiment return to his previously 'healthy' diet speedily reverses the health impacts of his temporarily excessive sugar consumption, and while he gains a substantial 8.5 kg during the experiment, even at his fattest, the weight never attaches to him in ways that are morally threatening. Towards the end of the experiment, he muses in the film on his current state of sugar-filled, bad-tempered exhaustion and reflects pityingly that some people live their lives like that 'and have never experienced anything different'. 'I have', he continues, 'and I'm really excited to get back to that point.' The provisional and purposeful nature of his weight gain sets him apart; in an echo of Oliver's claim to the 'clear view' of the middle classes, he knows a better reality that is affirmed rather than threatened by the experiment.

Throughout the film, we see him repeatedly exposing and rubbing his expanding belly in imitation of his partner's growing pregnancy – 'my little fructose baby'[46] – and in one scene, he grabs the fat with his hands and ventriloquises it. This reminded me of research I conducted several years ago among marathon swimmers, many of whom purposefully gain body fat before a long sea swim for added insulation against the cold. Previously lean male swimmers – but not women, because fatness can rarely be comedic for women – would manage the potential stigma of weight gain by engaging in physical comedy with their rounding stomachs, slapping the fat to make it wobble and making it 'speak' or demand food.[47] Like the swimmers, Gameau is playing at being fat while never allowing the moral stigma of fatness to attach to him. Instead, his growing stomach is a performance of fatness; it is a dramatic fat suit that can be quickly removed and order restored.[48]

For Oliver, his defiant expectations that he will get 'a bashing' are not without foundation, and despite his considerable fan base, he has long been a divisive figure who attracts charges of hypocrisy and of patronising interference. For example, following the reformulation of the soft drink Irn Bru, Oliver was described by furious fans of the drink as a 'lettuce shagger'[49] and in March 2016, *The Daily Telegraph* reported Ruth Davidson (then leader of the Conservative Party in Scotland) as calling him a 'rocket-munching millionaire'.[50] This opposition mirrors previous resistance to his campaigning interventions. For example, when, in *Jamie's Ministry of Food*, he attempted to transform the eating and cooking habits of the town of Rotherham, local pockets of resistance pushed back, including the launch of a 'Jamie Go Home' campaign.[51] In a similar vein, following the success of the sugar tax petition to which viewers were directed in *Jamie's Sugar Rush*, a petition to 'Ban Jamie Oliver' was launched (although it fizzled out quickly with fewer than 200 signatures). More ominously, Oliver has hinted that a series of burglaries and break-ins at his home and offices that started after *Jamie's Sugar Rush* aired was a malevolent industry response to his interventions – an unsubstantiated suggestion that can only boost his reputation as a risk-taker and truth-seeker who has touched a nerve.[52]

Oliver is also the subject of several 'gotcha' articles that seek to discredit him by highlighting his failure to live by his low-sugar, healthy-eating principles. For example, an article in *The Daily Telegraph* in 2013 reported a survey of celebrity chef cookbooks whose recipes fall short of government healthy eating guidelines, including recipes by Oliver.[53] And during his select committee evidence in 2015, he was forced to defend the fact that, although he had strongly advocated clear labelling, the nutritional information for his own restaurant menus did not specify sugar content. But just as Gameau is not discredited by his fattening stomach, nor is Oliver harmed in these attacks, which only serve to re-emphasise his position as a force to be reckoned with, whether positively or negatively, enhancing rather than diminishing his brand as a man who 'gets stuff done' where others have failed to act.[54]

'I'm not going to pretend to be a dietician or a nutritionist'

The second way in which both men position themselves as getting things done is by presenting themselves as non-expert experts for whom a lack of formal qualification is an asset rather than a limitation. In the films, both Oliver and Gameau are on a quest to learn about sugar for themselves, cultivating a naive non-expert persona on a journey of discovery, with the 'truths' of sugar exposed along the way. Having seen for themselves, they become lay experts who are then able, or even compelled, to share their message with others. This process of knowledge acquisition and then evangelism models good neoliberal citizenship, with social problems rendered resolvable through individual entrepreneurialism rather than structural change. They are heroes who set out to win people over to their point of view, but it is not a collective vision and quickly steps over work that is already being done at the community level.[55] This is exemplified by Gameau, who 'sets out to bypass confusion and find out for myself',[56] culminating not only in the film, but also in a book, more than half of which is dedicated to 'the good news' of how he recovered his health after the experiment ('If I can cut out sugar, anybody can').[57] In line with many of the self-help books discussed in Chapter 4, despite striking out so determinedly on his own journey of discovery, it yields little in the way of new insights, and his tips for relinquishing sugar are strikingly familiar: seeing sugar-free eating as gaining health rather than giving something up; writing shopping lists; reading labels; seeking out hidden sugar; calculating sugar content; and not listening to the doubters.

Gameau's acquired non-expert expertise is warranted by experience rather than qualification; he declares in *That Sugar Book*: 'I am not going to pretend to be a dietician or a nutritionist. I am just going to share what worked for me … .'[58] This is not a confession of weakness, but rather, since the experiment is premised on cutting through the confusion of competing dietary experts, is a claim to a different kind of non-scientific authority, with Gameau using his body to mediate expert advice and appealing instead to common sense. For example, writing of debates surrounding addiction, he observes: 'There are scientific terms and principles for what classifies a substance as being addictive, but the majority of people I have talked to since starting this adventure care little for the scientific wording.'[59] This echoes Paul McKenna's dismissal of scientific debates around addiction in arguing that 'I personally don't think that the process of definition matters', and reminding readers that 'you don't have to be an electrician to switch on a light and you don't need to be a mechanic to drive a car'.[60] The contingency and caution of scientific debates can be discarded in the interests of action, even while invoking science as offering incontrovertible truth about the wrongness of sugar, fatness and addiction (see Chapter 2). In casting off his 'addiction', Gameau mobilises the familiar rhetorics of the clean slate. He describes his recovery diet as a 'metabolic reset', recalling his earlier account of himself as the perfect experimental subject who consumed no refined sugar, alcohol, caffeine or medication. This enables his body to represent all bodies; his restoration 'provides great hope' for those whose health is being harmed by sugar.[61] The right to speak with authority – as a non-expert expert – is won in exchange for his entrepreneurial willingness to take risks for the greater good.

While Gameau draws authority from his own bodily experience of excessive sugar consumption, for Oliver, authority comes from the accumulated capital of his well-established profile as a celebrity chef and campaigner. Oliver has high and enduring public recognition both within and beyond the UK. In the academic literature dedicated to the study of the phenomenon of Jamie Oliver, he is described as a 'mega force'[62] and as a 'global celebrity megachef *extraordinaire*',[63] with his move from celebrity chef to food and health campaigner elevating his personal reputation as a force to be reckoned with. He operates as a cultural intermediary who is at once a 'Big Citizen' who speaks (albeit unelectedly) in influential circles on behalf of the general public and an intimate friend who invites us into his domestic space and to join him on exotic travels.[64] This is captured in his self-introduction when giving select committee evidence in 2015: 'I'm Jamie Oliver, chef, campaigner and author, and probably most importantly today, a dad.'[65]

His campaigning track record is central to his reputation in relation to sugar as a man who gets things moving. In particular, his 2005 series *Jamie's School Dinners* is widely perceived as having prompted the government to take action on the quality of school meals. Similarly, *Jamie's*

Sugar Rush and his subsequent campaigning around the sugar tax are routinely cited, including by Oliver himself, as playing a major role in the introduction and formulation of the sugar tax. For example, when Oliver gave evidence at the 2018 Health and Social Care Committee hearings on childhood obesity, he declared: 'I fought tooth and nail for the money from this tax to be a progressive tax for good. And a tax for good means you take it from Peter to pay Paul. Paul was education. It was primary schools and this money was ring-fenced. Although Mr Cameron hated the idea of hypothecation, we got it.' Earlier in the same hearing, he reassured the committee that 'I know that Mr Cameron sees [the childhood obesity strategy] as very important. I think that his senior team find it incredibly important.'[66] Oliver repeatedly positions himself as 'in the know' and able to wield influence in the higher echelons of public health decision-making, and he gains credibility and strengthens his brand by association with, and access to, politicians.[67] However, he is also careful to distinguish himself from the political elites, as well as from scientific and public health experts, reassuring the select committee that 'I don't think that I'm a rocket scientist' and 'I ain't no pro.'

In this way, like Gameau, he locates himself firmly within the safe ground of common sense, where the absence of detail and specialist knowledge gives way to instinct and feeling. For example, he told *The Guardian* in 2018 that 'it just feels like the right thing to do', insisting: 'If you analyse what I'm saying […] there's nothing clever and there's nothing really controversial; it's fucking really basic common sense.'[68] Similarly, both of his select committee appearances are short on specifics but punctuated with rambling declarations of being 'passionate' and of the need for unspecified 'holistic' solutions. In making such statements, he positions himself as an intermediary who can move between governing elites and the general public, telling it like it is to cut through uncertainty and hesitancy in the interests of action. As an article in *The Times* noted approvingly after his 2015 select committee appearance: 'Oliver is not your run-of-the-mill witness'; 'for a start, he answered all the health committee's questions with honesty, frankness and cockney chirpiness'.[69]

One consequence of this intermediary position is that he is easily, if anomalously, included in lists of expertise. These lists function in the newspaper reporting to illustrate weight of opinion and, in doing so, grant him equivalence. For example, an article in *The Guardian* in October 2015 noted that 'Cameron's refusal to consider a sugar tax puts him at odds with medical groups, health charities, the Labour Party, the campaigning celebrity chef Jamie Oliver and even some Conservatives.'[70] Similarly, that same month, *The Times* reported that the government had rejected the sugar tax 'despite support from Dame Sally Davies, the chief medical officer, the British Medical Association and celebrities such as Jamie Oliver'.[71] Not everyone is persuaded by these gestures of equivalence, and following his 2015 select committee appearance, a representative of the British Dietetic Association was reported in *The Times* as insisting that Oliver should never have been allowed to 'pontificate on what was nothing more than personal opinion', adding: 'it's the cult of celebrity debasing nutrition to see a celebrity chef feted as if he knew anything'.[72] Similarly, following the select committee appearance of Oliver and fellow celebrity chef Hugh Fearnley-Whittingstall in May 2018, political sketch writer John Crace described the committee's brush with celebrity as turning 'sharp brains to juicy pulp'.[73] But for most, his intermediary position instead makes any shortfall in recognisable expertise forgivable. For example, in the 2018 interview in *The Guardian* cited above ('it's fucking really basic common sense'), the journalist reflects that '[Oliver] seems to be coming at obesity as a diet problem rather than a social one, although it may be too much to ask someone as energetic and ambitious as him to fix society.'[74]

But regardless of the enthusiasm for Oliver's contribution, there are grounds for scepticism about the ways in which he is credited with driving policy. Writing of Oliver's school meals campaign, social policy consultant Asmita Naik argues that it is more accurate to say that he reflected and energised existing policies than that he drove the agenda.[75] Similarly, in relation to the sugar tax, there was already a gathering head of steam around the sugar tax by the time *Jamie's Sugar Rush* came out – for example, in the 2013 report by Sustain, which made an early case for a tax.[76] Consequently, while Oliver undoubtedly energised the campaign, he certainly did not initiate it and was, to some extent, jumping on a bandwagon that was already gaining momentum. As a result, and in common with much celebrity campaigning, both Gameau and Oliver are not instigating anti-sugar campaigning so much as wielding their non-expert expertise and sizeable media power to give the oxygen of publicity to a cause already established in the public imagination. This in turn boosts their own brands and entrepreneurial ventures, as well as expanding the boundaries of what constitutes expertise in relation to sugar.

Conclusion

Both *Jamie's Sugar Rush* and *That Sugar Film* are intensely watchable and attention-grabbing films starring two amiable, if naively self-satisfied, protagonists. They move expertly between shock, persuasion, intimacy and (especially in Gameau's case) humour, deploying swiftly moving narratives to carry their viewers along. They slide smoothly between intimate domestic spaces and exotically unfamiliar locations to simultaneously reassure and entertain the viewer, while shoring up the wrongness of sugar – and, by extension, the wrongness of the (over)consuming Other against whom viewers are invited to define themselves. In this way, the films are object lessons in governing at a distance; they communicate to viewers a socially endorsed way of being in the world. But the films' goals can be achieved only at the expense of nuance, and the short-term and constrained nature of their investment in the issue, alongside the spectacular gestures demanded by campaigning as entertainment, means that they can never really get to know it. Instead, they end up lionising individual acts (introducing a tax on sugary drinks in a restaurant or self-sacrificially overconsuming sugar) that are inevitably dislocated from wider structures of inequality or the wider social and cultural context in which food choices are made. This is exemplified by Gameau, who offers a message of empowerment in *That Sugar Book* to readers who are struggling to give up sugar: 'There is a great story about a circus elephant with a chain around its leg. If only the elephant realised how powerful it was, it would snap the chain and break free. You are that powerful – sugar is minuscule.'[77] The problem with the analogy is that once the elephant is free from the chain, it is still far from home, utterly alone and in an alien environment where it will be unable to thrive and be safe. Similarly, successfully breaking free of sugar does nothing to address the vast inequalities which constrain health and wellbeing and within which otherwise derogated patterns of consumption come to make sense. Accidentally, Gameau is correct: perhaps sugar is minuscule in the grand scale of things. The remainder of the book takes up this issue explicitly, arguing that the determined foregrounding of the problem of sugar, alongside the insistence that consumption is within the necessary remit of the individual regardless of economic or social constraints, not only obscures those backgrounded inequalities but also actively entrenches and solidifies them. This characterises not only the domain of entertainment or popular non-fiction, but also the policy domain, as will be explored in the next chapter in relation to the sugar tax.

6

Taxing sugar

In his budget speech on 16 March 2016, Chancellor of the Exchequer George Osborne announced plans to introduce a Soft Drinks Industry Levy – colloquially known as the 'sugar tax'. Anti-sugar and anti-obesity campaigners were jubilant, and Jamie Oliver was reported in *The Sunday Times* as having 'parked his Vespa on Parliament Square and strolled towards a scrum of television cameras' before removing his helmet to reveal 'a toothy grin' and dancing 'a jig of joy' for the watching press.[1] Both his presence outside Parliament when the decision was announced and his subsequent 'sugar tax dance' for the cameras were unconvincingly claimed as impromptu; but for Oliver, as one of the UK's most prominent and popular anti-sugar voices, it was a moment of vindication not to be missed. Meanwhile in Parliament, Osborne, faced with the potentially unpopular task of introducing a new tax, positioned himself as a brave leader fuelled by moral obligation to future generations, declaring: 'I am not prepared to look back at my time here in this Parliament, doing this job and say to my children's generation: I'm sorry. We knew there was a problem with sugary drinks. We knew it caused disease. But we ducked the difficult decisions and we did nothing.'[2] The tax, scheduled for implementation in 2018, would apply an additional duty of 24 p per litre for drinks with more than 8 g of sugar per 100 ml and 18 p per litre for those with 5–8 g per 100 ml. The goals were simultaneously to reduce consumption (or, more accurately, sales, which serve as a proxy for consumption), to drive the soft drinks industry to create lower sugar alternatives and to generate revenue to fund child health-related programmes. The announcement was hot news,[3] giving the newspapers an opportunity to reprise the debates that had been rumbling along since the delayed publication of the 2015 Public Health England (PHE) report *Sugar Reduction: The Evidence for Action*. But even while voices of opposition made for good copy, the tone of the reporting was largely positive. At last, something had been done.

Sugar taxes on soft drinks are premised on a cascade of convictions: that obesity constitutes a crisis against which action must be taken; that the consumption of sugar-sweetened soft drinks is increasing; that this increase constitutes a significant factor in obesity and its associated metabolic and chronic diseases; and that reducing their consumption, or at least reducing the amount of sugar consumed when they are drunk, will generate cost-saving public health benefits.[4] And the UK is not alone in its decision to introduce a sugar tax: by 2021, over forty-five countries, regions and cities had introduced some form of taxation on sugar-sweetened beverages.[5] Thus the UK sugar tax, alongside similar global interventions, marks a significant step in sugar's recent rise to infamy, aligning it firmly with other legal substances, such as alcohol and tobacco, whose regulation and taxation in the interests of public health and revenue generation enjoy high levels of public acceptance. It also marks a move away from a reliance on voluntary product reformulation on the part of industry, and it became a lightning rod for ongoing debates about the distribution of responsibility for food choices, particularly in the wider context of austerity (as discussed in Chapter 7). These debates were played out at length in the newspaper coverage both before and after the sugar tax announcement, and this coverage is the primary resource for this chapter.

In line with the over-arching aim of this book, and perhaps to the frustration of some readers, I am not making an argument here about whether the sugar tax 'works' or is the right thing to do, since to do so remains trapped within the narrow terms of the debate already set. Instead, the chapter explores how the sugar tax is constructed in these reports, to what effects (both intended and unintended) and in whose interests. I begin by exploring how the case for the sugar tax is made, including the wielding of the 'nanny state' to both contest and defend it. Then I look at the 'playbook' of industry responses and at the Responsibility Deal to which they appeal as an alternative to taxation. Finally, I consider the multiple ways in which the success of the tax is measured. I argue that despite the apparent singularity of the sugar tax – the suggestion that everyone is talking about the same thing – its discursive coherence obscures the multiple and often conflicting agendas and investments through which it is constituted. In this way, the tax congeals convictions around the wrongness of obesity and sugar's causative role in it in problematic and necessarily fat-phobic ways that limit the terms of debate to one of efficacy, but where even what counts as effective remains fluid.

The case for the sugar tax

The case against sugary soft drinks and in favour of their taxation rests on the wrongness of obesity; sugar's culpability in generating fatness; the positioning of sugar-sweetened drinks as a primary vehicle for the delivery of sugar; and, therefore, the need to both reduce the consumption of sugary soft drinks and reduce the sugar content of those drinks through reformulation. The promised benefits include: obesity prevention and reduction; reduced healthcare costs; increased revenues for the promotion of public health; and the distribution of the greatest benefits to those with the lowest incomes, since they are most likely to be suffering from non-communicable diseases (NCDs).[6] The drinks are also a perfect target for fiscal intervention because their nutritional emptiness already renders them non-essential, while enabling policy-makers to avoid the complexity of taxing foodstuffs where sugar is one ingredient among many. These rationales combine to give common-sense coherence to the case for the sugar tax and are reproduced time and time again in the newspaper coverage by commentators, anti-sugar activists, celebrity chefs, politicians and medical professionals. A key strategy through which this case is made is through the invocation of the case of Mexico, which has become totemic in sugar tax debates.

On 1 January 2014, Mexico introduced an excise tax of 1 peso per litre of soda, amounting to a price increase of approximately 10%. Mexico was not the first country to tax soft drinks – for example, France introduced a soda tax in 2012 of €0.0716 per litre – but it quickly became the touchstone case for arguments in favour of taxation, not only in the UK, but also internationally. This is exemplified in the newspaper data, where over a third of all the articles discussing the sugar tax also mention the Mexican case. The Mexican case captured global attention because of its unusually high rates of sugar consumption, often in the form of sugary drinks, alongside high rates of obesity and its associated NCDs.[7] It is, noted an article in *The Guardian* in appalled despair, 'a country where Coca-Cola is commonly consumed with breakfast'.[8] The facts about the seriousness of the problem in Mexico form a common contextualising preface to the many journal articles and newspaper commentaries about the tax, with high rates of consumption, morbidity and mortality adding a sense of urgency and human drama to the potentially dry topic of taxation.

After a year, first reviews of the effects of the tax showed a significant impact on purchasing (as a proxy for consumption).[9] By December 2014, studies reported an overall decline in purchasing of 12%, rising to 17% among low socioeconomic groups.[10] The tax is also credited with generating a 5.2% rise per capita in water sales,[11] with greater changes in purchasing associated with those who were high consumers prior to the tax.[12] Modelling studies optimistically anticipated significant health impacts, including predictions of 18,900 fewer deaths between 2013 and 2022,[13] and the prevention of 239,900 cases of obesity by 2024 with total healthcare cost savings of $3.98 per dollar spent implementing the tax.[14]

In the UK newspaper data, the 12% purchasing reduction in Mexico circulated as a viral soundbite that became increasingly untethered from the study itself, functioning rhetorically to persuade readers of the incontrovertible success of the tax in ways that would travel across contexts. In response, industry representatives and associations opposing the tax, such as the British Soft Drinks Association, circulated a viral figure of their own to counteract the 12% claim: that 'the tax in Mexico has led to a reduction of just 6 calories per person per day in a daily diet of over 3000' – a figure they describe as 'a drop in the calorific bucket'.[15]

But as with Jamie Oliver's easy appropriation of the Mexican case, there is a tone to much of the reporting that should give us pause for thought, with Mexico repeatedly figured as a 'traditional' culture that has been overwhelmed by the forces of modernity, as represented by Coca-Cola's ubiquitous presence. Reporters repeatedly invoke the image of babies sucking on Coca-Cola-filled bottles or of the incorporation of Coca-Cola imagery and products into religious ceremonies that we also saw in *Jamie's Sugar Rush* in the previous chapter. The reader is presented with an ignorantly Coke-guzzling population, blissfully bewitched by the pleasures of sugar and its paraphernalia and lacking the capacity to consume rationally. An article in *The Guardian* in November 2015 pushed the stereotype even further, arguing that 'excessive consumption of soda kills twice as many Mexicans as trade in the other kind of Coke that Mexico is famous for'.[16]

The Mexican population is figured in this reporting as the incontinently consuming Other, overwhelmed by a modern food system that it is unable to adapt to. The undertone of the argument is that if the tax can work in Mexico, it must be able to work in a context more at home with the values and practices of modernity that is less lost to the predations of sugar. Missing from these accounts is recognition of the paucity of safe drinking water in many regions; the enduring health impacts of high rates of poverty and inequality; and a long history of colonial occupation that has impacted in fundamental and detrimental ways on everyday lives and futures.[17] The primacy of the Mexican case in the UK reporting, then, is never only about the precedent-setting timing of the Mexican tax or the extremity of the health crisis the country faces; it also establishes the principle of a population, or sub-population, for whom the promises of modernity and the neoliberal compulsion to simultaneously consume and show restraint are simply too overwhelming to manage sensibly. Instead, compulsion through taxation is required. This underpins the

UK rationale for the sugar tax and accounts for the appeal of the Mexican example in making the case for the tax (as will be explored further in Chapter 7 in relation to austerity).

Invoking the 'nanny state'

The case for the sugar tax is always made with the opposing case in mind, with both sides attempting to pre-empt the arguments of the other. But nor is it a binary debate, and instead there are multiple agendas at work, provisionally and strategically congealing around positions for or against. One of the core oppositional discourses that haunts the case for the sugar tax specifically, and regulatory intervention in general, is the invocation of the 'nanny state'; that is, where intervention is read as a fundamental curtailing of individual freedoms to make informed consumption choices. It is used pejoratively to forestall regulation by shouting down contradictory views and forcing proposed interventions into a binary frame whereby individual rights are either protected or denied.[18]

In the newspaper coverage of the sugar tax, three key uses of the nanny-state accusation are visible. The first is direct accusations of nanny-statism designed to protest interference and to forestall regulation. The second is a re-appropriation of nanny-statism as something that the current crisis demands more of. And thirdly, and most commonly, the accusation is used to articulate an instinctive libertarian response that must be sacrificed in the face of a crisis. This allows those on the conventionally tax-averse political right to square the circle of supporting the tax while maintaining an ideological posture wedded to individual choice.

Outraged nanny-state expostulations feature most commonly around the March 2016 budget announcement, and particularly in the right-wing tabloid press. For example, in *The Sun*, Conservative MP Jacob Rees-Mogg is cited as denouncing the tax as 'absurd, nannying, puritanical cobblers'.[19] Campaigning group, the TaxPayers' Alliance – an 'astroturfing' organisation that gives the appearance of a third-party grassroots movement while promoting a neoliberal, pro-business agenda – has also been a vocal critic, freely wielding nanny-state accusations. For example, in response to the budget announcement, its chief executive, Jonathan Isaby, told the *Daily Mail* that Osborne had 'decided to cave in to the demands of the High Priest of the Nanny State in the public health lobby'.[20] In April 2019, on the first anniversary of the implementation of the sugar tax, the group issued a forthright summary statement about the tax and its failings, which it attributes to 'a bloated and patronising state':

> The sugar tax is the nanny state at its very worst. People should be free to decide what they eat and drink. It is nobody else's business – especially not an unaccountable quango such as Public Health England, whose entire reason for being appears to be stopping people doing anything fun. The sugar tax represents an unacceptable infringement on personal liberty and freedom of choice.[21]

The nanny-state attribution hits all the right notes, not only mourning the perceived erosion of freedom of choice but also positioning regulation as the enemy of fun. This aligns easily with the agendas of the food and drinks industry, for whom fun is an increasingly important tool for marketing food and drink to both adults and children.[22]

These protestations are never really about the sugar tax and are not being mobilised in relation to genuine losses of freedom, but instead relate to the principle of state intervention in public health more generally. As a result, those crying 'nanny state' and those advocating the sugar tax are not having a disagreement along a single axis, but rather are engaging in two separate (if related) arguments. The protestations force complex decisions around public health into an un-nuanced binary of free or unfree choices, pitching the individual against the state (a dynamic that is repeated in the COVID-19 pandemic around practices such as mask-wearing).

In contrast to attempts to weaponise the nanny state in order to forestall regulation, for others, the problem is not an over-reaching state, but rather an under-reaching one that is too cowed by the taint of nanny-statism to do what is necessary. For example, in June 2014, *The Guardian* reported the advice of psychologist Jane Ogden for tackling obesity: 'The government has to be much more nanny state in terms of policing the food industry, taxing snack food, taxing fizzy drinks, banning fizzy drinks, banning sugary foods and not just in school dinners but also in work canteens and hospital food.'[23] The claim freely wields verbs of coercion (policing, taxing, banning) in direct provocation to libertarian objections. In 2015, Jamie Oliver joined the chorus, insisting in an article in *The Times* that 'at the right time, we need a nanny state'.[24]

This strategic re-appropriation of the nanny state is exemplified by a series of events at the turn of 2018–19. In December 2018, England's Chief Medical Officer, Dame Sally Davies, issued her annual report, in which she recommended the expansion of the sugar tax to other products high in added sugar, such as milk drinks and shakes.[25] In the subsequent media coverage, Davies leaned into the nanny-state accusations that inevitably followed. Citing the failures of voluntary industry-focused sugar reduction schemes as a justification for the introduction of taxes, she declared: 'Do you want to call that nanny state? If so, I am chief nanny' – a soundbite that was widely reproduced.[26] In January 2019, PHE used the turn of the new year to launch the new Change4Life 'Sugar Swaps' campaign. This included not only the animated kitchen drama discussed at the beginning of Chapter 3, but also the headline-grabbing claim that by the age of ten, children have already exceeded the lifetime total sugar intake suitable for an eighteen-year-old.[27] The nanny-state soundbite from Sally Davies the previous month was recycled repeatedly in the subsequent newspaper coverage. For example, the National Obesity Forum chair, Tam Fry, told *The Times* that 'the medicine needed to tackle obesity is Nanny Sally's prescription …' .[28] It is hard to imagine a similar term of reference for a male chief medical officer – a simmering sexism that Davies herself raised in a BBC Radio 4 interview with journalist Nick Robinson in February 2019.[29] But her appropriation of the 'chief nanny' label nevertheless highlights a determined attempt to reclaim regulation as both positive and necessary.

The third and most common wielding of the nanny state in the newspaper reporting comes in the form of urgent exceptionalism; that is, in claims from commentators that while they would ordinarily oppose state intervention in consumption choices, in the case of the sugar tax, the urgency of the problem demands that they suspend their usual convictions. For example, journalist Ian Birrell considered the possibility of a sugar tax in a commentary in the *Daily Mail* in September 2014: 'Instinctively, I recoil at nanny-state diktats, lectures from politicians (of all people) over how to live our lives, and the idea of government intervention unless absolutely necessary. But the health crisis unfolding before our eyes demands urgent action even if it has been forced on us through legislation.'[30] Birrell's 'instinctive' horror in the face of government intervention is underlined by his contemptuous dismissal of politicians ('of all people'), who are figured as inadequate substitutes for the rational individual who knows their own mind and preferences. The sacrifice of his libertarian principles only amplifies the urgency of the problem.

In an editorial in *The Times*, columnist Kenny Farquharson recounted how the decision by the newspaper to support the sugar tax had led to some 'eye-rolling' in the office, with one colleague declaring frustratedly: 'It's not even lunchtime and we're banning something.' Farquharson's response is sympathetic but resistant: 'I see where they are coming from. When the government wants to curb something, a sound instinct is to say: "Cool your jets, bud. Is this really necessary?" But not every intervention is the nanny state rustling its petticoats.'[31] Instead, citing costs to the National Health Service (NHS) of doing nothing and the personal costs of chronic illness and death, he argues that the 'potential gains are too great to be lost because of squeamishness'. Intervention through taxation is rendered an undesirable but necessary act of political courage whose time has come.

The 'playbook'

For the food and drinks industry, the move towards sugar taxation marks a decline in influence over policy, a potential loss of revenue and the setting of a precedent that in the future could see taxation reach far beyond soft drinks into confectionery and other sugar-sweetened foods. According to *The Guardian* in 2015, the introduction of sugar taxes is what 'keeps soda executives up at night', not only threatening their bottom line, but also demonising a product whose reputation depends on its associations with healthful athleticism and harmless fun.[32] Consequently, as you would expect, the industry pushed back, continuing a long history of resistance to the demonisation of its products that has been both sustained and vociferous. Its strategies are closely associated with a 'playbook' developed by the tobacco industry, inadvertently solidifying the association with the tobacco industry even while determinedly resisting the idea that its products are the 'new tobacco'. These include: casting doubt on the science, including the co-option of scientists to give credibility to alternative, more favourable, findings; (re)framing the problem of energy balance to focus on the 'energy out' side of the equation; lobbying activities to influence policy; promoting personal responsibility in tandem with personal choice; promoting self-regulation in partnership with public health organisations; and advocating product reformulation and innovation.[33] The playbook enables companies to push back against the increasingly entrenched conviction that the industry is venally invested in covering up its role in creating the problem of sugar (and by extension, obesity) to protect its profits at any cost. It is an attempt not only to fend off regulation, but also to recapture consumer trust in an industry whose products are increasingly seen, as discussed in Chapter 3, as packed with both sugar and deception.

Confronted with a powerful consensus about the risks of its products, the soda industry's first move is to challenge those claims by planting seeds of doubt. One of the ways it achieves this is through the assertion of complexity, cultivating doubt about the presumed certainties that constitute the rationale for the tax. This strategy was also a mainstay of the tobacco industry's attempts to resist regulation, with the cultivation of doubt in turn creating space for alternative, more industry-favourable, interpretations of both the problem and its solutions.[34] For example, in 2014, *The Sunday Telegraph* told the history of the silencing of Yudkin's sugar research in favour of research on fat; a turn of events which Lustig describes in the article as a 'disastrous detour' of science.[35] Towards the end of the article, a representative of the UK business group AB Sugar is cited in response, insisting that obesity in Britain is a result of 'a range of complex factors'. They then sow further doubt by invoking opposing evidence wrapped in the authority of science, insisting that 'reviews of the body of scientific evidence by expert committees have concluded that consuming sugar as part of a balanced diet does not induce lifestyle diseases such as diabetes and heart disease'.[36]

The appeal to balance is doing a lot of discursive work here, casting doubt on the starting premise of the claims in the article about the toxicity of sugar by refusing the singular focus on sugar. This is a common tactic in the industry's responses to negative newspaper coverage. For example, in a critical article in the *Daily Mail* in 2015 about the Coca-Cola Christmas truck – 'a giant Coke truck touring Britain's fattest towns, plying children with free drinks' – a Food and Drink Federation representative, Tim Rycroft, counter-argues that 'Demonising single ingredients or products isn't constructive when we really need to be improving overall diets.'[37] These rebuttals directly co-opt the rhetorics of public health, for which the pairing of diet and lifestyle, the complexity of obesity and the need for a multi-faceted approach are also mainstays, lending them credibility. They also demonstrate what Scrinis describes as the 'corporate capture' of mainstream obesity science, which remains wedded to the notion of energy balance as a means of understanding, and intervening in, fatness.[38] This creates spaces for the claim that there is no such thing as a bad food in moderation ('a balanced diet'), especially when matched with high-profile corporate social responsibility activities on the 'energy out' side of the equation, such as sponsorship of sports activities from school teams to global mega events. The casting of doubt on the accepted science, then, is not rejection of science *per se*, but rather is the selective deployment of alternative conclusions that still lay claim to the authority granted by science.

A key function of the creation of doubt is to prepare the ground for alternative, industry-funded research that can then be wielded in rebuttal. This can take several forms, including in-house research facilities, industry-funded research groups and industry funding of established scientists and researchers. The aim is to grant authoritative equivalence to findings that go against the prevailing dietary grain, unsettling its certainties. In her book on industry-funded nutrition research, *Unsavory Truth*, Marion Nestle argues that these ventures are 'market research masquerading as basic science', and that their findings should always be treated with suspicion since they are predominantly favourable to the financial interests of the sponsors.[39] This is an effect that has already been well documented in relation to pharmaceutical research,[40] but in the context of nutrition-related research, it occurs in a much less regulated environment.

In *Unsavory Truth*, and consistent with a protracted career of meticulous documentation of, and advocacy against, industry-research relationships, Nestle takes a firm stand against researchers accepting any industry funding. This position is widely adopted in the newspaper coverage. Against the increasingly febrile atmosphere of suspicion about industry motives that characterises the attack on sugar, even the suggestion of an industry connection sends them into 'shocked exposé' mode, with the whiff of scandal and intrigue making for attention-grabbing headlines. For example, in 2014, a headline in the *Daily Mail* promised to expose 'the sugar tsars in bed with confectionery giants',[41] and in 2018, *The Sunday Times* led with 'Diabetes UK in tie-up with sugar giant'.[42] Big Sugar is figured here as a behemoth drawing even the most well-intentioned actors relentlessly into its orbit of influence to secure its own powerful interests. Despite the best efforts of industry to put the sanitising gloss of partnership onto its research practices, industry-funded research is treated routinely in the newspaper coverage as at best suspicious and at worst outright corrupt.

This is demonstrated by the media vilification of Ian Macdonald, a professor of metabolic physiology at the University of Nottingham who chaired the Scientific and Advisory Committee on Nutrition (SACN) working group on carbohydrates that delivered the revised recommendations for sugar consumption in 2015. In an article in *The Guardian* in September 2013 about industry funding of sugar-related research, Macdonald (alongside several other lower-profile working group members) was portrayed as inescapably compromised by his position on advisory boards for both Coca-Cola and Mars, as well as being the academic lead for the University of Nottingham's strategic relationship with Unilever.[43] This theme was picked up again in January 2014, when the Channel 4 current affairs programme *Dispatches* aired an episode on sugar addiction in which Macdonald's perceived conflicts of interest featured, prompting widespread and scandalised press coverage. 'Sugar watchdog works for Coca-Cola', declared *The Sunday Times*, including the widely reported soundbite from Action on Sugar's Simon Capewell that it was 'like putting Dracula in charge of a blood bank'.[44]

In the newspaper coverage of the *Dispatches* programme, Macdonald defended his industry involvement, citing the transparency of his declarations of interest, the inclusion of any personal funding on his tax returns and his conviction of the necessity of working with industry to influence its practices. In 2015, *The Times* published another exposé-style story headlined 'Fizzy drinks giant pays millions to diet experts', which highlighted the heavy investment by Coca-Cola in scientific research and healthy-eating initiatives. In the article, Macdonald once again defended the principle of industry-funded research, declaring, 'I do not regard links with both industry and the government as being in conflict [...]. Both the public and industry are entitled to access the best advice available.' In the same article, Marion Nestle offers the adamant counterpoint: 'In my opinion, no scientist should accept funding from Coca-Cola. It's totally compromising. Period. End of discussion.'[45]

In *Unsavory Truth,* Nestle acknowledges the heavy institutional demands on researchers to bring in external funding,[46] and in an earlier 'viewpoint' piece in *Journal of the American Medical Association,* she acknowledges the ways in which funding cuts make industry funding hard to resist for researchers, institutions and professional organisations. She refrains from attributing biased research to intentional malfeasance, arguing instead that the distorting effects of industry funding 'are almost always unconscious, unintentional and unrecognised, making them especially difficult to prevent'.[47] Nor, she argues, does industry funding inevitably corrupt the findings, although 'it invariably appears to do so'.[48] In an atmosphere of widespread suspicion towards sugar, for the companies profiting from it and the researchers with whom they collaborate, this taint of corruption sticks easily. It also extends to politicians, where reluctance to take firm action becomes evidence of being in the pockets of industry, and the delayed 2015 publication by PHE of the revised guidance on sugar is repeatedly attributed to Prime Minister David Cameron having been 'got at' by industry lobbyists. In the newspaper coverage of the sugar tax, the playbook is unable to recuperate the widely cultivated status of the sugar industry (along with sugar itself) as the manipulative and deceptive villain of the piece.

'The big stick is finally being wielded'

While the food and drinks industry has always needed to defend its products and practices – hence, the playbook – the announcement of the sugar tax and its subsequent implementation signal a new and significant downturn in the industry's fortunes and reputation. In particular, the increased support for the sugar tax, even among those who might otherwise be ideologically opposed to such interventions, marks a recognition of the limits to voluntary industry self-regulation. This interrupts the determined efforts of the food and drinks industry to position itself as part of the solution rather than the problem and therefore as warranting a seat at the policy-making table. This emphasis on solution-seeking partnership is a key element in the industry playbook, and one which found easy accommodation in the early years of the Conservative–Liberal Democrat coalition government (2010–15) in the form of the Public Health Responsibility Deal (more commonly known as the Responsibility Deal). This was launched by the Secretary of State for Health, Andrew Lansley, in March 2011, and its stated aim was to '[tap] into the potential for businesses and other organisations to improve public health and help to tackle health inequalities through their influence over food, physical activity, alcohol and health in the workplace'.[49] It consisted of five networks (food, alcohol, physical activity, health and work, and behaviour change), each of which developed a series of pledges to which companies could publicly sign up. In relation to food, with sugar still largely off the radar, the initial pledges related to salt reduction, the removal of trans fats (or trans-fatty acids) and the provision of out-of-home calorie labelling. But in March 2012, an additional pledge to cut 5 billion calories per day from the national diet (equating to 100 calories per person per day) was launched.[50] This created a clear space to bring sugar more explicitly into the remit of the Responsibility Deal, particularly in relation to soft drinks, with companies invited to commit to reformulating products and reducing portion sizes.

The logics of the Responsibility Deal were not left unchallenged, even before the early enthusiasm for it began to wane. For example, in an article in February 2013 in *The Guardian*, Tim Lobstein of the International Association of the Study of Obesity (IASO) argued that voluntary agreements like the Responsibility Deal are 'a very valuable opportunity for the government to play for time'.[51] In the same article, Terence Stephenson (chair of the Academy of Medical Royal Colleges) protested that 'it's like asking petrol companies to encourage people to cycle or walk rather than use cars'. Published evaluations of the Responsibility Deal also highlighted concerns about industry influence over the terms of the pledges; the lack of quantitative monitoring or clear targets; the paucity and inconsistency of progress reports; the fact that many of the reported actions were already under way at the time of pledging, rather than being instigated by the Responsibility Deal directly; and the absence of sanctions, including a clear pathway to regulation in the case of the failure to meet goals.[52]

Sceptics' concerns were confirmed in May 2018, shortly after the implementation of the sugar tax, when PHE issued an interim progress report on its 2015 sugar reduction strategy. The strategy had called for voluntary industry reductions in the sugar content of their products of 5% in the first year, with a target of 20% reductions by 2020. However, the report showed average reductions of only 2% across retailed own-brand and manufacturer-branded products, confirming for many that the decision to move away from voluntary agreements to regulation through taxation had been correct.[53] It was time for a new approach. As health journalist Sarah Boseley reported in *The Guardian* just days before the implementation of the tax, the days of the Responsibility Deal 'are long gone':

> Food companies just look back wistfully at the panels convened by Andrew Lansley, then health secretary, where companies would offer to cut a few calories here, do a bit of labelling there and never got called to account. There was no real measurement of what was being done because different companies made different pledges and comparisons were nigh impossible. This is different. The big stick is finally being wielded.[54]

Faced with the 'big stick' of sugar taxation, and with the threat of further taxes to come, the food and drinks industry mustered its resources and fought back, revivifying the logics of the Responsibility Deal in its own defence.

This can be seen, first, in appeals to a common enemy: obesity. As discussed in Chapter 2, the problem of obesity has been placed so thoroughly beyond contestation that it requires no specific articulation or justification. This means that it can serve as an accommodating platform for multiple competing positions and goals under the guise of shared endeavour. As Leendert den Hollander, UK general manager for Coca-Cola, argued in *The Guardian* in 2016: 'we don't believe the sugar tax is the right thing to be done. We are not debating the issue, we are debating the solution.'[55] This creates space for the industry to continue positioning itself as a partner in a shared struggle and a necessary player in finding a solution.

The second defensive appropriation of the logics of the Responsibility Deal can be seen in the emphatic industry endorsement of the effectiveness and economies of self-regulation. This point is driven home in the repeated showcasing of companies' own accomplishments, which are portrayed as exceeding government ambitions and as impossible in a more externally regulated environment. For example, in an article in *The Guardian* in 2016 about the proposed sugar tax, Gavin Partington of the British Soft Drinks Association observed: 'There are steps our industry is already taking and as a result has reduced calories by 7.5% since 2012 with plans to reduce a further 20% by 2020.'[56] Here, the industry is positioned as ahead of the government ('*already* taking'; my italic) in the search for a solution and as leaders whose capacity for problem-solving innovation will only be stifled by regulation.

The third strategy is the enthusiastic appropriation of the space that the Responsibility Deal created for the extravagant self-promotion of reformulation efforts. Public commitments to reformulate products so as to reduce sugar content (or saturated fat, or salt) lie at the heart of claims to self-regulation. In a study of industry responses to the sugar tax in Ireland, marketing scholar Norah Campbell and colleagues describe reformulation as the 'silver bullet', which allows companies to position themselves as problem-solvers.[57] It also enables them to narrow the distance between themselves and public health organisations, media and governments, for whom product reformulation also remains a key element of sugar reduction strategies. For example, as discussed in Chapter 3, the possibility of reformulation is the defining logic of Action on Sugar's hidden-sugar shock stories, and it aligns easily with a stealth strategy where subtle changes in sweetness are expected to slowly transform consumer tastes.

Reformulation is appealing for food and drinks companies because it enables them to reposition problematised products as 'healthy', creating opportunities to transform even small reductions into attention-grabbing cumulative totals that highlight their partnership role. For example, in June 2014, *The Guardian* reported that under the auspices of the Responsibility Deal, the Co-operative supermarket chain had pledged to remove 100 million teaspoons of sugar from its shelves by launching an own-brand, no-added-sugar fruit squash range.[58] The corporate mobilisation of arresting cumulative totals echoes the 'big, round and highly contestable numbers' which Michael Gard argues characterise the war on obesity (see Chapter 2) – for example, the announcement by the Department of Health and Social Care in the second year of the Responsibility Deal of the goal to remove 5 billion calories from the daily national diet. It is also an opportunity for companies to expand their range of products, since reformulations are more commonly launched as additions to their portfolio rather than as replacements. For example, in an article in June 2014 in *The Sunday Telegraph* about failures of the

Responsibility Deal to produce meaningful change, a representative of Coca-Cola GB defended the decision to leave the recipe for original Coca-Cola unchanged, saying: 'We have no plans to change Coca-Cola. We know that people love it and we provide two great-tasting sugar-free, no calorie options in Diet Coke and Coca-Cola Zero, which together comprise more than 40 per cent of the cola we sell in the UK.'[59] This potentially bifurcates supply chains to create new lines of reformulated products that can be coded as healthy and command a higher price, while simultaneously demonstrating a commitment to keeping reformulation front and centre. In this way, reformulation can be seen as performing not only a marketing function for food and drinks companies, but also an ideological and political one oriented towards convincing governments to support industry-friendly policies and regulations.[60]

But however enthusiastically wielded by the food and drinks industry to fend off regulation, the newspaper data clearly shows the changing reputational fortunes of both the Responsibility Deal and the companies relying on it. In the coverage from 2013 and 2014, while the rush to target sugar was still gathering steam, newspapers showcased reports trumpeting high-profile pledges such as the reduction of sugar in Lucozade and Ribena in January 2013;[61] the pledge later that year to remove 'the equivalent of one and a half Olympic-sized swimming pools of saturated fat from the national diet' by reformulating KitKats and Oreos;[62] or the boast by supermarket chain Waitrose, when challenged about the high sugar content of its upmarket drinks, that it had 'removed 7.1 million tons of sugar from its chilled juices and would turn its attention to carbonated drinks'.[63] Government endorsements of the Responsibility Deal are also given a high-profile voice in these articles. For example, in the same report in *The Guardian* about the Lucozade and Ribena pledges by GlaxoSmithKline, Public Health Minister Anna Soubry triumphantly declared that 'through the responsibility deal we are already achieving real progress in helping people reduce the calories and salt in their diet. Overall, more than 480 companies including many leading high street brands have signed up.'[64] In these early examples, these claims do not go unchallenged, but the challenges focus primarily on the limited nature of the changes and the need for more companies to sign up and to make greater changes. For example, Charlie Powell of the Children's Food Campaign complained that even after their reformulation, Lucozade and Ribena would still be 'red' in the traffic light labelling system, and the president of the Faculty of Public Health, John Ashton, raised concerns about the sugar and salt in KitKats and Oreos that remained in the products to compensate for the reduction in fat. As a result the critiques leave the principles of the Responsibility Deal largely intact, however underwhelming in practice.

But as time goes on, opportunities for companies to showcase pledges, and for the government to trumpet the achievements of the Responsibility Deal, recede. Instead, as calls for a sugar tax gather steam, the Responsibility Deal is increasingly relegated to a cautionary tale of failure that can be mobilised as justification for 'the big stick' of taxation. This decline in the fortunes of the Responsibility Deal, and along with it the industry claims to solution-focused partnership, are visible in the structure of the newspaper reporting. Where industry voices had previously taken centre stage with their pledge announcements only a couple of years earlier, these are gradually dislodged, and industry comment is relegated to the ends of the articles. Far from their offering an authoritative final word on the issue, the tail-end positioning of these ripostes is more commonly an act of tokenism; a gesture of balance or a right-of-reply opportunity for brands, products or professional associations implicated in the main body of the story. For example, following the launch of the 2018 PHE interim report, a *Daily Mail* article led with the headline 'Junk food firms fail miserably to meet a sugar reduction target set by Government to cut child obesity'. Gavin Partington of the British Soft Drinks Association defends the disappointing figures in a peripheral final sentence, noting that the drinks industry has cut sugar 'by almost five times as much as other categories'. Gesturing back to the Responsibility Deal, he observes that this 'correlates with the industry's strong track record in sugar reduction before the introduction of the soft drinks levy'.[65] These changes in the structure of the newspaper reporting to de-centre industry voices reflect a reconfiguration in the relationship not only between industry and government, but also between industry and popular opinion, which is increasingly intolerant of corporate claims to be acting in the best interests of public health.

Measuring success

But to be counted as a viable change of policy, the big stick of the sugar tax must do more than signal the failures of the Responsibility Deal which comes before it; it needs to make its own positive case by demonstrating, or at least promising, its own successes in reducing rates of sugar-induced obesity and its associated metabolic health problems. However, the absence of measurable reductions in either, or at least their relocation to an unspecified future, means that alternative measures are needed to warrant the tax. Consequently, success is instead measured by three key proxies for the promised health benefits: (1) reduced sugar consumption; (2) increased revenue to invest in health-related programmes; and (3) raised awareness of the risks of sugar. These render the category of success so broad as to be virtually meaningless; by these measures, it is almost impossible for the sugar tax to fail. This highlights the performative nature of the sugar tax, whose primary function is to be seen to be taking action rather than its specific outcomes.

Sugar reduction

One of the key aims of the UK sugar tax was to pick up where the Responsibility Deal had failed and motivate companies to create lower-sugar iterations of familiar products, while generating price incentives for consumers to move to lower-sugar products unaffected by the tax. This expectation sets up both product reformulation and reduced sales to function as proxies for obesity reduction, which is presumed to be an inevitable consequence of reduced consumption. Using theoretical modelling in advance of the tax, the predictions are varied but relentlessly optimistic. For example, in 2013, an article in the *British Medical Journal* predicted that a 20% tax on sugary drinks would reduce obesity prevalence by approximately 180,000 people[66] – a figure that was reproduced virally over the next couple of years as concerns around sugar intensified. In 2014 in the *Daily Mail*, journalist Ian Birrell sets the figure at an even more ambitious 250,000 (vaguely attributed to 'one government agency'),[67] and in February 2016, Cancer Research UK predicted that a 20% tax could result in 3.7 million fewer cases of obesity by 2025.[68] Caught in a whirlwind of optimism inflation, the big round numbers become increasingly meaningless as they float free from their origins to become facts.

The two-year gap between the announcement of the tax in 2016 and its 2018 implementation meant that companies could avoid the levy by reformulating products before it came into force. This meant that by the time the tax was implemented, the scheme could pronounce itself a success even before it started. For example, a Treasury press release announcing the implementation of the tax in 2018 trumpeted that 50% of manufacturers had already reformulated products to take them below the threshold of the levy, removing an estimated 45 million kilos of sugar from the food supply annually.[69] Subsequent evaluations of the levy have been similarly celebratory. In 2020, PHE published its third sugar-reduction progress report, which was hailed in a press release as highlighting the success of the tax.[70] The report included the headline figure of a 43.7% reduction in the total sugar content of drinks subject to the tax and a fall of 35.2% in the calorie intake likely to be consumed in a single occasion.[71] These falls occurred alongside a purchasing shift towards products not subject to the tax and exceed any previous voluntary reductions.

The outcomes of the UK sugar tax in terms of reduced purchasing (as a proxy for consumption) are in line with reviews of similar interventions globally. For example, in a review of fifteen studies across ten jurisdictions, public health scholar Andrea Teng and colleagues found taxes to be 'effective in reducing SSB [sugar sweetened beverage] purchases and dietary intake', with a 10% SSB tax associated with a decline in purchases and intake of 10% (although with considerable variation across studies and contexts).[72] They also identified a modest 1.9% increase in the consumption of non-taxed beverages such as bottled water. Similarly, a review of twenty-seven studies across eleven jurisdictions published by the Institute for Fiscal Studies found that taxes led to price increases and reduced purchases of taxed products.[73]

But despite the projected health improvements anticipated because of this sugar reduction, evidence of those health impacts has been underwhelming. For example, an evaluation of impact of the tax on the weight of young people living in an urban region of Mexico found no change in body mass index (BMI) on average, with a mean BMI reduction among heavier girls (but not boys) equivalent to a weight loss of only 0.35 kg over a two-year period.[74] Nevertheless, the lack of evidence of measurable health improvements is no obstacle, since the determined future-orientation of the attacks on both sugar and obesity (as discussed in Chapter 2) means that the certainty that they will manifest themselves compensates for the fact that they haven't manifested themselves yet. This creates a space where sugar reduction can stand in as a proxy for success in the meantime, providing proof of concept. This in turn fuels calls for the gap between sugar reduction and the anticipated, but as yet unseen, health improvements to be bridged both by increasing the level of tax and by extending it to other categories of sugary foods. As the National Obesity Forum chair, Tam Fry, told the *Daily Mail* in July 2018: 'I think cereals, milkshakes and all the drinks which have a superfluity of sugar are all now eligible for the levy.'[75] Where tax-induced sugar reductions can act as a proxy for future health impacts, the tax's only failure can be that it doesn't go far enough.

New funds for good causes

A second alternative measure of success, particularly in the debates preceding the introduction of the sugar tax, is financial. This includes both the anticipated savings in healthcare costs – up to £10 million in the year 2025 alone according to Cancer Research UK[76] – and in the direct generation of revenue which can be ring-fenced for health-related interventions. This is key to securing public support for taxes, and social policy researcher Malene Bødker and colleagues argue that one of the reasons why the Danish 'fat tax' failed was that it was seen by the public as a means of simply filling the government's coffers rather than as a serious public health intervention.[77]

In his 2016 budget speech, George Osborne promised to use the sugar tax revenue to 'double the amount of funding we dedicate to sport in every primary school',[78] and the Treasury press release in 2018 announcing the implementation of the tax anticipated 'a funding boost for healthy school breakfast clubs'.[79] The 2013 Sustain report proposes multiple uses, including providing free, high-quality school meals, improving food education and skills, offering free fruit and vegetable snacks in schools and installing fresh drinking water fountains.[80] Meanwhile, the newspaper data reveals a host of further possible uses for the funding, including additional doctors and nurses, health education programmes and treatment facilities. The anticipated funds are spent many times over in the reporting and public announcements, offering up an alibi for the potential absence of measurable health impacts in the form of health gains by other means. Furthermore, it insulates the tax against both over- and under-achieving in terms of sugar reduction, with high revenues compensating for low levels of reformulation or minimal changes in consumer behaviour, and low revenues signalling success in the form of high levels of reformulation or reduced purchases. In this way, the tax is always able to occupy a position as a social good regardless of the amount raised.

For all the promises, though, there is no guarantee that the hypothecated taxes will reach their declared destination, and in 2021, Sustain protested angrily that since 2018, £700 million of the revenue raised by the tax was unaccounted for.[81] This followed a report in 2019 in the trade journal *The Grocer* under the headline 'Javid admits Treasury has swallowed sugar tax cash', claiming that the Chancellor of the Exchequer, Sajid Javid, had dropped earlier commitments to ring-fence the revenue raised by the tax and that the money was now being 'pocketed' by the Treasury.[82] This disappearing cash also speaks to the ways in which the multiple agendas underpinning the sugar tax congeal around a singular measure while meeting divergent goals. For example, as discussed in the next chapter, the (unfulfilled) promise that revenues will be used to fund public health interventions and services provides political cover for the devastation of those same public services under austerity (see Chapter 7).

'The noise will do more than the tax'

The final, and most nebulous, marker of success is the very fact of the tax, including the controversies surrounding it. As commentator Alex Renton noted in *The Observer* in March 2016, 'the noise will do more than the tax', which, in his view, is a tokenistic gesture that will have little effect on 'British waistlines or on type 2 diabetes rates for years, if ever'. Instead, he argues that the noise of debate means that 'every mention [of the danger posed by sugar] is another warning to a parent buying a Britvic Drench for a thirsty toddler'.[83] Jamie Oliver used a similar tactic to deflect critical attention when reminded during his 2015 select committee appearance that his own restaurants sell Coca-Cola, declaring evasively: 'I'm not sure if it's the action or the conversation that's more powerful. Probably the latter.'[84] This recalls Abigail Saguy's argument, discussed in Chapter 2, that debates around the precise nature of the problem of obesity and what to do about it solidify it as a problem. Similarly, any debate around the sugar tax solidifies rather than discredits the problem of sugar.

Outside the noise of debate, simply having a sugar tax in place is seen as sending a powerful message. For example, in *The Times* in January 2016, the head of Public Health at the Organisation of Economic Co-operation and Development, Franco Sassi, is quoted as saying: 'The most valuable contribution taxes can make to a public health strategy is the signal they give to consumers and the food system that a government is concerned about the harms associated with unhealthy diets and is serious about tackling them.'[85] For Sassi, taxes communicate seriousness, in terms of both government intent and the seriousness of the problem at hand, but the move of evaluations of success away from measurable health improvements and towards message signalling widens what constitutes success to the point where it is stripped of meaning. Signalling is also important to Jamie Oliver, for whom the sugar tax is a powerful shot across the bows for the soft drinks and junk food industries. For example, in a feature on him in *The Guardian* in April 2018, Oliver explains: 'the best bit is that it's the first time government has put someone on the naughty step and said "there's a few more of you out there and if you don't reformulate your products, we're watching"'.[86] The infantilising reference to the 'naughty step' – a disciplinary technique for misbehaving children popularised by the TV show *Supernanny* – echoes his earlier insistence on the need for a nanny state in addressing the problem of sugar. This builds on his 2015 select committee testimony, where he insisted that 'we need to be big, bold, brave and frankly, act like a parent'.[87] For Oliver, the naughty child in this scenario is the food and drinks industry, for whom the tax acts as a potent warning of worse to come if they fail to reform ('we're watching').

In this way, we can see that success for the sugar tax enjoys an almost infinite elasticity, ranging from reduced sugar sales and consumption as a proxy for imagined future health benefits, to the generation of ring-fenced funds for public health interventions, to raised awareness on the part of both consumers and producers of sugary foods and drinks. This elasticity is made possible by the urgency that attaches so easily to obesity and, by association, sugar; it is the lowest common denominator which enables multiple motivations to hang together. In short, the sugar tax can't fail because it already meets the imperative to do something that drove the implementation of the tax in the first place.

Conclusion

The introduction of the sugar tax is a central issue in the narrative arc of the social life of sugar in the second decade of the twentieth century. It marks out sugar as a pernicious and urgent problem about which something must be done; it offers a 'big stick' where voluntarism has failed and brings with it endlessly optimistic promises of dietary and health transformations. It marks a shift in the relationship not only between governments and industry, but also between industry and the consumer on whom its living depends. And most of all, it is a chance for governments to demonstrate that they are doing something about sugar, even in the absence of the measurable health impacts on which it is premised. In offering this commentary on the sugar tax, I am not aligning myself with its opponents, and especially not with a food and drinks industry whose motives, environmental impacts and disregard for social, economic and cultural inequalities are deeply problematic. However, I'm also aware that my resistance to the foregrounding of sugar to the exclusion of other considerations gives the unfortunate appearance of synergies between my own critique and the appeal to complexity offered by the sugar industry. This superficial point of commonality is one explanation for the many times I have been asked in talks and interviews whether I have accepted, or would accept, industry funding for my research. I always laugh when asked, since the flow of money from a large soft drinks corporation to a feminist sociologist with a background in critical fat studies is an astoundingly unlikely prospect. But the serious answer is a categorical 'no' because our positions are fundamentally divergent, because when food and drinks companies appeal to complexity, they are still restricting themselves to dietary complexity. As such, they remain safely embedded in nutritionist and fat-phobic thinking. This enables them to duck the embeddedness of what we eat in a complex network of social and economic inequalities that they push firmly into the background in their own interests. This is a tactic that they share with those advocating and implementing the tax, and this erasure of the wider social, economic and political context is the focus of the last two chapters of the book, beginning with the context of austerity, without which the attack on sugar cannot gain purchase.

7

Sweetening austerity

In response to the 2008 financial crisis, the Conservative–Liberal Democrat coalition government (2010–15) under Prime Minister David Cameron set about a programme of public spending cuts resulting in a raft of austerity measures that were made concrete in the 2012 Welfare Reform Act. These policies aimed to shrink the welfare state and enacted punitive sanctions against those unable to conform to the proliferating demands of welfare conditionality. This situation created conditions of profound precarity and poverty in some of the most disadvantaged sections of society.[1] In June 2019, the Institute for Public Policy Research issued a report estimating that from 2012 to 2017, austerity measures had led to 130,000 excess preventable deaths,[2] and in May 2019, Philip Alston, a United Nations (UN) Special Rapporteur on extreme poverty and human rights, issued an uncompromisingly critical report on the devastating impact of austerity measures in the UK. He described the measures as a fundamental restructuring of the relationship between the people and the state, concluding: 'British compassion has been replaced by a punitive, mean-spirited and often callous approach apparently designed to impose a rigid order on the lives of those least capable of coping'.[3] The British government described the findings of the report as 'barely believable' and as of 'an extraordinary political nature', confirming what the report describes as 'a striking and almost complete disconnect between the picture painted by the Government and what people across the country told the Special Rapporteur'.[4]

These well-documented material consequences of austerity occurred alongside, and were facilitated by, a hardening of attitudes towards those dependent on the welfare system. This sedimented a binary between feckless 'scroungers' and 'skivers', who were seen as irresponsibly taking more than their fair share and giving nothing in return, versus deserving 'strivers' who work hard and take responsibility for themselves and dependent others. This facilitates what social policy scholars John Clarke and Janet Newman describe as the 'alchemy of austerity', transferring blame for the financial crisis away from the elite-dominated global finance system and onto public spending in general, and those reliant on welfare in particular.[5]

Austerity and its consequences constitute an important piece of context for the attack on sugar. The first hint of this lies in the intensifying focus – as measured by increased newspaper coverage – on sugar as a health threat in 2012–13. This increase fails to correlate with a rise in rates of either obesity or sugar consumption, raising questions about why the increased coverage happened then, to what ends and in whose interests. The most obvious answer lies in the constant need for revivification and reinvention of the war on obesity to escape its own failures. From this perspective, the attack on sugar was just the next in a long line of re-animations. But this cannot answer the question of 'why then?', or even 'why sugar?' In this chapter, I argue that austerity provided a context within which an attack on sugar makes sense, particularly via narratives of irresponsible overconsumption (of sugar, of healthcare services, of public resources). In this context, a war on obesity spearheaded by an attack on sugar, with all its associations of emptiness, intemperance and instant gratification, can thrive with an intensity that neither obesity nor dietary fat can achieve. Conversely, the attack on sugar shores up the figure of the feckless and abject Other, who sociologist Imogen Tyler argues is central to securing consent for the cruelties of austerity.[6] This is not to argue for a causative relationship between the two, but rather to suggest that they are mutually endorsing with each providing fertile ground for the other. This mutuality is inflected through the intensifying focus on sugar in four key ways: (1) the classed construction of fatness as overconsumption; (2) the strategic deployment of 'the poor' in relation to the sugar tax; (3) the rhetorics of thriftiness; and (4) the depoliticising individualism of the attack on sugar.

Trimming the fat

The discourses of austerity and the demonisation of fatness are deeply bound together, with the fat body seen as bearing literal witness to its own overconsumption and in urgent need of restraint. This is embedded in the rhetorics of austerity, which are awash with exhortations to 'tighten our belts' and 'trim the fat'. Fat here is a dead weight that doesn't belong to the body and is dragging it down, taking everybody else with it.[7] Furthermore, fatness is coded as signifying being working class, which in turn serves as a red flag for undeserved welfare dependence. For example, in a study of the images used in BBC reporting of obesity stories, Elaine Graham-Leigh observes that not only do those images code people as working class on the basis of clothing, location or food choices, but also there is a marked absence of images of fat people at work.[8] This renders fatness and worklessness synonymous and places fat bodies firmly in austerity's firing line alongside the benefits broods, welfare queens, feral parents, scroungers and skivers who populate the austerity pantheon of abject Others.[9]

The focus on sugar intensifies these sentiments because it is seen both as dietarily unnecessary and as an unsophisticated source of instant gratification. In contrast to fat, which has been partially rehabilitated through the concept of healthy fats, the nutritional emptiness of sugar renders it always already in excess. To consume it is to overconsume it. This is particularly true for a population already under close surveillance for the slightest hint of taking more than their share or for not using scarce resources in accordance with prevailing middle-class norms and priorities. In the same way as possession of material goods by benefits claimants such as flat-screen TVs, gaming consoles and mobile phones is commonly used in discrediting accounts to signify profligate spending,[10] perceived dietary and bodily excess can then be used to discredit claims of poverty and need.

This discrediting is compounded by the easy pleasures of sugar, which are framed not only as excessive in themselves, but also as irresistible to those already understood as liable to intemperate consumption if left to their own devices. Such a framing is evident in the 2017 campaign by celebrity chef and anti-sugar campaigner Hugh Fearnley-Whittingstall, who targeted the high-street newsagent WHSmith under the hashtag #WHSugar. The vociferous campaign began as part of a BBC documentary, *Britain's Fat Fight*, where he focused his ire on the canyons of cheap chocolate and multi-buy confectionery deals through which customers are funnelled to reach the checkouts. He argued that customers are unable to resist temptation and should therefore be protected by the restocking of the displays with 'healthy' alternatives. This is an archetypal nudge strategy, setting new defaults to the choice architecture in an attempt to influence purchasing behaviour without eroding the freedom to choose.[11] But the rationale for the apparently benign replacement of confectionery with snacks of nuts and fruit rests on profoundly classed assumptions that tap directly into the logics of austerity. There is, for example, a sharp contrast between the imagined appetites of the primarily working-class customer base of the store and the privileged figure of Fearnley-Whittingstall, who remains secure in his white, middle-class, masculine command over his impulses. Even when surrounded by walls of sugary treats, he never displays the vulnerability to their allure that he presumes governs the store's customers. Not everyone can be trusted with sweet treats or to make sensible choices.

The perpetual perils of working-class dietary incontinence in the face of sugar were demonstrated again in November 2018, when Action on Sugar launched the results of a survey of out-of-home and supermarket milkshakes culminating in calls for a 300-calorie limit to all milkshake products.[12] The campaign was the organisation's opening gambit for Sugar Awareness Week, and in line with the hidden-sugar shock genre, it had a headline-grabbing worst offender ready: the freakshake.

Freakshakes are spectacularly excessive concoctions of milkshake, ice cream, sweets, cookies and cake; or what *The Sun* described in its second day of coverage of the story as 'a mega milkshake mash-up of a drink and a pudding'.[13] The most extravagant freakshakes contain well over 1,000 calories and over thirty teaspoons of sugar, and the enthusiastic media coverage made the most of the spectacle, decorating its reporting with lurid images of the tall, brightly decorated shakes oozing with chocolatey sauces and overflowing with sugar-filled toppings. The campaign, and its subsequent media coverage, focused on products sold by the Harvester and Toby Carvery chains, both of which cater to a working-class demographic.

The day after the campaign was launched, to keep the story alive, Action on Sugar tweeted that daily consumption of freakshakes by children would cause tooth decay and obesity but without offering any evidence of how frequently they were consumed, and by whom. For example, at over £5 per shake, it is highly unlikely that children are consuming these daily, and Action on Sugar's hyperventilating horror cannot account for the sociality of eating – the possibility that people might club together with multiple spoons to share a freakshake as a sociable treat. It could be argued that the cultivated alarm around the freakshakes was never intended to be taken too seriously and instead is better understood as strategic hyperbole; just a fun story designed to engage readers with the wider problem of sugary milk-based drinks and to grab people's attention at the beginning of a week of campaigning. But even as a piece of attention-grabbing fun, the underlying message is disturbingly clear: that working-class people (where working-classness is treated as synonymous with fatness) are dietarily incontinent in the face of sugary foods, the most excessive of which should either be banned (as in the case of freakshakes) or strongly calorie-limited as a result. Just as a war on obesity inevitably becomes a war on those categorised as obese, moralising attacks on particular foods slide easily into attacks on the people presumed to eat those foods, with hierarchies of taste setting up distinctions between us and them.[14]

Weaponising 'the poor'

The reproduction of discourses of working-class bad taste and uncontained appetite is central to austerity policies and their justification. This is never more evident than in debates surrounding the sugar tax, where 'the poor' are repeatedly invoked both in support and in opposition in ways that directly reproduce and rely on the logics, rhetorics and practices of austerity. In these debates, people who are poor figure in two intersecting, but contrasting, ways, depending on how the tax is conceptualised. First, where the tax is understood as a punitive measure designed to compel behaviour change, 'the poor' find themselves positioned on either side of a deserving/undeserving binary; they either warrant protection from additional taxation or they should be punitively subject to it. And second, they are positioned not as the subjects of taxation but as its beneficiaries. In both cases, the neoliberal logics of austerity, in tandem with fat-phobia, position people who are poor as both the cause of the problem of insufficient public resources and its solution.

The deserving/undeserving poor

For those ideologically opposed to the sugar tax, people who are poor commonly feature as its victims. This argument rests on the regressive nature of the tax, which impacts disproportionately on lower-income groups. In March 2016, for example, a vocal opponent of the tax, MP Jacob Rees-Mogg, was reported in *The Sun* describing it as 'a tax on the poorest in society',[15] and in July 2020, during its 'Hands Off Our Grub' campaign, *The Sun* reported fears that Prime Minister Boris Johnson might choose to extend the sugar tax as part of his anti-obesity campaign following his COVID-19 hospitalisation. Journalist Matt Dathan protested that '[…] making treats more expensive for all would hit the low-paid hardest' and breathed a sigh of relief that Johnson had 'emerged from his ordeal with his marbles intact' and ruled out further taxes.[16]

These protestations in defence of the poor can be hard to swallow, given that they sit alongside simultaneously held convictions that social welfare, designed to provide a safety net for the most vulnerable, cultivates indolence and scrounging in its recipients. For example, Rees-Mogg is an enthusiastic supporter of the austerity policies and practices which have consistently eroded the benefits and services relied upon by those who are already disadvantaged economically with the purported aim of fending off an imagined something-for-nothing culture. Similarly, while *The Sun* protested the loss of affordable treats for the low-paid, it has simultaneously pursued a vociferous and sustained campaign publicly shaming those judged to be making unwarranted claims on the welfare state. For example, its 2015 'Welfies' awards 'recognising the country's scroungers and dossers' included award categories for benefits claims based on fatness, over-reproduction, fraudulent disabilities and 'job dodging'.[17]

These competing sentiments hinge not on a general concern for the poor, but rather rest on the binary of the deserving and undeserving poor, which underpins the distinction between the exemplary hard-working strivers and the indolent, overconsuming Other that is central to public consent for austerity measures. As a result, the positions adopted by Rees-Mogg or by *The Sun* are not so much contradictory as mutually endorsing: the deserving poor who should be spared a price rise on hard-earned treats are always defined against their undeserving counterparts, and vice versa. It is a precarious binary, with the most disadvantaged slipping easily into the scrounger category as the cuts progress and as the common-sense understanding of austerity as necessary (and of those claiming benefits as having created that necessity) gains everyday purchase.[18]

The construction of classed, fat bodies as the legitimate targets of austerity is never more evident than in the declarations of nanny-state exceptionalism discussed in the previous chapter, with the fecklessness of fat overconsumers forcing the abandonment of libertarian instincts in favour of the 'big stick'. This exemplifies what Clarke and Newman describe as the framing of austerity as 'virtuous necessity'; that is, 'we must do this because we cannot afford it; we must do this because it would be morally right'.[19] For example, in an article in *The Daily*

Telegraph in August 2015, commentator Philip Johnston adopted a posture of reluctant acquiescence to government intervention in the form of a sugar tax. The tension between his libertarian impulses and the need to address the financial implications of a health crisis finds reconciliation in his undisguised classed fat-phobia:

> My instinctive reaction to stories like this is to rail against the Nanny State and tell the fat police to mind their own business. Let people make their own mistakes. If they want to waddle through life in elastic, 50in-waist 'leisure pants' and subsist on a diet of pizza and cola, that's up to them. But when I have to pay for the injurious consequences of their poor lifestyle choices, then that is another matter.[20]

On a roll now, he continues:

> The problem, though, is that hectoring does not work because those people who are most likely to become dangerously obese are the least likely to heed the warnings. The newspapers, TV and radio are full of advice about healthy eating and dieting has become a national obsession – but mainly among those for whom, almost by definition, obesity will never be an issue even if they could do with losing weight [...] No-one wants to see the big fiscal stick wielded to force people to behave differently. But if those most prone to obesity simply won't listen and the costs to the NHS [National Health Service] continue to soar, a fat tax might be the only answer.[21]

The figure summoned by Johnston is inescapably classed as workshy (sitting around in 'leisure pants') and wilfully oblivious to healthy eating messages. Pizza and cola operate here as emblems not only of poor dietary choices, but also of laziness, requiring no forethought or preparation. Johnston's use of the term 'fat tax' allows for a slippage between taxing foods coded as unhealthy and a tax on fat bodies themselves; under austerity, the two can be treated synonymously, with dietary excess presumed to be readable off the fat body. For Johnston, 'those people' are not only making poor choices, but also 'won't listen', and this perceived refusal transforms fatness into an unforgivable act of wilful destruction of the NHS. His disgust at the poor, fat bodies that cause this destruction rests on a privatised vision of the welfare state whereby he should only ever have to pay for what he personally needs, and where the needs of some (for healthcare, income support) can be delegitimised as unwarranted desires. Their failure to make the 'right' choices can be met only with abandonment and coercion.

In these crudely caricatured accounts, the fat body is barely human, waddling with animalistic clumsiness rather than walking. Journalist Peter Foster used similarly derogatory terms in an article in *The Sunday Telegraph* in 2014, in which he urged readers to set aside nanny-state defences of personal choice in favour of implementing a sugar tax: 'Go to a child's sporting event and it is astonishing how many children come waddling off the pitch and immediately guzzle a bottle of Gatorade or similar. And even worse, their parents seem oblivious to the self-destructive folly of it all.'[22] Like the leisure-pant-wearing Other of Johnston's imaginary, these abject Others 'waddle' and 'guzzle', constrained by their immobility and incontinent appetites. Elsewhere, fat people 'gobble', 'gorge', 'scoff' and 'slurp' in classed invocations of unmannered, animalistic and tasteless consumption. Alongside this dehumanising rhetoric, Foster also introduces yet another stalwart of the abject Others on austerity's hit list: the failed parent.[23] In an echo of the horrified accounts in Chapter 5 of Mexican women nursing babies with bottles of Coca-Cola, no space is left to consider the conditions under which parenting takes place and the constraints within which food decisions are made.

The explicit fat-phobia that both Johnston and Foster display is foundational to the impulse to force less responsible (over)consumers to comply with the behavioural and dietary norms against which their behaviours are measured. There is no hint that these men too might need to modify their own behaviour, which is constructed in contrast as governed by rational self-control. This reflects one of the defining traits of austerity: that despite claims by Chancellor George Osborne at the 2009 Conservative Party conference that 'we are all in this together',[24] the weight of austerity falls disproportionately on those who already have the least. It is they, and not the elites making the case for austerity measures, who are expected to change.[25] Using the fat body as a proxy, the taxation of sugar becomes the perfect vehicle for marking out austerity's undeserving, failed citizens.

Win-win

Both those for and those against the sugar tax, regardless of position on the political spectrum, widely acknowledge that its regressive nature means that it impacts most heavily on those with the fewest resources. But for most commentators, this is not a failing of the tax but rather its primary asset. As discussed above, for some, this is because it will punish the poor into compliance. But for those less punitively oriented, the regressive nature of the tax offers a reassuring win-win scenario whereby the position of the poor at the sharp end of health inequalities means that they will also benefit disproportionately from the tax's anticipated (but undemonstrated) health benefits as a result. Sustain made this point explicitly in making its case for the sugar tax in 2013: 'Since people on low incomes suffer disproportionately from diet-related diseases, a duty that encourages people to drink fewer sugary drinks can help to improve their health [...].'[26] While for Johnston, the tax is primarily for his own good (to avoid incurring additional healthcare costs that he might have to contribute to because of others' failings), in this framing, the tax is to the benefit of the poor and must be implemented on their behalf. In the newspaper coverage, research showing that the Mexico sugar tax led to the highest purchasing reductions among the poorest groups acts as a touchstone for this claim.[27]

From this perspective, the sugar tax promises a social and financial win-win, with impacts among poorer communities giving the biggest returns against the costs of implementing the scheme. For example, in March 2016, *The Guardian* cited Simon Capewell in his role as vice-president of the UK's Faculty of Public Health, offering this back-of-an-envelope calculation:

> If you apply a sugary drinks tax across the board and everyone consumes 10% less, that produces a 1% reduction in disease overall. But in poorer areas, that would be a three-times-bigger reduction compared with more

affluent areas, because poorer people are two to three times more likely to get heart disease, diabetes, cancer or have a stroke. [...] Poorer people would benefit more from a sugary-drinks tax, so it would be progressive in health terms and not regressive in financial terms to any significant degree.[28]

As with all austerity measures, people who are poor are targeted as both the problem and the solution. In this way, it was possible in 2015 for Boris Johnson, then Mayor of London, to tell an audience of NHS leaders that sugar taxation 'is a matter of social justice', since 'overwhelmingly the people most affected by an obesity problem will be those on the lowest incomes'.[29] This claim separates the poor from their poverty and obscures the austerity measures in which Johnson himself is heavily implicated. He backtracked on this position in 2019 during his campaign to become Conservative Party leader, calling for a review of 'sin taxes' in light of recent calls to extend the sugar tax to milk shakes – a move which he argued 'seems to clobber those who can least afford it'.[30] This widely reported turnaround was a transparent attempt to mollify the right wing of his party in the service of his leadership bid, but it also highlights the discursive utility of 'the poor' to meet multiple political agendas without any accompanying need to address the causes of poverty itself.

A commentary in *The Times* in June 2016 by columnist Oliver Kamm makes a similar claim to the win-win effects of the sugar tax, but this time, one that is embedded much more explicitly in the logics of austerity:

If you don't want to pay a sugar tax, you stop buying sugary drinks and drink something else instead. [...] The distributional effects of a sugar tax are wider than [the] simple picture of poorer consumers suffering a blow to their income. If the revenues are devoted to improving public health then this will benefit lower income consumers in particular. If they suffer sudden health problems because of excess sugar consumption, they're less able to afford time off work or to pay for private healthcare.[31]

This defence of the sugar tax uncritically reproduces the retraction of the welfare state as an inevitable necessity – for example, in the loss of sickness benefits or threats to the provision of healthcare free at the point of use.[32] The extraordinary suggestion that the excessive consumption of sugar is preventing poorer people from paying for private health-care betrays an obliviousness to the realities of poverty, as well as to his own privilege. By reducing to sugar the problems faced by people who are poor, the multiple threats to health and wellbeing that accompany poverty and that have nothing to do with sugar, or at least far exceed sugar's impacts, are washed away. Furthermore, the suggestion that people could simply avoid the tax by choosing not to buy sugary drinks shifts the focus firmly onto individual choices and behaviours and away from those structural and systemic issues. Where disease is seen as diet-related, as in the Sustain report, responsibility falls easily onto the consuming individual. Consequently, following the work of sociologist Tracey Jensen on parent-blaming, the poor are defined here by their poor choices, presuming a culture of poverty to the exclusion of the lived experience of poverty itself, especially under conditions of austerity.[33] As will be discussed in Chapter 8, this is exacerbated in the reporting by the absence of the voices of those who are poor, who are consistently spoken about, but not spoken to or given space to articulate their own experiences.

Commentator Alex Renton reproduced this act of washing away, albeit more sympathetically, in an article in *The Observer*, claiming, 'The sad truth is that the people who are dying earlier because of the diseases that are triggered or exacerbated by sugar are largely the poor. They pay the human cost of cheap sugar and addiction to it.'[34] Appeals such as Renton's to the win-win promise of the sugar tax to reduce sugar consumption among those with the least resources and the highest rates of non-communicable diseases (NCDs) adopt a more benevolent stance, superficially at least, than those baying for the punitive shaming of the feckless poor. Jamie Oliver took a similar position in his 2018 select committee testimony, declaring paternalistically that 'this is a tax for love. This is designed to protect and give to the most disadvantaged communities.'[35] But the elevation of sugar to what Robert Lustig calls the Darth Vader of the Empire, and the sense of urgency that this creates, brush over the fact that poverty and social inequalities are supremely damaging to health.[36] As a result, the poor are paying the costs of that poverty and inequality, exacerbated by austerity, rather than the costs of simply eating too much cheap sugar. Consequently, even this more sympathetic invocation of the poor remains thoroughly embedded in the twinned logics of austerity and fat-phobia, whereby the problem lies in the overconsuming behaviours of the sugar-fattened poor and the solution lies in reducing their sugar consumption, not just for themselves, but for the financial wellbeing of everyone. Thus the sugar tax aims to make 'those people' less expensively fat and overconsuming (of sugar, of healthcare, of benefits), while deferring the need to address their poverty and its effects directly.

In praise of thrift

The third way in which austerity and the attack on sugar are mutually endorsing is through the neoliberal ideology of thrifty restraint. In the context of sugar, this is repeatedly framed as a means of saving the NHS, which, as discussed in the previous section, is seen as imperilled by irresponsible overconsumption, with the selfishly sugar-fattened body operating synonymously as unnecessarily expensive ill-health. This was made explicit in July 2020 when Prime Minister Boris Johnson, fresh from his own brush with COVID-19, launched his anti-obesity initiative, which aimed to 'get the nation fit and healthy, protect themselves against COVID-19 and protect the NHS'.[37] The slogan 'Protect the NHS' became a government mantra throughout the pandemic, performing a feat of distraction from the catalogue of missteps in the government's pandemic response, including an expensively ineffectual 'world-beating' test, track and trace system and a rushed return to 'business as usual'.[38] In both cases, responsibility for the survival of the NHS is placed firmly at the mercy of the choices and behaviours of individual members of the public and away from questions of investment at the state level.

Specific appeals to protect the NHS in relation to obesity make discursive sense because of the easy alignment between common-sense understandings of obesity as a threat to health and of healthcare services as struggling to meet the demands placed on them. This relation far precedes the attack on sugar and has always been a justification for the war on obesity. However, both the logics of austerity and the specific problem of sugar give this alignment additional purchase via the discourse of household economy. Elaine Graham-Leigh argues that commonly used phrases like 'balancing the budget' equate the national budget with our personal finances, underlining the notion that the financial crisis was the fault of over-spending individual consumers. This provides the rationale for austerity: 'If "we" have all over-spent, it follows that "we" have to cut back.'[39] Framed in this way, austerity makes (common) sense because we are already familiar with the idea of 'tightening our belts' at the household level. This also facilitates the notion of shared sacrifice in the face of a crisis, where we all must do our part.

The endorsement of thriftiness as an aspirational virtue is central to this invoking of household economies. Writing about sustainable consumption, economic sociologist David Evans distinguishes between thrift and frugality. He argues that to be frugal 'is to be moderate or sparing in the use of money, goods and resources with a particular emphasis on careful consumption and the avoidance of waste'. This means that frugality is at odds with normative consumer culture and is often appropriated as a virtue by those seeking environmentally sustainable ways of living. Thriftiness, on the other hand, also implies restraint, but is 'the art of doing more (consumption) with less (money) and so thrift practices are practices of savvy consumption, characterised by the thrill and skill of "the bargain"'.[40] As such, it aligns with the neoliberal imperative to consume, with savvy consumption creating more opportunities to consume rather than fewer, although always held in tension with the imperative to restraint.

Appeals to thriftiness in the era of austerity are a strong presence in popular culture. For example, during the 2020 pandemic lockdown, both TV celebrity Kirstie Allsop's home-crafting show *Kirstie: Keep Crafting and Carry On* and Jamie Oliver's *Jamie: Keep Cooking and Carry On* mobilised the 'make do and mend' rhetorics of creative thriftiness.[41] In their respective TV shows, Allsop and Oliver both promise to 'make the most' of what they have to hand (items around the home or kitchen staples) while neither blowing the budget nor sacrificing the opportunity to make delicious food, or decorative gifts to beautify the domestic space. These shows explicitly mobilise the austerity nostalgia of wartime Britain via the aesthetics and rhetorics of the 'Keep Calm and Carry On' propaganda poster. According to writer and journalist Owen Hatherley, the poster was never mass-produced in the 1940s, but it has found new life in the contemporary era of recession and austerity,[42] invoking an implied message of collective resilience in the face of a crisis. In difficult times, thrifty resilience promises more for less for the savvy consumer, leaving no excuse for hardship.

While amplified by the extraordinary conditions of the pandemic, the celebration of thrift precedes the COVID-19 crisis and is central to the austerity project. For example, sociologist Kim Allen and colleagues describe the figure of the happy, thrifty housewife – 'a contemporary exemplar for recessionary times' – as embodied in the figure of Kate Middleton, who married into the royal family but is widely portrayed as true to her humbler roots, re-using dresses, wearing high-street brands and living in a modest house, all while fulfilling a busy schedule of public duties.[43] Contrasting with celebrity Kim Kardashian, whose fame is commonly seen as lacking merit and whose body and lifestyle are figured as excessive, Middleton has cultivated a domestic femininity which signals a nostalgic retreat into home-making and childcare that both coincides and colludes with the political and economic imperatives of austerity.

More specifically in relation to food, media scholar Abigail Wincott describes the rise of 'foodie austerity', which rests on a preference for homely and simple foods, emphasises the pleasures and virtues of self-restraint and places an emphasis on care and labour in food production.[44] TV shows and cookbooks by celebrity chefs such as Nigel Slater, Hugh Fearnley-Whittingstall and Jamie Oliver showcase the virtues of rustling up dishes from home-grown and store-cupboard ingredients they have to hand. It is a fundamentally nostalgic vision of a return to the land and the reclamation of lost culinary skills, suggesting the possibility of creating healthy meals accessible to all, with the work of preparation too pleasurable to even count as work (see Chapter 4). Wincott argues that this resonates with the widely held conviction that the poor could eat well if only they cooked simple foods from scratch.

These mediated celebrations of thriftiness, alongside the wider circulating ideologies of austerity in which they are embedded, provide clues for understanding the mutual alignments of austerity and the attack on sugar. We can see sugar itself rendered a currency to be spent thriftily through 'Sugar Smart' consumption, which in turn is framed as opening possibilities for further consumption; for example, through an expanded repertoire of home cooking and eating or by cultivating new tastes and food pleasures. But a closer look at this celebration of sugar thriftiness also exposes the exclusions upon which that valorised thrift is premised.

The first of these exclusions is the ways in which, as discussed previously, the work of thrift is discounted as work. These are exemplified by the ways in which primarily women are encouraged to make 'smart swaps' to eke out the family's sugar budget while enhancing rather than sacrificing deliciousness and nutrition (see also Chapter 8). These gendered familial household economies of sugar rely on an endless series of micro-reductions in sugar that can be parsed by the gram, cube and teaspoon. The 'added' nature of sugar and the easy visualisation of cubes and teaspoons render sugar countable in ways that fat is not, making it the perfect target for dietary thrift. For example, in a series of tweets for Sugar Awareness Week in November 2018, Action on Sugar posted a series of suggestions for lowering sugar consumption with small swaps: for example, mixing up a jar of ready-made pasta sauce with a tin of tomatoes to reduce the sugar content per portion,[45] or mixing low-sugar whole-grain breakfast cereal in with a high-sugar one to dilute the sugar content.[46] These normative sugar economies and their invisible food work align comfortably with what sociologist Tracey Jensen calls the 'romance of austerity', where, replete with nostalgia for wartime rationing, thrift stands in joyful contrast to the impulsive overconsumption of socially abjected individuals.[47] The fear of the stain of bad motherhood makes this careful budgeting of sugar a far cry from the casual pleasures of rustling up food from the garden.

The second exclusion occurs around relations of class inequality, with displays of thriftiness accruing cultural capital most readily to middle-class consumers who already have ample social, economic and cultural capital on which to build. The freedom to rustle up meals or to craft decorative household items with whatever ingredients or materials are to hand presumes an unplanned superfluity that is already a marker of privilege. For example, Kirstie Allsop's series is filmed at her second home,[48] and Hugh Fearnley-Whittingstall's *River Cottage* brand showcases his own extensive home and gardens.[49] Even on a more mundanely domestic scale, to 'make the most of our kitchen staples', as Jamie Oliver promises to do in the promotional blurb for *Jamie: Keep Cooking and Carry On*, not only requires a well-stocked kitchen but also a functioning fridge and stove. As observed in Chapter 4, lists of essential kitchen staples are a mainstay of sugar-free living advice. The ready supply of staples is intended as a bulwark against snacking on sweets, but these are resources that are beyond the reach of many of those living in poverty compounded by austerity cuts. This shortfall is exacerbated by time poverty, which many of those living under conditions of severe constraint experience, juggling multiple low-paying jobs and caring responsibilities in the struggle to put food on the table.

Under these conditions, the valorised spontaneity of creatively 'making do' gives way to the arduous work of 'getting by', replacing thrift with desperate frugality to survive. But while those seeking to distance themselves from consumer culture in the interests of environmentally sustainable consumption are engaging in a voluntary frugality that is status-bearing,[50] those for whom frugality is the only survival option are commonly viewed under austerity as failed citizens, brought low by the failure to manage their resources effectively. Consequently, none of the capital that attaches to either the thrifty austerity foodie or the frugal sustainable consumer accrues to the mother trying to feed her children from the last remnants of a foodbank parcel. Instead, the struggling mother remains austerity's abjected Other, against whom the valorised thrifty citizen is celebrated.

In the case of the attack on sugar, the presentation of 'smart swaps' and micro-reductions as simple acts of dietary budgeting accessible to all transforms the failure to implement those changes into a wilful refusal, marking out austerity's failed citizen. This masks the realities of living in conditions of poverty and precarity, where the selection of a (more expensive) low-sugar alternative, cooking stove-top porridge instead of having a cereal bar, or carefully calculating a daily budget of grams or spoons of sugar may simply be unaffordable diversions of time and resources when compared with the imminent imperative to assuage hunger in the face of scarcity. This is not just an innocent oversight, but rather the direct consequence of pulling sugar so firmly into the foreground and obscuring the lived realities of food insecurity. Furthermore, as will be discussed in the next chapter, this also normalises middle-class tastes and practices as the standard to which everyone should aspire, leaving no space for preferences, acquired tastes or familial food cultures that diverge from that norm. In this way, we can see that the normative micro-counting of sugar rests on middle-class privilege in ways that are both disguised and enabled by the austerity discourses of shared sacrifice promoted by elites.[51] This leads to the final section of this chapter, which highlights the ways in which both austerity and the attack on sugar cultivate a depoliticised individual responsibility that contributes to the absolution of those elites for their political choices and their unevenly borne consequences.

Individualising responsibility

The fourth point of connection between austerity and the attack on sugar can be found in their repeated invocations of individual responsibility, both for the crisis and for its resolution, and their depoliticising effects. As we have already seen, the abject figure of the workshy, overconsuming scrounger meets the discursive needs of both austerity and the attack on sugar, with the consumption of sugar and welfare treated as proxies for each other. The nutritional emptiness of sugar, its common association with illicit and addictive drugs, its added use in food and the presumed vulnerability of the lower classes to the instant and unsubtle gratifications of sugary foods all align the attack on sugar easily with the discourses and practices of austerity. Writing of the figure of the 'welfare queen' (as opposed to the 'thrifty housewife'), Kim Allen and colleagues describe the ways in which celebrity Kim Kardashian's lack of cultural capital makes her 'a convenient vessel for anxieties and moral judgements circulating within austerity'.[52] The same can be said of sugar, which operates as a lightning rod for anxieties around what Graham-Leigh describes as 'ruling-class fears about the demands and appetites of the poor'.[53] This focus on individual responsibility gains purchase in the context of the alliance between austerity and the attack on sugar because it is already embedded in circulating neoliberal ideologies that insist that we make our own luck in a meritocratic world through the exercise of self-entrepreneurship, adaptability and resilience.[54] It is also continuous with the neoliberal rhetorics and practices of anti-obesity, which insist that good citizens become responsible partners in the governance of their own bodies through weight loss.

One effect of this individualisation is the depoliticisation of deeply political choices, emphasising adaptation over proactive structural change and maintaining a silence around those who benefit the most from the social inequalities that are maintained by the prevailing social, economic and political systems. As a result, the attack on sugar is not only embedded in the rhetorics and practices of austerity, but also shores up austerity and its entrenchment of inequalities by focusing on choices rather than opportunities. This depoliticisation through individualisation is exemplified in the case of sugar, first, in the refusal of inequalities as political choices; and second, in the portrayal of individual action to reduce sugar consumption as a form of politics.

Depoliticising inequality

The sugar tax provides a host of stark examples of the depoliticisation of inequalities under austerity. As discussed earlier in this chapter, people who are poor are mobilised discursively to support both the case for and the case against the tax, but their poverty remains a self-evident fact of life whose origins require no further enquiry. For example, earlier I cited Simon Capewell's claim in *The Guardian* in 2016 that 'Poorer people would benefit more from a sugary-drinks tax' since they suffer more NCDs and therefore are expected to enjoy greater health benefits from taxation-induced reductions. From this perspective, the tax stands as an intervention into the health problems experienced by those who are poor to minimise the costs that they generate, rather than into their poverty itself. It is a position that at best suggests that there is nothing to be done about poverty beyond ameliorating some of its selected consequences; and at worst, it presumes a behavioural explanation whereby their poverty is of their own making, with an intervention into consumption habits marking one step towards redirecting their self-destructive behaviours. Urgent appeals to health give neutralising cover to these acts of political forgetting, leaving space 'for a set of moral assumptions that are allowed to fly stealthily under the radar'.[55]

This same lack of curiosity about the underlying causes of inequality can be seen in the spending plans for sugar tax revenues. For example, in April 2017, *The Guardian* reported an interview with Barry Popkin, a researcher from the University of North Carolina who has published extensively on the impacts of the sugar tax.[56] Popkin describes the introduction of a sugar tax in Philadelphia – a poor city with high rates of soda consumption – the revenues from which were ring-fenced for daycare centres. Popkin notes: 'That was how they sold it [to the public] [...] The revenue has been double what they expected. Daycare centres have doubled and tripled in size.'[57] Similarly, towards the end of *Jamie's Sugar Rush*, as part of the Mexico segment, Oliver reports on a survey where residents were asked whether they would support a sugar tax if the money was used to put clean drinking-water fountains into schools. The proposal gained 80% approval, which Oliver cites as evidence of the effectiveness of, and public support for, sugar taxes. However, in both cases, the political decisions that left daycare and potable water underfunded go unexamined, with deficits in provision instead functioning as leverage for 'selling' the tax and providing philanthropic cover for the primary motivation of instigating behaviour change.

In the same vein, in the UK case, consent for the sugar tax was secured with the promise that some of the revenue would go towards breakfast clubs to ensure that disadvantaged children get a healthy meal before school. This act of sugar tax-funded largesse leaves unexamined the political choices that have led to rising numbers of impoverished and hungry children in the UK under austerity. It also stands in sharp contrast to a parliamentary vote in October 2020, which, during the devastations and hardships of the pandemic, saw the rejection of a proposal to further extend free school meal provision over the holiday period.[58] This was later reversed after a public outcry led by footballer Marcus Rashford, but Conservative MPs opposing the measure justified their votes with familiar austerity-fuelled, stigmatising tropes of irresponsible poverty, citing the fear that providing free meals would discourage parents from taking responsibility for their children and the risk that parents might use the vouchers to buy alcohol or cigarettes, or trade them for drugs.[59] Strikingly, even where voices of political dissent appear, they risk being neutralised by the depoliticising and individualising discourses of austerity. For example, sociologist Jessica Martin describes the case of blogger, cook, activist and mother Jack Monroe, who has built on her own experiences of devastating poverty and food insecurity under austerity to become an 'austerity celebrity'. However, her overt critique of austerity is repeatedly subjugated in news reporting to narratives of resilience, resourcefulness and the overcoming of adversity in ways that silence her political message and provide the perfect complement to ideological justifications of austerity.[60] The depoliticisation of inequality, then, is never simply a matter of oversight, but rather is integral to austerity itself.

'Join the low sugar revolution'

The second aspect of the depoliticisation through individualisation, this time specifically in relation to sugar, is the framing of sugar reduction as political action. This is achieved by mobilising the rhetorics of 'revolution' and 'movements' while amplifying the anticipated transformative impacts of individual consumer choices, which are seen as accumulating to become something greater than their parts. These changes are seen as reaching far beyond the domain of the individual, striking a blow against the food and drinks industry and leading others towards the sugar-free path.

As discussed throughout the book, despite the ubiquity of the attack on sugar, the sense of the self as bravely going against the dietary grain by giving up or significantly reducing sugar consumption is a staple of anti-sugar advocacy. This reflects a defiant pride in being able to see through the faithless practices of Big Sugar and the unreliable 'truths' of conventional dietary guidelines and lends itself easily to the rhetorics of revolution. Giles Fraser exemplified this in a declaration in *The Guardian* that giving up sugar is 'a form of protest';[61] in Goran and Ventura's call to 'grow the Sugarproof movement';[62] and in Mowbray's invitation to 'join the low-sugar revolution'.[63] Individual food choices are positioned here not simply as divergent from a dietary mainstream which tolerates sugar in moderation, but as disruptive of it, with sugar-free choices credited with generating positive change through their cumulative force. This imagined work of changing the world one low-sugar meal at a time echoes environmental campaigns that focus on widely accessible, highly individualised changes and consumer choices such as re-usable shopping bags, meat-free Mondays or buying Fair Trade goods.[64] But as sociologist Eva Giraud observes in the context of the promise of empowerment through food that characterises the increasingly mainstream availability of plant-based products, 'the primary danger of individualised solutions is if they come at the expense of other possibilities'.[65]

Nevertheless, in the anti-sugar domain, the power to change is placed firmly with the individual consumer. For example, in *Get Control of Sugar Now!*, McKenna argues that individual purchasing decisions are central to achieving social change, particularly in relation to the food industry. He argues that to change what companies make, 'We just stop buying their junk [...] The companies that get good food to you will prosper.

Those that don't will die. So, in the end, we have the power to change our own environments.'[66] The 'just' imposes a normative simplicity onto the proposed action; it is a change that everyone can (and therefore should) make. Similarly, in answer to the question 'What can you do now, as an individual?', Goran and Ventura urge readers to 'take immediate responsibility for improving the American diet' through purchasing and consumption choices, alongside educating children about the dangers of sugar and modelling good dietary habits for them.[67] Unusually among anti-sugar self-help books, they also encourage an engagement with a wider, albeit locally oriented, politics. For example, they urge readers to vote for initiatives promoting positive food policy change at school, community or state levels or to plant fruit trees or fund the creation of a school garden – a step that has the added benefit of helping to 'fight climate change'. But the scope of these interventions remains firmly limited to sugar reduction, and even where poverty is discussed, they do not engage with its wider causes, complexities or implications. For example, reproducing the neoliberal logics of austerity in the UK, they lament the fact that the US food stamps programme, SNAP, allows recipients to use the vouchers to buy sweet foods like soda with 'your tax money' and identify food assistance programmes as a prime target for policy change to ensure sugar reduction.[68]

In the case of sugar, the claim to a revolutionary politics through consumption choices is further bolstered by the insistence, as discussed in Chapter 4, that giving up sugar is not a diet. This locates it beyond the feminised, narcissistic weight loss domain into something of much greater portent. However, while the more-than-a-diet discourse aims to give gravity to anti-sugar evangelism, the political scope remains contained by strategies of personal empowerment and the determinedly narrow focus on sugar as the primary problem. This is rooted in what social and political theorist Alexis Shotwell calls 'purity politics'; that is, the conviction that it is possible to 'access or recover a time and state before or without pollution, without impurity, before the fall from innocence, when the world at large is *truly beautiful* [sic]'.[69] As discussed in Chapter 2, nostalgia for a time before sugar is fundamental not only to conceptualisations of the problem of sugar but also to the work of holding competing conceptualisations together. Furthermore, as explored in Chapter 4, the restoration of a 'clean slate' of tastes and appetites is a core enticement to the work of giving up sugar. But as Shotwell argues, 'the slate has never been clean'; 'there is no food we can eat, clothing we can buy or energy we can use without depending on our ties to complex webs of suffering'.[70]

Instead, Shotwell argues that these 'personal purity pursuits' represent a politics of despair that displays acquiescence in the face of complex situations that are out of our control, shutting down 'precisely the field of possibility that might allow us to take better collective action [...]'.[71] Despite the relentless optimism about the revolutionary impacts of relinquishing sugar, this despair is inescapable in anti-sugar self-help (and other) texts. For example, DeFigio warns that readers should not 'try to save the world all at once', warning readers to 'remember that you can't change other people; you can only change yourself'.[72] This despair is to some extent ameliorated by the expectation that transformation of the self will rub off on others and recruit them to the cause. For example, Carr urges readers emphatically to 'DO IT FOR YOURSELF',[73] arguing that 'being free from BAD SUGAR leaves so much amazing, nutritious, healthy food in your life – your family won't even notice if you help them by influencing their eating for the better'.[74] In a similar vein, Jones encourages her implicitly female readers to make themselves a priority, reminding them that 'everyone close to you will benefit in the long run when you reach your health goals'[75] while DeFigio promises that 'your good example (and better mood!) will start to rub off on other members of your household'.[76] For others, the process of converting others is more overt. Goran and Ventura, for example, advise involving the whole family in a time-limited 'No-Added Sugar Challenge' to win them over,[77] while Wilson urges readers not to become 'an anti-sugar bore', but rather to 'be your message'; 'live it, radiate it, be an inspiration'.[78] The hoped-for collateral effect on others in part ameliorates the moral hazard for women of doing anything just for themselves, but at best, the revolution can only ever persuade others to also make the individual choice to relinquish sugar. As revolutions go, it is despairingly modest in both its field of vision and its ambition.

This despair is particularly marked in appeals to sugar reduction as the one thing that everyone can agree on and as the change that everyone can (and therefore should) make. As Goran and Ventura argue: 'Despite all the complexities and understandings about what constitutes a healthy diet, there is one simple common denominator: Almost everyone agrees that reducing sugar would be a good place to start.'[79] This appeal to the lowest common denominator obscures the multiplicity and complexity of the problems that sugar has come to denote and constitutes an attempt, as Shotwell describes it, to 'step outside of relations of entanglement that are also always relations of suffering'.[80] This maintains a sense of control through self-exemption and purposeful action in the face of a crisis about which, above all, something must be done. But it ultimately offers an illusory purity whose success is defined against the abjection of those who have failed to make similarly 'good' choices and which rests on the denial of the complex entanglements and political choices that determine which choices make sense to whom and to whose unequally distributed benefit. In this way, the act of giving up sugar emerges as a far from a revolutionary movement, instead sedimenting the neoliberal status quo, the discourses and practices of austerity and the relations of privilege enjoyed by its strongest advocates.

Conclusion

Austerity did not cause the attack on sugar and vice versa, but together they make perfect partners. The emptiness of sugar, its ascribed role in a wide range of expensive health conditions and the easy way in which sugar lends itself to the discourses of household economies and thrift mean that it sits comfortably with the imperatives of austerity to trim the fat, to centralise individual (over)consumption as the cause of structural problems and to secure public consent for the erosion of welfare, health and other public services by offering up abjected Others who can shoulder the blame. Consequently, even where giving up sugar is claimed as a radical act that flies in the face of conventional nutritional wisdoms and everyday consumption practices, its reality is profoundly conservative, holding prevailing relations of power and privilege (and the vast inequalities on which they rely) in place.

This argument makes me vulnerable to charges of 'whataboutery'; that is, the disingenuous discrediting of one action (giving up sugar) because it fails to do something else I am more invested in (address inequality) – as, for example, when anti-feminists attempt to derail feminist arguments with cries of 'but what about men?' But I am not suggesting that because we cannot do everything in the face of a complex problem we should do nothing (although we might disagree about the nature of the problem in the first place). Nor do I think that those advocating against sugar are necessarily without compassion for those less privileged than themselves or are insincere in their desire to improve health and wellbeing. But the despairing abandonment of complexity in favour of the lowest common denominator – the need for sugar reduction – means that sugar reduction always becomes an end in itself rather than a starting point for something more transformative. Facilitated by the neoliberal logics of austerity, this setting aside of complexity in the interests of expediency is always an act of foreclosure, blurring out the wider social context in which giving up sugar has come to make sense. This invisibility is the focus of the next, and final, chapter of the book.

8

The (in)visible inequalities of sugar

In *Jamie's Sugar Rush*, Jamie Oliver visits London's Royal Free Hospital, where he meets patients whose type 2 diabetes has led to foot amputation. Like the dental scene that opens the film, this scene includes graphic footage, showing healing post-amputation stumps; Oliver comments that 'it all feels quite medieval to me'. Immediately after the hospital scene, with the images still fresh in our minds, Oliver goes to meet Becky – a fifteen-year-old mixed-race girl who lives with her white mother and who has had type 2 diabetes since she was thirteen. We see Becky walking alone on the street and then sitting, alone again, at the bus stop. In the family kitchen, Oliver asks Becky's mother: 'As a mother, I'm sure you were tracing back – what on earth happened?' Becky jumps in before her mother can answer, confessing that she had made 'some really poor choices', spending her pocket money on soft drinks and confectionery at the corner shop. Her mother counters Becky's confession with one of her own:

> Looking back, I kind of fell out of the habit of cooking meals every day and got more into the habit of buying something that's quick and easy, or buying a takeaway. As a parent, it is my responsibility to take care of my children. I mean, I had half an idea and was trying to get healthy things but maybe if the packaging on the …

Oliver interrupts her to observe, 'But you were still getting it wrong.' The interjection is designed to reinforce her speculation about the misleading packaging, but simultaneously affirms her culpability. 'Yes', she agrees sadly, 'I was still getting it wrong.'

In the next scene, we see Oliver and Becky sitting on her bed while she lays out the equipment that she uses to test her blood sugar, which she then demonstrates to Oliver. 'So you have to do this to yourself every day?' he asks, and she explains her regimen of multiple tests per day, observing, 'it's quite annoying to have to be so responsible'. The film cuts back to Oliver and Becky's mother looking through old photos of Becky on the computer, identifying the point at which her weight gain begins to show. Becky's mother worries about the potential future health consequences of Becky's diabetes, and for the viewer, the memory of the healing amputation stumps hangs unspoken in the air as the portent of Becky's imagined future.

The scenes are powerful and drive home the point about the spread of a disease traditionally associated with older people to younger populations. But they also leave a lot unspoken. First, of the three children featured in the UK segments of the film, all are either Black or mixed race: Becky, Mario (whose teeth were pulled at the beginning of the film) and Ori, who appears in an experiment involving camera glasses that track her eye movements in shops 'to see the world from a child's perspective'. Ori's eyes bounce predictably to the bright arrays of confectionery and soft drinks; 'Mum's got no chance', declares Oliver. This reflects a broader trend in the representation of the war on obesity, and writing in the US context, sociologist Priya Fielding-Singh observes that Black and brown children are 'the faces of childhood obesity, the mascots of a public health crisis'.[1] These representational trends are never innocent, with media studies of reporting on obesity showing that individuals are much more likely to be held responsible in articles that discuss African Americans, Latinos or the poor than in those that don't.[2] While the racial dynamics of the UK are different from those in the US, the focus on non-white children in Oliver's film acts as tacit shorthand for failures and vulnerabilities in the face of sugar.

The second unspoken element to these scenes is their gendering, particularly in their cultivation of maternal blame. We learn nothing about Becky's mother other than her well-intentioned failures. In the same way as Oliver fails to ask more questions about the feeding of Coke to babies (see Chapter 5), he never asks why she 'fell out of the habit of cooking meals every day' or what competing demands on her time and finances she might be facing while raising her children. Coded as working class, she is unnamed in the film; she is there to represent well-meaning, naive maternal failure at the sharp end of a health crisis. Becky too is similarly one-dimensional, and we learn nothing about her other than her diabetes; nor is she praised for having risen to the demands of her testing and treatment regimen so capably. Always sitting or walking alone, she is never seen hanging out with friends or engaging in other activities. Instead, we are offered a life defined (and ruined) by diabetes alone. In this way, class, race and gender are absently present, intersecting in ways that become simultaneously (if selectively) both highly visible and invisible.

This strategic (in)visibility around intersecting axes of social inequality is the focus of this final chapter. Throughout the book I have highlighted multiple points where the wider social, economic, cultural and political contexts of sugar consumption are blurred into the background in the rush to target sugar. In this chapter, by focusing on the intersections of race, gender and class, I explore what the substance of those erasures might be and how their foregrounding might change the way we think about sugar. In doing so, I am confronted with the problem of writing about what isn't there in the data as well as what is. To bridge this gap, I draw on the wider literature on experiences of food and fatness as a resource for imagining what is missing from mainstream sugar talk. Consequently, some of this material is not explicitly about the attack on sugar, but rather provides the context within which that attack comes to makes sense. I start by looking at the (in)visible racialisation of sugar; then at its gendering; and finally, at sugar's inflection in its wider social life through the lens of class. As discussed in the previous chapter, I argue that the absence of a sustained consideration of how intersecting identities frame sugar consumption is not merely a matter of oversight, but rather an act of strategic simplification and discursive shorthand to keep the focus firmly on sugar consumption as a matter of individual self-discipline.

Racialising sugar

In spite of repeated warnings that 'we are eating too much sugar', this generalising 'we' obscures the profound unevenness of the distribution of risk and blame in the attack on sugar. Race and ethnicity are a key dimension to this unevenness, albeit in strategically (in)visible ways. This section explores this absent presence, first, by considering the racialisation of the risky body; and second, in the use of modern hunter-gatherers as both proxies for an idealised diet of the distant past and cautionary tales for the sugar-consuming present.

Risky bodies

One of the most striking absences from the dataset I collected for this project is that of overt discussions of race and ethnicity. In the newspaper data, there is only a handful of direct mentions, all focusing on the firmly entrenched idea of a South Asian predisposition to obesity and metabolic illness. For example, an article in *The Guardian* in 2015 argues that 'South Asian adults need not reach high body weights to experience the dangerously elevated risks for cardiovascular disease, stroke and diabetes of a much heavier Caucasian person.'[3] The article warns menacingly: 'For the wrong person, a chocolate kiss could literally provide a pre-taste of an early death.' The explanation for this heightened risk, we are told, lies in the familiar idea of a mismatch between bodies adapted to traditional ways of living and the encounter with modernity: 'This picture of human metabolism in India evolved against a background of starvation combined with rigorous physical activity outdoors. It makes sense that the sudden metabolic imbalance that emerged in South Asia over the past 15 years as economies improved has upset the calorie-activity equilibrium of centuries.' The explanation is disturbing for its nostalgic portrayal of a life of starvation and hard physical labour as one of 'equilibrium' and fails to account for the metabolic legacies of starvation across generations. As Harris Solomon explains in his study of metabolic disease in India, the familiar theme of bodies outpaced by a rapidly changing diet is 'an abiding analytic that is out of alignment with all the things that metabolisms are and do across shifting arrangements of bodies, substances and environments'.[4] He argues that the 'mismatch' discourse inevitably reduces the problem to one of (over)consumption – a move which 'closes doors when it comes to metabolic matters because it becomes mired in proportion and excess'.[5] We can see this clearly in the story in *The Guardian*; it is the chocolate kiss that will kill.

In the UK context, culture-bound beliefs are commonly seen as holding ethnic minority populations back from implementing the pre-scribed changes to consumption patterns that are seen as the key to a healthy lifestyle. This re-instates the 'mismatch' discourse in the form of a clash between cultures. For example, citing research with Bangladeshi, Pakistani and Black African communities, the 2009 marketing strategy for Change4Life singles out ethnic minority families as 'at-risk'. This risk is attributed to a range of cultural factors including faith, traditional gender roles, parenting styles, a reactive approach to health, intergenera-tional households, a lack of stigma associated with fatness and 'cultural foods' that are high in fat.[6] The latter is endorsed by Gillespie who, in a section on meal planning in *The Sweet Poison Quit Plan*, warns: 'You don't have to go cold turkey on Asian food; you just have to know that it is dangerous territory […].'[7] A presumed culture of misplaced body satisfaction is also a key barrier to overcome, although always with the neutrality of the category of health as a buffer against suggestions of fomenting disordered body image. For example, the Change4Life mar-keting strategy encourages people to connect fatness and health using the model statement: 'This isn't about how I or my children look; it's about type 2 diabetes, cancer, heart disease and lives cut short.'[8]

The misconceived body satisfaction of the racialised Other also fea-tures in Lustig's *Fat Chance*, this time in the form of a proudly 'politi-cally incorrect disclosure', in which he cites Latina mothers who bring fat children to his clinic complaining that they aren't eating enough. He explains: 'The immigrants view their obese children as the epit-ome of health and an affirmation of their ability to provide for them. In their countries of origin, thin children were sickly and at risk of premature death. Unfortunately, they aren't yet familiar with the fact that the opposite is true in America.'[9] Missing from these knowledge deficit accounts is any recognition of the experience of those being spoken about. For example, Fielding-Singh describes the struggles of Teresa, an undocumented immigrant from Sinaloa in Mexico who was raising her son, Esteban, in conditions of hardship and precarity. She took pride in his enthusiastic consumption of the traditional Sinaloan dishes that she prepared, but also celebrated his growing taste for processed American food, even while knowing it was not the healthiest option. Like other low-income parents, she often had to deprioritise nutrition in favour of a cheap, filling meal, but his growing taste for American food was also a sign of him fitting in and building a life in the US. This gave her the hope that he would experience security and belonging in contrast to her own experiences of precarity and exclusion.[10] Knowledge deficit cannot begin to capture the multiple motivations and constraints that constitute her and Esteban's food choices, nor her more expansive definition of what constitutes 'health' for her son.

There is an unmistakably racialised dimension to these appalled encounters with minoritised Others who don't demonstrate sufficient concern about fatness. For example, Lustig warms to his theme with 'more political incorrectness': this time, teenage African American girls who 'tip the scales at 300 pounds' but describe themselves as 'thick' and well-proportioned.[11] Sociologist Sabrina Strings argues that through slavery and its brutal objectification of Black bodies, Black people, and particularly Black women, were turned into 'the shadow figures of modernity', seen as governed by unconfined appetites and irrationality and growing fat through indolence and gluttony. As body size became increasingly linked to racial categories, the fat Black body became a marker of primitiveness against which white superiority, good taste and morality could be measured. Strings observes that contemporary studies showing high body mass index (BMI) rates among Black women have re-ignited these associations, rendering Black women once again 'the focus of fear, anxiety and degradation over the size of their bodies'.[12] Lustig's insistence that the bodies of the 'thick' African American girls can be properly known only in relation to a medicalised standard of (white) thinness leaves them beyond recuperation, since it is a standard that is already defined against their own derogated Black bodies. In this context, the girls' contentment with their bodies can only ever constitute indulgent self-deception.

This case exemplifies the common use of minoritised bodies, and especially fat minoritised bodies, as a signifier not only of risk, but also of the failure to take responsibility for the body. Just as Oliver's documentary uses Black and mixed-race children's bodies to signify vulnerability to the lure of sugar, *Fat Chance* quietly mobilises racialised Others to signify poor choices and as sites for coercive state intervention. Sixteen of the book's chapters opens with short, illustrative case studies of children, six of which focus on non-white children. The ethnicity of the non-white children is noted in the case studies, alongside potent markers of their social status. For example, the book opens with the case of 'Juan, a 100-pound six-year-old Latino boy whose mother is a non-English-speaking farm worker from Salinas, California'.[13] Whiteness is not explicitly marked – 'Sally is a beautiful thirteen-year old girl'[14] – but more significantly, while the non-white cases showcase incidences of poor parenting and ill-informed food choices, obesogenic medical conditions such as hypothalamic tumours, genetic defects and abnormally high insulin release account for six out of the ten white children's cases (and none of the non-white case studies). Furthermore, while all but one of the white children achieve positive outcomes (as assessed primarily via weight loss), only one of the non-white cases achieves resolution. Even in this instance, while the white children's successes are the result of successful medical interventions and informed parent-involved lifestyle changes, salvation for an eleven-year-old African American, DeShawn, comes only after Child Protective Services become involved, forcing his mother 'to face up to her own sugar addiction'.[15] With mothers figuring as the primary carers in the case studies, an implied model of good and bad dietary citizenship emerges along racialised, classed and gendered lines, with one-dimensional, racialised Others operating as a shorthand for the failure to exercise the informed self-efficacy demanded of good neoliberal citizens in the face of sugar.

Paleo-proxies

A second site for the absent presence of race lies in the paleo fantasies introduced in Chapter 2. These provide a model for the dietary 'before' which is central to the discourse of dietary mismatch, exercising an inescapably colonial and racialised gaze through their use of modern hunter-gatherer societies as the closest proxies for our distant ancestors. These are known primarily via colonial anthropological studies, and as proxies, modern hunter-gatherer societies are defined and selected according to their diets alone, which were based on a shared reliance on hunting, fishing and gathering for subsistence. Even where differences between Paleolithic people and their modern proxies are acknowledged, these are quickly set aside in favour of dietary similarity. As paleo diet advocates Boyd Eaton and Melvin Konner explain:

> In comparison with the majority of paleolithic human beings, existing hunter-gatherers occupy marginal habitats and their lives differ in many ways from those living before the advent of agriculture. Nevertheless, the range and content of foods they consume are similar (in the sense that they represent wild game and uncultivated vegetable foods) to those that our ancestors ate for up to 4 million years.[16]

The diverse cultural and social practices of these societies are erased in this presumption of dietary commonality, positioning them as pristine pre-agricultural societies whose imagined dietary patterns represent a pure 'before' on which we should model our own diets. Alongside this erasure of diversity, the dark history and present of the colonialist and racist oppression suffered by those societies, and in which much of the data they are drawing on is entangled, are set quietly aside. For example, Eaton and Konner note that of the fifty or so modern hunter-gatherer societies that have been studied, 'only a handful have survived into the second half of the 20th century and have had their diets analysed'.[17] The decimation of these societies figures as a methodological inconvenience rather than as a sign that these populations are far from untouched proxies for distant ancestors. Similarly, their observation that they occupy 'marginal habitats' says nothing about the traumatic processes of dispossession that led to that territorial marginality.[18] This erasure also overlooks the troubled history of the ideologically driven geneticisation of racial difference and sameness upon which many of those anthropological knowledge claims rest.[19] Instead, rather than recognising this long history of exploitation and its embodied, cross-generational impacts, their use as proxies extends and intensifies that exploitation through a process of strategic and selective extraction. This reduces complex societies and their devastating histories to diet alone in the interests of constructing coherent dietary 'just-so stories' in the present.

Cautionary tales

As proxies, modern hunter-gatherers serve as models of an idealised lost dietary past to which we should aspire to return. But this is so only up to the time of their encounter with the Western diet, when they are appropriated instead as cautionary tales of the harms of sugar (and refined carbohydrates more generally). For example, Taubes describes a contemporary epidemic of sugar-induced diabetes among historically unaffected indigenous populations including Inuit, Native Americans, Polynesians, Micronesians, Melanesians, Australian aboriginals and New Zealand Maoris, whose catastrophic health problems he attributes to adopting Western diets and lifestyles.[20] Gillespie proffers a similar list of populations who 'seem particularly susceptible to the effects of prolonged insulin resistance', including Polynesians, Aboriginal Australians and Native Americans.[21]

Although this is not named explicitly by Gillespie, the attribution of susceptibility gestures to the thrifty gene hypothesis, first posited by James Neal in 1962. The hypothesis suggests that some bodies are 'exceptionally efficient in the intake and/or utilisation of food'.[22] This gives them a survival advantage in environments characterised by periods of feast and famine but is seen as having devastating consequences in a context of the sustained abundance of high-energy foods associated with modern Western food environments. Postcolonial scholar Margery Fee notes the remarkable ease with which, over time, this 'rather unclear scientific hypothesis was transformed into a clearcut racializing account that is now a popular, free-floating "explanation" for the high incidence of diabetes among Aboriginal peoples'.[23] As anthropologist Emily Yates-Doerr observes, this positions those described as suffering diseases of modernity as irretrievably 'not quite modern enough to truly master the refinement and restraint required by "modern" civilisation', holding (post)colonial relations of power in place.[24]

The concepts of the thrifty gene and more generally of the perceived mismatch between bodies adapted to traditional ways of living and their clash with modernity are exemplified in the anti-obesity and anti-sugar domains by what Julie Guthman and Melanie DuPuis describe as 'the saga of the south-western Pima'.[25] Now living primarily on three reservations in Arizona, the Pima are a highly studied population because of the devastatingly high rates of diabetes in their communities, which make them the perfect cautionary tale for the harms of the Western diet in general and of sugar in particular. Taubes takes up their case in all three books in his trilogy, describing them as 'among the best-studied indigenous populations in the world'.[26] He narrates their tragic history of exploitation, destitution and territorial marginalisation, including the over-hunting of game, the diversion of essential water sources and a devastating famine in the late nineteenth and early twentieth centuries.[27] Loss of traditional food sources, even as early as the mid-nineteenth century, led to increased reliance on sugar, coffee and canned goods from settler trading posts, and in times of famine, they were reliant on government rations, including large quantities of white flour and sugar, to fend off starvation.[28]

In *Why We Get Fat*, Taubes draws on early twentieth-century anthropological studies of the Pima to illustrate his claim that their 'weight problem' reaches back to a time 'when there was nothing particularly toxic about their environment at all, or at least not as it would be described today'.[29] He illustrates the segment with a picture taken by

Harvard anthropologist Frank Russell, who published a landmark study of the Pima in 1908.[30] The picture is of a rotund Pima woman sitting up against a tree, staring into the distance away from the camera. She does not make eye contact and we don't know whether she consented to the image being taken; all we know of her is that Russell named her 'Fat Louisa'. In his subtext to the image, Taubes notes that 'she surely didn't get fat because she ate at fast food restaurants and watched too much television'.[31] Instead, he argues that her fatness while living under conditions of poverty that her community faced at the time when the picture was taken can be explained only by the type of food being consumed: in this case, government rations heavy in white flour and sugar. Russell made a similar observation, noting that 'certain articles of their diet appear to be markedly flesh producing',[32] although he also attributed this with unabashed colonial confidence to indolence induced by the semi-tropical climate and a general slovenliness, particularly among women.[33]

The problem with Taubes' account is twofold. First, it rushes too quickly to his desired conclusion about the evils of refined carbohydrates, including sugar, skipping quickly over the historical, economic, social, cultural and environmental factors that constitute health among the Pima. The romantic discourse of pre-modern Others dietarily corrupted by modernity overlooks the conditions of that encounter and the imposed terms of their forced integration into a market economy in which they were perpetually left on the losing side of the exchange.[34] The conviction that there was 'nothing particularly toxic' about the Pima living environment at the time Russell was doing his research is directly contradicted by their everyday struggles with poverty, violence, racism and dispossession, all of which have long histories and enduring impacts which reach into the present. As anthropologist Amy Moran-Thomas observes in her study of communities living with diabetes in Belize, 'diabetic sugar's normalised losses emerge from a machine 500 years in the making'.[35]

This is not to argue that the subsequent reliance on cheap refined carbohydrates, including sugar, is not a contributor to poor health, but rather that viewing their lives so relentlessly through the singular lens of sugar consumption inevitably sets aside the enduring and embodied impacts of those histories and rebounds to solutions reliant on individual food choice. This, in turn, pushes (over)consumption into the foreground while obscuring the many other factors that impact on health and access to healthcare. These not only constrain individual choice but may be experienced as more pressing than food choice (for example, hunger, unemployment or violence). As Moran-Thomas notes of the nutritional education interventions that she witnessed: 'I watched white doctors from foreign countries lecture these same women about why preventative health was important, seemingly without realising how entire lives were already being lived in a mode of preventative care.'[36]

The second problem with Taubes' account of the Pima is that his engagement with them is problematically extractive. He discusses them in the book as a cautionary tale about the connection between sugar and insulin resistance, but in doing so, he reproduces a familiar pattern of the exploitation of indigenous at-risk populations as a research resource. As Moran-Thomas notes, 'People living with diabetes in villages around the world today are much more likely to have their genomes sequenced for risk than to have access to dialysis that might actually mitigate its consequences.'[37] This renders those people one-dimensional, defined only by their risk and stripped of their history and culture. As anthropologist Carolyn Smith-Morris observes, the Pima are known throughout the global scientific community for their diabetes and obesity, but not 'for their agricultural genius and long history of hospitality towards the Anglos'.[38] More broadly, this approach positions indigenous cultures as having moved from idealised simplicity and stasis to complexity and too-rapid change, but as an elderly Guatemalan woman cautioned Yates-Doerr:

> You spend a fixed amount of time with us, and think you understand change in our communities. You start to see the complications in our lives and you mistakenly conclude that our lives were once simple and are just now becoming complicated – you do not realise they have always been this way. You mistake changes in your own amount of knowledge about our community for changes we are undergoing ourselves.[39]

This matters because, as Moran-Thomas observes, 'the setting of any narrative already establishes certain terms for its unfolding plot and will have much to do with what will count as its resolution'.[40]

Throughout this section, we can see that race and ethnicity are strategically (in)visible in the anti-sugar domain, which is run through with social inequalities that are at once conspicuously absent and starkly present. 'Dangerous' South Asian food, culture-bound parents, misplaced body satisfaction, the fat minoritised body and the ailing indigenous body are all mobilised to signify ignorance, irresponsibility and being 'not quite modern enough'. As such, they serve as one-dimensional figures against which white, middle-class norms of diet, embodiment and taste can be measured and found superior. The next section takes up this (in)visibility again, this time in relation to gender.

Gendering sugar

Food is about many different things, but whatever else it is about, it is always about gender. Entangled with expectations of care, health and the family, what, where and how we eat is inescapably gendered, with food work and all its accompanying responsibility and shame falling disproportionately onto women.[41] This section explores the gendering of sugar by looking, first, at the gendered distribution of work and responsibility in going sugar free; and, second, at the construction of women as especially vulnerable to sugar.

A woman's work ...

In February 2017, *The Sun* published a mortified mother article headlined 'the hidden risks of a spoon of sugar', where a stay-at-home mother of three, Gemma, responded to a nutritionist's evaluation of her children's daily diet:

> I'm really surprised and shocked by how much sugar all the children have been eating. It's been a real eye-opener. I always thought cereal bars were a good option for breakfast but I've already started making Findlay toast

and porridge instead. I was told to put Macie on a high-calorie diet when she was a baby, but it's my fault she's ended up on a high-sugar one as well. I'm going to make sure she eats a lot more nutritious foods. All the kids love spaghetti Bolognese but since doing this diary I've started making my own pasta sauce […] I've also started shopping online as the nutritional information is much easier to see and add up which is making a difference. And we've switched from full fizzy drinks to diet versions.[42]

For the reformed Gemma, sugar content is carefully calculated and accounted for, with higher-sugar items swapped out for lower-sugar alternatives to stretch out the daily sugar allowance. This is achieved primarily by home-cooking from scratch (porridge, pasta sauce), alongside the additional work of reading labels and calculating nutritional content online. This is a process that generates significant domestic labour for Gemma but, as discussed in previous chapters, is cast as part of her maternal duties and therefore as pleasurable (being a good mother, acquiring new cooking skills) and is never therefore coded as work. All this is performed against a background of burning maternal guilt and without any discussion of the redistribution of domestic and reproductive labour in the household.

The case of Gemma illustrates what I have returned to repeatedly throughout the book: that the obligations to do something that come with the crisis of sugar fall unevenly and disproportionately onto women. While the authoritative voices of the anti-sugar domain are overwhelmingly male, the workhorses of the movement are women, whose job it is to adapt, swap, shop, prepare and cook, all while cajoling children and male partners to get on board by inconveniencing them as little as possible. At times, as in the mortified mother stories, the focus on women is clear; a parallel 'mortified father' story is narratively impossible since expectations in relation to family food and nutrition don't fall directly onto men. At other times, women, particularly as mothers, are simply the default setting, unspoken until those norms are breached. For example, in January 2014, an article in *The Sunday Times* reported on a survey of sugar-laden foods claiming to provide at least one of 'five-a-day'. Action on Sugar's Graham Macgregor warned: 'Mothers are being deceived into thinking they are not giving sugar to their children when in fact they are because apple juice concentrate is the same as sugar.'[43] Similarly, in June 2015, an article in *The Daily Telegraph* reported on a study debunking the commonly held belief that children experience a 'sugar rush' leading to unruly behaviour after consuming sweet food and drink. Instead, psychologist David Benton is reported as saying that rather than being over-stimulated by sugar, children are responding to maternal expectations: 'Because the mother anticipated a problem, they put their child on a much shorter rein and interpreted behaviour differently and saw what they wanted to see.'[44] In both of these cases, mothers are responsible but also gullible, requiring constant advice and correction. While the naming of mothers here at least makes their responsibility explicit, this act of taken-for-granted naming holds that distribution of work and responsibility in place as inevitable and unremarkable.

One of the effects of this is to understate the labour involved in food work, which is never only the (already onerous) task of putting food on the table but also the invisible work of planning and delegating. For example, in March 2017, *The Daily Telegraph* published a story by dietitian and nutritionist Sarah Schenker, in which she documents her efforts to persuade her husband and two children to follow in her footsteps and eliminate sugar from their diets. 'After eliminating the sweet stuff from her diet', we are told in the sub-headline, 'Dr Sarah Schenker got her husband and two sons in on the act.' On top of the immediate food work of eliminating sugar, the task of 'getting' her husband on board adds yet another layer of work for her:

> I immediately felt a difference [after giving up sugar]. I was more alert, energetic and looked trimmer. But eating is such a family treat and I wanted my husband, Ronnie, 46, a barrister, to be on board too. To say he was reluctant is an understatement. He's a chocolate fiend and with decades of bad eating habits behind him, it was much harder to wean him off sugar. When I sent him to get groceries, he's invariably come back with bars of Toblerone hiding at the bottom of the shopping bags.[45]

Even though her efforts eventually 'won him round', he is infantilised by his lack of direct responsibility; he is weaned off sugar and he buys himself a stash of chocolate bars when he is 'sent' grocery shopping. In these stories, male disinterest in the sugar-free project is forgivable; his acquiescence to the project is enough. Similarly, in an epilogue to Eve Schaub's *Year of No Sugar*, her husband, Stephen, declares his respect for her growing vision, noting approvingly that she 'still makes most meals from scratch'.[46] I found no cases where a radical change in eating had also led to a transformation of the division of domestic labour, which remains firmly the domain of women, however unspoken.

The male infantilisation that we see in Schenker's account is also a noticeable feature of Gameau's *That Sugar Film*, where he displays an impishly disinterested masculinity as a counter to the potentially emasculating effects of dietary concern. His account in *That Sugar Book* of meeting his wife, Zoe, and winning her over makes this clear:

> The years passed and, as often happens with a man just before it's too late, he meets a sensational woman. That woman will iron out a few creases, tame his wandering eye and give him a gentle reminder that he is, in fact, an adult. For me, it happened at 32. My body and my behaviour reflected years of sugar abuse. Then along came Zoe [...] She understood that the food we put into our bodies is instrumental to the way we appear, feel and view the world. In the formative weeks of a relationship, men will pretend to be interested in a whole range of things to win the affections of their new love. For me, it was pretending to enjoy cucumber and kale smoothies, quinoa salads with chia seeds, and plain yoghurt with berries. Love really does work miracles though and as I got used to this new way of eating – and, crucially, as I began to feel better in both body and mind – I discovered I actually enjoyed it.[47]

This narrative of playful dishonesty enables Gameau to circumvent the threat to masculinity that is posed by concern about diet, and particularly by eating food that might be associated with the feminised domain of weight loss. Zoe's role here is not simply to recalibrate his diet and palate, but also to civilise him ('iron out a few creases, tame his wandering eye'). Once he is convinced of the virtues of the transformation of his diet, his experiment enables him to reclaim it for the masculine domain through risk-taking and his alignment with the authoritative domain of science. However, a woman's work is never done, and the meals he eats during his post-experiment recovery are devised by Zoe in collaboration with recipe developer Michelle Earl and nutritionist Sharon Johnston. Reproducing the familiar trope of food work as too pleasurable to be counted as work and of women as taking responsibility for domestic labour by preference rather than expectation, he describes Zoe as someone 'who has always loved cooking and does it with a simple ease and flair'. The meals, he explains, allowed his body to heal, but 'were also designed to help stabilise my moods, making the whole post-sugar period beneficial for everybody'.[48] Even the work of managing his mood can be delegated to women.

Jamie Oliver displays a similarly boyish 'naughtiness' in an article in *The Sunday Times* in November 2015. He describes the happy routine of taking his children to a local old-fashioned sweet shop where they are allowed to spend 50p on sweets, which he acknowledges are 'full of sugar, no nutritional value', before countering that 'it's important for the kids to have their own money and be able to choose how to spend it'. This is followed by a cheeky confession: 'Technically, I'm not allowed to give them sweets until after lunch, but sometimes one slips in.'[49] The childish 'I'm not allowed to …' enables Oliver to adopt the role of the playful father who is 'technically' not allowed to let the children have sweets before lunch, but occasionally lets them anyway, with a treat made forgivable by being wrapped up in a lesson in financial responsibility. He never says whose rule he is breaking, but we are left to assume that it comes from the children's mother, reinstating a gendered division of responsibility for family nutrition between the everyday and treats. As Fielding-Singh observes, fathers are more able to break the dietary rules precisely because mothers take responsibility for setting and enforcing the rules most of the time.[50] This is not to suggest that Oliver does not prepare food for his family or that he does not engage in concerns about their everyday nutrition, but rather that he is able to draw light-heartedly on a gendered discourse of parenting that would not be so readily available to a mother. This enables him to walk the fine line between 'new lad' and 'new man' that is central to his brand,[51] while inadvertently demonstrating that the possibilities for parental failure in relation to sugar remain inescapably higher for women than for men.

A weakness for sugar

One of the reasons why Oliver can position himself as a permissible rule-breaker is that his white, privileged masculinity enables him to portray himself as able to exert rational control over sugar. However, as we also saw in relation to race, vulnerability to sugar's allure is highly stratified and attaches easily to women, who are commonly imagined, like children, as innately incapable of resisting sweet foods. For example, in his book *Addicted to Food*, journalist James Erlichman identifies women as uniquely vulnerable and as finding refined carbohydrates 'especially seductive', including 'the ultimate seduction ... chocolate'.[52] This editorialised claim comes at the end of a three-paper chain of citation beginning with a paper that found that overweight or obese women, when induced into a negative mood, chose a carbohydrate drink over a carbohydrate and protein alternative.[53] This initial finding travels along the citation chain.[54] By the time it reaches Erlichman, it has morphed into a generalised claim about women and refined carbohydrates, which presumes an innate difference between men and women and which aligns comfortably with gendered assumptions of emotional instability, comfort eating and vulnerability to sweetness.

A further dimension to this gendering of sugar is demonstrated in an article in *The Times* in October 2013 reporting on David Gillespie's *The Sweet Poison Quit Plan*. On the topic of withdrawal symptoms, the article notes: 'These symptoms lasted two to three weeks [for Gillespie], although women in their thirties and forties following his programme say that it takes up to two months for withdrawal to end; no-one knows why men tend to find it easier.'[55] This theme is pursued with a light touch in the book, and there is a striking absence of curiosity about this anecdotal difference, which is presented as simultaneously too bewildering and too self-evident to explain. Hormonal fluctuations and menstruation are the go-to explanations, and Gillespie notes that pre-menopausal women appear to be protected from some of the worst effects of fructose, laying down fat on the legs and bottom rather than abdominally. He notes this as a health advantage, before adding in a flourish of fat-phobic misogyny: 'except for the looking bad in swim-suits bit'.[56]

Sociologist Deborah Lupton argues that women's presumed suscep-tibility to sweet foods reflects normative gender attributes. Sugary, light and delicate foods, she argues, are seen as 'indulgences, easy to eat and digest, as decorative and pretty, pale coloured, the foods of child-hood. So too, women are often represented as decorative, anodyne, delicate, less intelligent and far more childlike than men.'[57] But there is also a darker side to this perceived attraction: 'that which associates their pleasures with addiction, guilt and furtiveness, with losing control over one's desires, and even to irrational behaviour as a result of the "sugar high" induced from eating sweet foods'.[58] Women's relation-ship to sugar, then, reflects the contradictions of normative feminin-ity, whereby women are coded as gentle, sweet and restrained, yet also unpredictable, governed by emotions, susceptible to temptation and unable to transcend the body in the way that men are presumed to do. This explains Gillespie's comfort with women's apparent inability to go 'cold turkey'; they simply cannot be expected to exercise the same tight control over the body as men. He observes that the need to take withdrawal more slowly risks allowing sugar to creep back in, warning women: 'Don't kid yourself.'[59] Around sugar, women can't quite be trusted.

Women emerge in these accounts as vulnerable to sweet food and the imperatives of their unpredictable bodies, with gender differences written into the body in intractable ways. However much 'we' are all at risk, then, not all bodies are seen as equally salvageable from the inef-fable lure of sugar. Just as the attack on sugar shores up racial inequali-ties by rendering them strategically (in)visible, it also sediments gender inequalities in equally absently present ways. This is also true in rela-tion to relations of class, which is the focus of the final section of this chapter.

The classed inequalities of sugar

In January 2017, *The Guardian* reported on the reality TV show *Sugar Free Farm*, where a group of minor celebrities identified as sugar addicts were taken to a rural retreat where sugar was completely removed from their diet. The article exposes the classed assumptions about who the archetypal sugar addict is:

> As the series began, one of those who was consuming the most sugar was the actor Peter Davison, a charming, sensible-seeming man who did not appear to me to be vastly over-weight. He eats [...] 52 kilos of sugar a year. Just imagine it. Piled up, it would fill your downstairs loo. Two days into cold turkey, it was Davison, rather than, say, Gemma Collins from TOWIE, who came over all dizzy. The paramedics took him away in an ambulance, just another pitiful, trembling addict.[60]

As a working-class woman and star of the reality TV show *The Only Way Is Essex* (*TOWIE*), it is Collins who is assumed to be unable to control her sugar intake rather than Davison. The use of the toilet bowl as a comparator for the quantity of sugar consumed serves to emphasise just how far Davison has strayed from proper middle-class masculinity in his acquiescence to sugar. The (over)consumption of sugar always carries the weight of class distinction.

This final section explores the classed assumptions (and their intersections with race and gender) that underpin the attack on sugar in both their explicit and implicit forms. I argue that although class is perhaps the most strategically visible axis of inequality in the anti-sugar domain, the lived experiences of poor or working-class people are largely absent, instead serving as one-dimensional signifiers of dietary failure against which middle-class norms of informed self-efficacy can be established. The section explores three aspects of this: (1) the embeddedness of the attack on sugar, and the war on obesity in which it is entrenched, in middle-class norms of taste and consumption; (2) the classed relations of interventions into the obesogenic environment; and (3) knowing the poor.

Middle-class aspiration

Even more than race and gender, class is perhaps the most strategically (in)visible axis of inequality in the anti-sugar domain. As shown in the previous two chapters, 'the poor' have a vigorous discursive life in relation to sugar, serving as a shorthand for the fecklessness, overconsumption, low self-control and bad taste against which middle-class norms of taste, consumption and self-efficacy can be measured. This middle-class standard is equally (in)visible, never explicitly stated as such but unmistakably present, even while being actively denied. For example, the Change4Life marketing strategy document discussed earlier in this chapter notes the concern from 'at risk' groups that healthy living is a 'middle class aspiration' that is not relevant to them. This is adamantly refused as a misperception to be overcome; they are instructed instead to 'believe that change is possible'.[61] But as Robert Crawford observes, 'Health *is* the language of class',[62] and by extension, so is food, with the incitement to self-control over consumption not only serving as the path to health but also acting as a site of distinction.

This tacit middle-classness is also visible in the food recommendations that run through the anti-sugar domain. For example, in an article in *The Daily Telegraph* in March 2014, journalist Hazel Southam described her own experience of giving up sugar, including its unexpected economies: 'my food bill has halved since I gave up sugar in all its forms. I can no longer be seduced by supermarkets' three-for-two offers and bottles of sparkling wine at the end of the aisle. I'm more likely to buy a brace of pheasants, a decent Camembert, and some salad from the farmers' market.'[63] Her choices – framed as both economically and nutritionally shrewd – speak directly to the privileged tastes and preferences of the paper's readership but are unmistakably classed in the framing of what constitutes the 'good' diet. Less overt examples abound: for example, the prevalence of recommendations to replace sugary cereals with stove-top porridge; the repeated invocation of fresh food and farmers' markets; or advice to treat yourself to a single square of quality dark chocolate rather than cheap confectionery. All are run through with classed expectations of good taste and restraint, and the act of giving up sugar marks a move away from foods coded as tastelessly excessive towards the tastefulness of the sugar free life (see Chapter 4).

The obesogenic environment

The discourse of the obesogenic environment is another way in which class is made (in)visible, this time under cover of benign concern for people who are poor and the desire to move away from blame-filled discourses of individual responsibility. This approach begins from the conviction that obesity and chronic health problems among the most disadvantaged are the result of a built environment which determines unhealthy food and activity behaviours, which in turn are seen as causing obesity. Issues of concern commonly include a high prevalence of fast food outlets, easily accessible arrays of soft drinks and confectionery, limited supermarket access ('food deserts') and a lack of access to parks and other exercise spaces in areas characterised by high levels of poverty, obesity and chronic illness. Policies in response include measures like the taxation of targeted food and drinks, advertising bans, food labelling and removing confectionery from checkouts, as well as limiting the presence of fast food outlets, improving supermarket access and providing educational programmes in targeted areas. It is an appealing approach for many because it appears to move the focus away from punitive discourses of individual blame, relying instead on a structural account of health inequalities.

However, even with the best intentions, this approach reproduces classed assumptions and expectations about how to live and eat well, as well as about the role of the built environment in achieving those ends. Julie Guthman argues that it is a prime case of problem closure, presuming cause and effect to the exclusion of other possibilities – for example, that the built environment might reflect social relations rather than producing them; that other factors than overconsumption might affect weight and health among those populations (e.g. sleep debt, environmental pollutants, stress, weight discrimination); or that obesity might not be the most pressing among the threats to health and wellbeing that those living in environments categorised as dangerously obesogenic face (e.g. violence, drugs, unemployment, hunger, poor housing). In short, she argues that 'these are attempts to make obesogenic environments more like the kind in which thin people live, without questioning whether people were made thin by living there'.[64] Through this problem closure, the environmental approach is rendered politically palatable, focusing reassuringly on those most in need while skirting the need for structural change to address fundamental inequalities. But in doing so, it also reproduces the very classed relations of power that it purports to avoid.

There are two dimensions to this reinstatement of relations of class. First, even while appearing like a benign collective intervention, it falls back repeatedly onto what gender studies scholar Anna Kirkland calls 'the micropolitics of food choice'.[65] In an imagined world where 'unhealthy' foods were successfully driven out of the environments where they had previously dominated and affordable 'healthy' foods have taken their place, the firm expectation that individuals will (and should) then choose the 'right' foods intensifies. This in turn creates new possibilities not only for failure, but also for punitive and intrusive state interventions to which those who are socially and economically disadvantaged are already most exposed. We don't need to look far to imagine this possibility; for example, in February 2015, Prime Minister David Cameron was widely reported as considering withdrawing benefits from fat people who refused to seek treatment for their size.[66]

And second, the transformed environment that is imagined in these interventions is built around 'elite norms of consumption and movement' which affirm the assumption that middle-class health and wellness is the direct result of the control they exercise over their bodies through their lifestyle.[67] The imagined transformed food environment is one built affirmingly in their own image, and the message to poor fat people is always to learn to be less like themselves in their tastes and practices and more like their middle-class role models. This was made explicit in the 2008 *Healthy Weight, Healthy Lives: Consumer Insight Summary*, which set out six clusters of people to identify appropriate types and levels of intervention for each.[68] The first three clusters mark out the 'at risk' groups most in need of intervention, including (1) 'struggling parents who lack confidence, knowledge time and money'; (2) 'young parents who lack the knowledge and parenting skills to implement a healthy lifestyle'; and (3) 'affluent families who enjoy indulging in food'. Clusters 5 and 6 are low priorities for intervention, showing 'strong family values' while just needing a few tweaks to their diet or exercise levels. But it is Cluster 4 – 'Already living a healthy lifestyle' – that provides the role model. The descriptor of the cluster offers an unashamedly middle-class (and gendered) summary of healthy lifestyle perfection:

> [They] take food very seriously. They are interested in organic, environmentally friendly and Fair-trade products and check labels for additives and E-numbers. They work hard to feed their children healthy food and successfully limit their consumption of processed foods and carbonated drinks. One of the reasons for their success is that their mothers in particular provide a positive role model: they don't eat when bored or view 'bad' foods as a treat.[69]

The cluster consists of 'affluent older parents', and as good neoliberal citizens, we are told, they are 'constantly looking for additional information and new strategies to increase activity levels and improve their diet'. Aside from the suggestion that they are over-inclined to drive their children to school because of a misplaced nervousness, all we can do is 'learn from the successful techniques used by this cluster' in their successful navigation of the obesogenic environment. The document precedes the attack on sugar by several years, and on the few occasions when sugar is mentioned, it is usually alongside fat and salt as nutrients to be restricted. But even though the next iteration of the strategy document highlighted the limitations of the clusters, which did not provide a clean fit for many, the scheme retained its commitment to 'improving the health of the poorest, fastest', holding the principles of segmentation in place.[70] As such, it sets the scene for the environment into which the attack on sugar came to make sense and remains pertinent for the vision of the imagined sugar-free future that we can see both in the popular domain and at the level of policy.

One of the key assets of Cluster 4 is not that their social status enables them to live outside the obesogenic environment, but rather that they are able to resist its temptations. This exposes what Kirkland calls the 'hidden moralism' of environment-centred approaches which rest on the conviction 'that some people are impervious to bad environments (the elites, who still manage their bodies properly) while others are more fully constituted by their environments (poor fat people)'.[71] This recalls the case of celebrity chef Hugh Fearnley-Whittingstall, as discussed in Chapter 7, whose #WHSugar campaign relied on the vulnerability of working-class Others to the temptations of checkout chocolate while he remained untouched by its allure. However much it is wrapped in the rhetorics of concern, it is a posture grounded in contempt for the imagined poor, fat Other. As Kirkland asks provocatively: 'what if it is the case that many elites find the terms of the environmental account to be simply a more palatable way to express their disgust at fat people, the tacky, low-class foods they eat, and the indolent ways they spend their time?'[72]

Knowing the poor

At the heart of the (in)visibility of class in the attack on sugar, and the war on obesity more generally, is the assumption that we know what poor (and by extension, fat) people eat and why. We see this in the stereotypes of overconsuming Others and in interventions into the obesogenic environment, which aim to remove the foods considered complicit in the fatness of those inhabiting those environments. But the reality is that we know relatively little about what people eat, and even less about the reasons behind those food choices.[73] So in the last part of this chapter, I want to turn to the growing sociological and anthropological research on what, how and why people make particular food choices. In particular, I want to focus on the ways in which arguments and prohibitions that focus on the nutritional content of foods assume that those foods are consumed for nutritional reasons to the exclusion of the many other social and cultural functions that food performs. I begin with a story from research by sociologists Megan Warin and Tanya Zivkovic in a disadvantaged community in an Australian suburb.[74]

In a local foodbank where people could purchase affordable portions of basic foods, the workers had begun to sell chocolate and biscuits, even though they knew that this might be frowned upon by their bosses from the programme funding the intervention (the Obesity Prevention and Lifestyle Programme, or OPAL).[75] A few weeks after the reintroduction of the chocolate and biscuits – all top sellers – one of the workers receives a phone call from her manager, who is coming to visit. She quickly instructs her colleagues to 'Hide the chocolate!', which they do, deciding to leave just one pack of chocolate biscuits out because it is a legitimate 'sometimes food' in the programme's advice materials. A customer watches in bemusement, asking: 'What do they think? That poor people can't have anything nice?' The workers explain that 'everything in the council is about health these days', before conceding that 'we like to be able to provide something nice for the customers and at a good price, but well – it's just a tricky position that we're in'.[76] The exchange exposes the complex ways in which sugar figures in the food lives of the people using the OPAL services, and the women in the shop demonstrate what a nutrient-oriented anti-obesity programme can never accommodate: that regardless of its unhealthy designation, sugar is also a valued form of care – both for the self and for others – and constitutes an accessible means of comfort and gratification in times of difficulty. As in the case discussed in Chapter 3 of Nyah, who spends her last dollars on syrupy, creamy coffee-shop drinks for herself and her daughter, sugary treats become a way of saying 'yes' and affirming social connections; it offers an affordable moment of pleasure in a life in which there is little prospect of a dramatic improvement in their circumstances in the foreseeable future.

Significantly, then, these dietary 'transgressions' are not because consumers don't know that these are foods categorised as unhealthy (as labelling and nutrition education initiatives assume). Indeed, studies of family food consumption repeatedly demonstrate an awareness of mainstream 'healthy eating' messaging.[77] Instead, this nutrient-focused knowledge sits in tension with the many other functions that food performs and the priorities that people are navigating in their daily lives: it is a means of establishing identity, creating social connections, maintaining links to a distant home, showing love and distinguishing yourself from others. Furthermore, for many, and particularly for those living on a low or precarious income, 'healthy eating' may have to be subjugated to the more immediate demands of empty stomachs and bills to pay. For example, many are forced to buy non-perishable processed food to avoid waste; to purchase calorie-dense foods that provide more food for less money; and to buy predictably palatable foods that they know their children will eat so that food will not go uneaten with nothing to replace it.[78]

This highlights the clash between the future-orientation to health that privilege affords and the present-orientation of having enough to eat now. In its list of barriers to change among consumers, the 2009 marketing strategy for Change4Life notes critically that 'parents prioritise their children's immediate happiness over their long-term health (indeed, the link between poor diet and sedentary behaviour today and future health concerns is not understood)'.[79] Knowledge deficit fills the space between prescribed and actual behaviours, but as Fielding-Singh observes, 'too little money, not enough time, unpredictable work hours, absent social support, unstable housing, more pressing needs or a lack of other comforts' all conspire to place the future-oriented healthy-eating ideal out of reach in exchange for health in the present.[80] Given the firm future-orientation of both the war on obesity and the attack on sugar, those struggling to live safely and happily in the present are inevitably relegated to the position of failed Other.

This no-win situation means that low-income families, and particularly mothers, are readily seen as consuming irresponsibly and are held to different standards from their middle-class counterparts. For example, Fielding-Singh notes how exactly the same foods take on very different meanings when given to children, depending on socioeconomic status. For middle-class mothers, a meal of less nutritious, processed foods enables them to be seen as fun parents who are practising moderation rather than exercising extreme control. However, for working-class mothers, the same foods signal their failures as mothers.[81] Similarly, she notes that 'people sing the praises of kale but not collard greens', with their stigmatised associations with soul food and Black culture,[82] and Anna Kirkland observes that 'a baguette is not junk food, but sliced white bread is'.[83] As targets in the war on obesity and the attack on sugar, the most disadvantaged have the deck stacked against them from the start.

Conclusion

This final chapter has returned to a theme that has run throughout the book: that the foregrounding of sugar as the primary problem to be solved necessarily erases the wider social, economic political and environmental context within which an attack on sugar has come to make sense. However, the intersecting social inequalities of race, gender and class are not simply erased, but rather are mobilised strategically to shore up the attack on sugar (and by extension, obesity), which can then remain firmly in the foreground. As such, they appear selectively as one-dimensional tropes that variously signify ignorance, indolence, a lack of self-discipline and excessive vulnerability to sugar in ways that reaffirm normatively gendered, white middle-classness as the ideal, future-oriented responsible citizen. This is achieved by pushing into the background the health priorities and lived experiences of those most immediately in the firing line of the attack on both sugar and obesity. In the anti-sugar domain, the voices of people who are fat, poor and racially minoritised are missing. They are spoken about but not with; they are known but are never allowed to be the knowers. As such, they are (in)visible, simultaneously absent and present. Just as discourses of obesity, addiction and nostalgia smooth out the differences between understandings of the problem of sugar, these simplified caricatures of race, gender and class flatten out the complexities and nuances of social inequalities to provide a language through which the singularity of the problem of sugar can be made legible. This makes way for the self-congratulatory tone of so much of the anti-sugar domain, where giving up sugar can be claimed as a triumphant act of self-mastery and self-making. As Julie Guthman observes of the alternative food movement, this self-congratulation is 'perhaps the most consequential for social justice, since it limits what is put on the table politically'.[84] The absence from our everyday sugar talk of those who are spoken about matters, then, because to leave the task of articulating the problem of sugar to those already best positioned to accrue capital through its repudiation is always to risk sedimenting health and social inequalities rather than ameliorating them.

Conclusion

In the second decade of the twenty-first century, sugar was placed at the centre of a gathering storm of anxiety around bodies, consumption and citizenship. Taking over the mantle from saturated fat, sugar was positioned as a superlative threat to health about which something must be done. Voices from the domains of biomedicine, public health, popular science, the news media, entertainment and the self-help industry joined the chorus, creating an inescapable swirl of sugar talk that left no room for doubt that 'we are eating too much sugar and it is bad for our health'. Where overconsumption is named as the problem, then the solution can lie only in reducing consumption, which in turn always rebounds to questions of individual choice, no matter how softly couched in sympathetic accounts of obesogenic environments and the machinations of devious food companies. This is the preoccupying concern of the attack on sugar and the prevailing theme of its social life: how to compel or persuade those deemed to be overconsuming sugar to make 'better' choices.

It is a goal that appears both benign and uncontroversial, especially when wrapped in the neutralising rhetorics of health; as I have found to my cost, any challenge is easily read and dismissed as being in the pockets of Big Sugar. But this is the point where *Sugar Rush* intervenes, arguing not that sugar is or isn't 'bad', but that the attack on sugar rests on a cultivated singularity of purpose that can maintain coherence only by forcefully narrowing the field of vision until all we can see is sugar (and the fat bodies it is deemed to cause). As in the introductory montage to *Jamie's Sugar Rush*, sugar is flung in our faces, blurring everything else into the background. This insistent focus on sugar over-weights it with expectation and alleviates the pressure to look elsewhere, obscuring and exacerbating the inequalities upon which the attack on sugar relies.

Perhaps the most immediate of these integral inequalities can be found in the fat-phobia that is central to the attack on sugar. The wrongness of the fat body is an enduring assumption that is not exclusive to the attack on sugar but is inseparable from it, and while fatness, like sugar, is problematised through discourses of health that give the veneer of morally neutral concern, contempt and disgust for fat bodies seep steadily from the anti-sugar domain. Ailing sugar-fuelled fat bodies litter the anti-sugar landscape as cautionary tales and as failed citizens who are unable and unwilling to take responsibility for themselves in prescribed ways. Confronted with the assumption that people who are fat could lose weight if they applied themselves, and with sugar firmly in the foreground as the primary culprit in the cultivation of fatness, the only way people who are fat can be seen or heard in the anti-sugar domain is as the willing subjects of conversion to the sugar-free cause. Otherwise, the fat body can only ever figure one-dimensionally as the Other against which the disciplined sugar-free subject can be measured. This matters because where sugar is seen as a cause of fatness (or even as the only cause of fatness), and where fatness is unforgivable, an attack on sugar easily slides into an attack on people who eat sugar (or whose bodies are read as overconsuming sugar regardless of what they eat). This is an invitation to stigmatisation and exclusion, which not only is an assault on basic human dignity but is in itself a threat to health and wellbeing.

Second, the foregrounding of sugar both distracts from and exploits relations of gender, race and class in order to establish white, middle-class dietary norms as universally desirable and attainable, but without recognising them as such. Normative expectations of dietary thrift, a rigorously nutricentric outlook, tasteful consumption and the relentless surveillance of sugar are treated as a matter of choice rather than circumstance, setting up those who fall outside those standards as the failed citizens against which the self-efficacy and good citizenship of those going sugar-free can be established. In this way, those disadvantaged in this exchange are rendered simultaneously visible and invisible; they are present as the one-dimensional abject Other yet absent as people with meaningful and nuanced food lives. This is not simply a benign oversight but instead acts as a direct delegitimisation of the tastes and food practices of those already navigating multiple disadvantages. Furthermore, the future-orientation of both the war on obesity and the attack on sugar means that the health priorities of those struggling to survive poverty, violence, drugs, racism and hunger in the present are discredited. This discrediting of the bodies, tastes and practices of those who fail to live up to unspoken white, middle-class norms of the attack on sugar is one of its most pernicious effects, especially when dressed as concern for those same groups.

This in turn points to a third erasure enacted by the foregrounding of sugar: the multiple functions that food performs in our lives beyond its nutritional content. The attack on sugar is crushingly nutricentric, privileging sugar content in the evaluation of the food we buy and eat. But even while food can feel like a very individual matter, it is irretrievably social; it sits at the heart of social organisation and it can be a source of comfort, pleasure and care. It is also a means of signalling belonging, marking milestones and structuring everyday social interactions. The attack on sugar positions nutritional content, and more specifically sugar content, as the primary arbiter of food choice, but in the end, this offers up an impoverished vision that can see the consumption of nutritionally suspect food only as a dietary failure rather than, for example, a legitimate act of self-care or a valued moment of sociality. This constitutes a further act of discrediting, especially of those for whom the accrual of social capital through sugar reduction or abstention is already off the table.

One of the defining features of anti-sugar advocacy is its self-portrayal as a radical departure from the dietary mainstream. Advocates position themselves as bravely going against the grain and speaking hard dietary truths; they are mavericks and apostates leading a revolution in times of great urgency. But this is not borne out by the reality of the attack on sugar, which, for all its protestations, offers a very conservative vision that entrenches rather than disrupts social hierarchies. This is another consequence of the foregrounding of sugar, which in focusing so intently on a single nutrient holds everything else in place as either unproblematic or too complex to address. It also demonstrates a paucity of new ideas, falling back repeatedly on generic dietary advice that has been demonstrably unsuccessful in the wider war on obesity of which it is part. As revolutions go, then, the attack on sugar is disappointingly modest in vision and ambition. As a result, anti-sugar advocacy can be understood as embodying a politics of despair, inciting followers to pursue individual dietary purity as the one thing that can be done, but in doing so foreclosing other possibilities. By centralising and foregrounding sugar so firmly, this makes sugar reduction an end in itself, precluding more ambitious possibilities for social transformation and entrenching the same social relations that enable those advocating sugar reduction to accrue social capital from it in the first place.

This is not to argue that because it's not possible to change everything we should not try to change anything, and nor is a strategically tight focus on a particular issue necessarily problematic. For example, in her work on nutritional epigenetics (as discussed in Chapter 1), Hannah Landecker argues that she is focusing on 'this small corner of biomedical endeavour' to 'offer purchase on much broader scientific and social transformations that might otherwise be rather hard to fathom or narrate'. She likens it to using a pinhole camera to produce a sharp image that can 'hold away much of the welter of the world of change in contemporary life science, just long enough to think a few things through'.[1] The attack on sugar, then, misses the opportunity to use this moment of focus to 'think a few things through' as a prelude to gaining purchase on broader issues. This is the primary message of *Sugar Rush*: the importance of stepping back and widening the field of vision; of always asking the next question.

Sugar Rush offers a snapshot in time when, during the second decade of the twenty-first century, sugar found extraordinary infamy as the latest enemy in the war on obesity. As such, it provides a window into the workings of the war on obesity, which endlessly reinvigorates itself in the face of its own palpable failures by finding new enemies to blame and fight. Bolstered by the politics of austerity and stepping into the space left by the changing fortunes of dietary fat, the nutritional emptiness of sugar and its easy associations with feckless overconsumption brought it into comfortable alignment with the molecularisation of the body, anxieties around the overconsumption of public resources and the intensification of healthism. However, as I write this conclusion in early 2022, the attack on sugar is now visibly losing momentum. The debates surrounding the sugar tax galvanised the attack on sugar and fuelled the newspaper reporting, but following the implementation of the tax, there has been a distinct loss of pace, with sugar dropping slowly out of the headlines. Where the war on obesity requires constant renewal, this prompts the question: what next? The attack on sugar invites us to think about how social context makes a particular target plausible and to ask what erasures this alignment enacts; learning from the attack on sugar, an alertness to the next iteration of the war on obesity prepares us to be suspicious of the terms of the debate we are being offered and to keep in view that which might otherwise be pushed into the background. If I were to hazard a guess, a likely candidate is ultra-processed foods, which are increasingly placed in opposition to 'real' food in ways that rest upon a binary of authentic/inauthentic consumption (and consumers). This not only lends itself well to the war on obesity but also allows the attack on sugar to be folded in, creating continuities rather than ruptures. Time will tell, but the given the extensive investment, both politically and financially, in the war on obesity, the ongoing need for revivification in the face of its own failures and flagging momentum means that a new enemy will need to be found (or an old one resurrected).

A second question is: if not sugar, then what is to be done? From the outset of the book, I have argued that questions about sugar's place in our diets are not only impossible to answer straightforwardly but also the wrong questions to be asking. They are already premised on a good/bad food binary that narrows both the terms of the debate and the field of vision, rebounding endlessly to discourses of individual overconsumption that distribute approval and opprobrium in predictably uneven and socially consequential ways. The analysis presented in this book shows that the stories that we tell about public health – in this case, in the form of sugar talk – not only set the terms of the debate but also demarcate the solutions that we can imagine. Evading the trap that sugar talk sets for us, then, requires a change of question from 'How can we get people to eat less sugar / lose weight / eat better?' to 'How can we achieve social justice?' In Julie Guthman's terms: what needs to be put on the table politically to achieve meaningful, healthful change for those most disadvantaged by the current economic, social and political systems?[2] For Guthman, this places capitalism in the firing line, while for anthropologist Charles Briggs and public health physician Clara Mantini-Briggs, 'the most deadly fiction' is the belief that 'social justice can be achieved without uprooting the distribution of wealth and human dignity according to hierarchies of race, gender, class, sexuality and nature'.[3] *Sugar Rush* joins these calls, insisting that social inequality and injustice are not incidental or collateral to the attack on sugar but, rather, are baked into it from the start. This points to the need to focus on political choices rather than food choices and on inequalities as failures of social justice and not simply as barriers to be circumvented to get people to make the 'right' food choices.

In response to those who will still insist that I at least concede that 'sugar is bad for you', my position at the end of my journey through the world of anti-sugar is this: I believe that food is an important contributor to health, although it is by no means the only one or even the most important one. I believe that some foods are more healthful than others, but most of all, I want everyone to have enough of the food that they want to eat. Beyond that, food prescriptions and proscriptions in the name of health can only ever be a distraction that creates superficial ripples in the dietary status quo rather than a fundamental social

Conclusion

transformation. *Sugar Rush* shows the inadequacy of single-nutrient interventions and instead points to the need for ambitious new points of departure that refuse the comforting sense of individual control and self-transformation brought by dietary restriction in favour of something much more unsettling.

Notes

Introduction

1 Freidberg, S., *French Beans and Food Scares: Culture and Commerce in an Anxious Age* (New York: Oxford: Oxford University Press, 2004); Levenstein, H., *Fear of Food: A History of Why We Worry about What We Eat* (Chicago: University of Chicago Press, 2012).

2 See, for example, Bowen, S., Brenton, J. and Elliott, S., *Pressure Cooker: Why Home Cooking Won't Solve Our Problems and What We Can Do about It* (Oxford: Oxford University Press, 2019); Cooper, V. and Whyte, D., eds, *The Violence of Austerity* (London: Pluto Press, 2017); Frazer, E., 'Teenage girls reading *Jackie*', *Media, Culture and Society* 9, no. 4 (1987): 407–425; Garthwaite, K., *Hunger Pains: Life inside Foodbank Britain* (Bristol: Policy Press, 2016).

3 Johnson, J. and Baumann, S., *Foodies: Democracy and Distinction in the Gourmet Foodscape*, 2nd edition (London: Routledge, 2015).

4 Bowen, Brenton and Elliott, *Pressure Cooker: Why Home Cooking Won't Solve Our Problems and What We Can Do about It*, 15.

5 Fischler, C., 'The nutritional cacophony may be detrimental to your health', *Progress in Nutrition* 13, no. 3 (2011): 217–221.

6 Public Health England, *Sugar Reduction: The Evidence for Action* (London: Public Health England, 2015); Scientific Advisory Committee on Nutrition, *Carbohydrates and Health* (London: The Stationery Office, 2015); World Health Organization, *Guideline: Sugars Intake for Adults and Children* (Geneva: World Health Organization, 2015).

7 Action on Sugar, 'Worldwide experts unite to reverse obesity epidemic by forming "Action on Sugar"', news release, 9 January 2014, www.actionon sugar.org/news-centre/press-releases/2014/items/worldwide-experts-unite-to-reverse-obesity-epidemic-by-forming-action-on-sugar.html [accessed: 9 July 2018].

8 Throsby, K., 'Pure, white and deadly: sugar addiction and the cultivation of urgency', *Food, Culture and Society* 23, no. 1 (2020): 11–29.

9 Public Health England, 'New Change4Life campaign encourages families to make sugar swaps', news release, 5 January 2015, https://www.gov.uk/government/news/new-change4life-campaign-encourages-families-to-make-sugar-swaps [accessed: 4 March 2022].

10 See, for example, Aronson, M. and Budhos, M., *Sugar Changed the World: A Story of Magic, Spice, Slavery, Freedom and Science* (New York: Mifflin Harcourt Publishing Company, 2010); Macinnis, P., *Bittersweet: The Story of Sugar* (Crows Nest, NSW: Allen & Unwin, 2002); Warvin, J., *Sugar: The World Corrupted from Slavery to Obesity* (London: Robinson, 2017).

11 Mintz, S., *Tasting Food, Tasting Freedom: Excursions into Eating, Culture and the Past* (Boston, MA: Beacon Press, 1996), 186.

12 Ibid., 214.

13 Affeldt, S., *Consuming Whiteness: Australian Racism and the 'White Sugar' Campaign*, Racism Analysis, Series A: Studies (Zurich: Lit Verlag, 2014); Aronson and Budhos, *Sugar Changed the World: A Story of Magic, Spice, Slavery, Freedom and Science*; Banivanua-Mar, T., *Violence and Colonial Dialogue: The Autralian-Pacific Indentured Labor Trade* (Honolulu: University of Hawai'i Press, 2007); Walvin, J., *Sugar: the World Corrupted from Slavery to Obesity* (London: Robinson, 2017).

14 Richardson, B., *Sugar* (Cambridge: Polity, 2015).

15 Aronson and Budhos, *Sugar Changed the World: A Story of Magic, Spice, Slavery, Freedom and Science*.

16 See, for example, Gilman, S., *Obesity: the Biography* (Oxford: Oxford University Press, 2010); Stearns, P. N., *Fat History: Bodies and Beauty in the Modern West*, 2nd edition (New York: New York University Press, 2002).

17 National Audit Office, *Tackling Obesity in England* (London: National Audit Office, 15 February 2001); National Institute for Health and Clinical Excellence, *Obesity: The Prevention, Identification, Assessment and Management of Overweight and Obesity in Adults and Children. NICE Guideline. First Draft for Consultation, March 2006* (London: National Institute for Health and Clinical Excellence, 2006); World Health Organization, *Obesity: Preventing and Managing the Global Epidemic. Report of a WHO Consultation,* (Geneva: World Health Organization, 2000).

18 Theis, D. R. Z. and White, M., "Is obesity policy in England fit for purpose? Analysis of government strategies and policies, 1992–2020", *Milbank Quarterly* 99, no. 1 (2021): 126–170.

19 Gard, M., *The End of the Obesity Epidemic* (London: Routledge, 2011).

20 Throsby, K., 'Sweetening the "war on obesity"', in *Routledge Handbook of Critical Obesity Studies*, ed. M. Gard, D. Powell and J. Tenorio (London: Routledge, 2022), 126–134.

21 See, for example, Guthman, J., *Weighing In: Obesity, Food Justice and the Limits of Capitalism* (Berkeley: University of California Press, 2011); Hayes-Conroy, A.

and Hayes-Conroy, J., eds, *Doing Nutrition Differently: Critical Approaches to Diet and Dietary Intervention* (London: Routledge, 2013); Warin, M. and Zivkovic, T., *Fatness, Obesity and Disadvantage in the Australian Suburbs: Unpalatable Politics* (Cham, Switzerland: Palgrave Macmillan, 2019) (Kindle).

22 Metzl, J., 'Introduction: why against health?', in *Against Health: How Health Became the New Morality*, ed. J. Metzl and A. Kirkland, Biopolitics: Medicine, Technoscience and Health in the 21st Century (New York: New York University Press, 2010), 10.

23 Metzl, J. and Kirkland, A., eds, *Against Health: How Health Became the New Morality* (New York: New York University Press, 2010).

24 Keys, A., *Seven Countries: A Multivariate Analysis of Death and Coronary Heart Disease* (Cambridge, MA: Harvard University Press, 1980).

25 'Medicine: the fat of the land', *Time Magazine*, 13 January 1961, http://con tent.time.com/time/subscriber/article/0,33009,828721–1,00.html [accessed: 5 January 2022].

26 Teicholz, N., *The Big Fat Surprise: Why Butter, Meat and Cheese Belong in a Healthy Diet* (Melbourne and London: Scribe, 2015), 67.

27 Lustig, R., 'Sugar: the bitter truth', 2009, https://www.youtube.com/wat ch?v=dBnniua6-0M [accessed: 18 September 2017]; Lustig, R., *Fat Chance: The Hidden Truth about Sugar, Obesity and Disease* (London: Fourth Estate, 2014); Yudkin, J., *Pure, White and Deadly: How Sugar is Killing Us and What We Can Do to Stop It*, 2012 edition (London: Penguin Life, 2012 [1972]).

28 Moss, M., *Salt, Sugar, Fat: How the Food Giants Hooked Us* (London: Random House, 2013).

29 De la Peña, C., *Empty Pleasures: The Story of Artificial Sweeteners from Saccharin to Splenda* (Chapel Hill: University of North Carolina Press, 2010).

30 Throsby, K., 'Giving up sugar and the inequalities of abstinence', *Sociology of Health and Illness* 40, no. 6 (2018): 954–968.

31 National Obesity Forum, *Eat Fat, Cut the Carbs and Avoid Snacking to Revserse Obesity and Type 2 Diabetes* (London: National Obesity Forum, in association with Public Health Collaboration, 2016).

32 Kromhout, D., 'National Obesity Forum report is flawed', *British Medical Journal* 353 (2016): i3342.

33 Campbell, D., 'National Obesity Forum faces backlash over "dangerous" diet advice', *The Guardian*, 28 May 2016, https://www.theguardian.com/soci ety/2016/may/28/national-obesity-forum-advice-fat-dangerous [accessed: 6 March 2022].

34 'Anti-obesity campaigners resign over low-fat diet report', *The Guardian*, 3 June 2016, https://www.theguardian.com/society/2016/jun/03/anti-obesity-campaign ers-resign-over-low-fat-diet-report [accessed: 19 February 2022].

35 Scrinis, G., *Nutritionism: The Science and Politics of Dietary Advice*, Perspectives on Culinary History (New York: Columbia University Press, 2015), 2.

36 Ibid., 12.

37 Ibid., 5.

38 Rose, N., *The Politics of Life Itself: Biomedicine, Power and Subjectivity in the Twenty-First Century*, Information Series (Princeton, NJ, and Oxford: Princeton University Press, 2007), 5.

39 Hatch, A. R., *Blood Sugar: Racial Pharmacology and Food Justice in Black America* (Minneapolis: University of Minnesota Press, 2016), 2–3.

40 Lustig, *Fat Chance: The Hidden Truth about Sugar, Obesity and Disease*, 7.

41 Crawford, R., 'Healthism and the medicalization of everyday life', *International Journal of Health Services* 10, no. 3 (1980): 365–388; Crawford, R., 'Health as a meaningful social practice', *Health: An Interdisciplinary Journal for the Social Study of Health, Illness and Medicine* 10, no. 4 (2006): 401–420.

42 Tyler, I., *Revolting Subjects: Social Abjection and Resistance in Neoliberal Britain* (London: Zed Books, 2013).

43 *The Guardian, The Observer, The Times, The Sunday Times, The Daily Telegraph, The Sunday Telegraph, Daily Mail, The Mail on Sunday* and *The Sun*.

44 Brookes, G. and Baker, P., *Obesity in the News: Language and Representation in the Press* (Cambridge: Cambridge University Press, 2021), 71.

45 The decision to focus on articles of 500-plus words may also have skewed the distribution of articles in favour of broadsheet coverage. However, a test search to include articles of 100-plus words produced very little new content and a lot of repetition (for example, a tabloid might include a short teaser article to grab the reader's attention and then a fuller article in the main body of the newspaper).

46 Jordan-Young, R. M. and Karkazis, K., *Testosterone: An Unauthorized Biography* (Cambridge, MA: Harvard University Press, 2019), 10.

47 Ibid., 10–11.

48 Barker, M.-J., Gill, R., and Harvey, L., *Mediated Intimacy: Sex Advice in Media Culture* (Cambridge: Polity Press, 2018); Gupta, K. and Cacchioni, T., 'Sexual improvement as if your health depends on it: an analysis of contemporary sex manuals', *Feminism and Psychology* 23, no. 4 (2013): 442–458.

49 Jordan-Young and Karkazis, *Testosterone: An Unauthorized Biography*, 23.

50 Twine, R., 'Vegan killjoys at the table – contesting happines and negotiating relationships with food practices', *Societies* 4 (2014): 623–639.

51 Jordan-Young and Karkazis, *Testosterone: An Unauthorized Biography*, 23.

52 Rich, E., De Pian, L., and Francombe, J. M., 'Physical cultures of stigmatisation: health policy and social class', *Sociological Research Online* 20, no. 2 (2015): 8.

53 Beagan, B. et al., *Acquired Tastes: Why Families Eat the Way They Do* (Vancouver, British Columbia: UBC Press, 2015), 2524 (Kindle).

Chapter 1

1 Public Health England, *Sugar Reduction: The Evidence for Action*, 5.

2 Public Health England, '5 year olds eat and drink their body weight in sugar every year', news release, 4 January 2016, https://www.gov.uk/government/news/5-year-olds-eat-and-drink-their-body-weight-in-sugar-every-year [accessed: 6 March 2022].

3 Public Health England, *Sugar Reduction: The Evidence for Action*, 43.

4 The universalising 'we' of this claim is also problematic, obscuring the ways in which the weight of the attack on sugar falls unevenly on disadvantaged social groups. I return to this in the later chapters of the book.

5 Public Health England, *Sugar Reduction: The Evidence for Action*, 5.

6 Law, J., 'Collateral realities', in *The Politics of Knowledge*, ed. F. D. Rubio and P. Baert (London: Routledge, 2012), 174.

7 Guthman, J., 'Too much food and too little sidewalk? Problematizing the obesogenic environment thesis', *Environment and Planning A* 45, no. 1 (2013): 143.

8 Supski, S. et al., 'The ineffable allure of sugar – hammer cake, *That Sugar Film* and contradictory pleasures', *Food, Culture and Society*, 29, no. 1 (2021): 44–65; Warin and Zivkovic, *Fatness, Obesity and Disadvantage in the Australian Suburbs: Unpalatable Politics*.

9 Saguy, A. C., *What's Wrong with Fat?* (Oxford: Oxford University Press, 2013), 10.

10 World Health Organization, *Guideline: Sugars Intake for Adults and Children*, 1.

11 Nestle, M., *Soda Politics: Taking on Big Soda (and Winning)* (Oxford: Oxford University Press, 2015), 3.

12 Avansino, C., 'The sugar trap: part one', *The Times*, 5 January 2014, https://www.thetimes.co.uk/article/the-sugar-trap-part-one-szfjbxfvmtp [accessed: 6 March 2022].

13 Campbell, D., 'Extend sugar tax to biscuits and cereals, says government adviser', *The Guardian*, 19 March 2016, https://www.theguardian.com/society/2016/mar/19/extend-sugar-tax-to-biscuits-and-cereals-says-government-adviser [accessed: 2 January 2021].

14 Gault, A., 'Cereal killers; fears over sugar levels', *The Sun*, 28 January 2015 (print edition).

15 Carpenter, L., 'Life without sugar: one family's 30-day challenge', *The Guardian*, 14 March 2014, https://www.theguardian.com/lifeandstyle/2014/mar/14/life-without-sugar-family-challenge-diet [accessed: 6 March 2022].

16 Scrinis, *Nutritionism: The Science and Politics of Dietary Advice*.

17 Dunbar, P., 'Mood swings, the shakes. What happened when this sugar addict tried to quit', *Daily Mail*, 9 June 2013, https://www.dailymail.co.uk/femail/

article-2338586/Mood-swings-shakes--happened-sugar-addicted-POLLY-DUNBAR-tried-quit-sweet-stuff-good.html [accessed: 2 January 2021].

18 Scrinis, *Nutritionism: The Science and Politics of Dietary Advice*, 8.

19 Scientific and Advisory Committee on Nutrition, *Carbohydrates and Health*, 31.

20 Public Health England, *Why 5%? An Explanation of SACN's Recommendations about Sugars and Health*, Public Health England (London, 2015).

21 Public Health England, *Sugar Reduction: The Evidence for Action*.

22 Ibid., 20.

23 Calorie Reduction Expert Group, *Calorie Reduction Expert Group Statement* (2011), https://assets.publishing.service.gov.uk/government/uploads/system/uploads/attachment_data/file/215561/dh_127554.pdf [accessed: 6 March 2022].

24 Hill, J. O. et al., 'Obesity and the environment: where do we go from here?', *Science* 299, no. 5608 (2003): 853–855. James Hill is a co-founder of the Global Energy Balance Network (GEBN). The GEBN (disbanded in 2015) received substantial funding from Coca-Cola and was perceived by many to be cynically invested in moving the research focus away from diet (energy in) towards physical activity (energy out) (although this is contested by the GEBN leaders). For a detailed discussion of the GEBN, see Nestle, M., *Unsavory Truth: How Food Companies Skew the Science of What We Eat* (New York: Basic Books, 2018).

25 Hill et al., 'Obesity and the environment: where do we go from here?', 855.

26 Scrinis, *Nutritionism: The Science and Politics of Dietary Advice*, 114.

27 World Health Organization, *Guideline: Sugars Intake for Adults and Children*.

28 Ibid., 20.

29 Ibid., 16.

30 World Health Organization, *WHO Handbook for Guideline Development*, 2nd edition (Geneva: World Health Organization, 2014), 126.

31 British Medical Association, *Food for Thought: Promoting Health Diets among Children and Young People* (London: BMA Board of Science, 2015).

32 Siddique, H., 'Sugar should be no more than 5% of daily calories, say nutrition experts', *The Guardian*, 17 July 2015, https://www.theguardian.com/society/2015/jul/17/cut-recommended-daily-allowance-sugar-5-percent-daily-calories-report [accessed: 3 January 2022].

33 'Horrified to find our kids eat so much sugar', *The Sun*, 21 July 2015.

34 'How to teach … sugar', *The Guardian*, 21 September 2015, https://www.theguardian.com/teacher-network/2015/sep/21/how-to-teach-sugar [accessed: 3 January 2022].

35 Public Health England, *Why 5%? An Explanation of SACN's Recommendations about Sugars and Health*, 21–23.

36 Public Health England, *Sugar Reduction: The Evidence for Action*.

37 Saguy, *What's Wrong with Fat?*, 8.

38 Public Health England, *Why 5%? An Explanation of SACN's Recommendations about Sugars and Health*, 21.

39 Landecker, H., 'Postindustrial metabolism: fat knowledge', *Public Culture* 25, no. 3 (2013): 495–522.

40 See, for example, Apple, R., *Vitamania: Vitamins in American Culture* (New Brunswick, NJ: Rutgers University Press, 1996).

41 Landecker, H., 'Food as exposure: nutritional epigenetics and the new metabolism', *Biosocieties* 6, no. 2 (2011): 172.

42 Scrinis, *Nutritionism: The Science and Politics of Dietary Advice*, 59.

43 Mudry, J. J., *Measured Meals: Nutrition in America* (New York: SUNY Press, 2009), 452 (Kindle).

44 Ibid., 590.

45 Coveney, J., *Food, Morals and Meaning: The Pleasure and Anxiety of Eating*, 2nd edition (London: Routledge, 2000), 61–62.

46 Mudry, *Measured Meals: Nutrition in America*, 527.

47 Ibid., 168.

48 Coveney, *Food, Morals and Meaning: The Pleasure and Anxiety of Eating*, 62–63.

49 Biltekoff, C., *Eating Right in America: The Cultural Poltiics of Food and Health* (Durham, NC: Duke University Press, 2013), 17.

50 Department of Health and Social Care, 'New obesity strategy unweiled as country urged to lose weight to beat coronavirus (COVID-19) and protect the NHS', news release, 27 July 2020, https://www.gov.uk/government/news/new-obesity-strategy-unveiled-as-country-urged-to-lose-weight-to-beat-coronavirus-covid-19-and-protect-the-nhs [accessed: 21 September 2021].

51 Donnelly, L. and Rayner, G., 'Lose 5lbs and save NHS £100m, Matt Hancock says after UK's coronavirus "wake-up call" on obesity', *The Daily Telegraph*, 27 July 2020, https://www.telegraph.co.uk/politics/2020/07/26/lose-5lb-save-nhs-100m-says-matt-hancock-coronavirus-wake-up/ [accessed: 6 March 2022].

52 Herndon, A. M., 'Collateral damage from friendly fire? Race, nation, class and the "war against obesity"', *Social Semiotics* 15, no. 2 (August 2005): 128.

53 Gard, M. and Wright, J., *The Obesity Epidemic: Science, Morality and Ideology* (London: Routledge, 2005), 41–42.

54 World Health Organization, *Guideline: Sugars Intake for Adults and Children*, 20.

55 Gard and Wright, *The Obesity Epidemic: Science, Morality and Ideology*, 43.

56 Ibid., 3.

57 Gillespie, D., *Sweet Poison: Why Sugar Makes Us Fat* (London: Penguin, 2008).

58 Lustig, *Fat Chance: The Hidden Truth about Sugar, Obesity and Disease*, 7.

59 Taubes, G., *The Case Against Sugar* (London: Portobello Books, 2017), 16–17.

60 Throsby, 'Giving up sugar and the inequalities of abstinence'.

61 Gillespie, *Sweet Poison: Why Sugar Makes Us Fat*.

62 Gillespie, D., *Teen Brain: Why Screens Are Making Your Teenager Depressed, Anxious and Prone to Lifelong Addictive Illnesses – and How to Stop It Now* (Sydney: Macmillan, 2019).

63 Gillespie, D., 'David Gillespie', 2017, http://davidgillespie.org [accessed: 13 September 2017].

64 Gillespie, *Sweet Poison: Why Sugar Makes Us Fat*, 9.

65 Carlyle, R., 'The sweet stuff: what sugar is really doing to your body', *The Times*, 12 October 2013, https://www.thetimes.co.uk/article/the-sweet-stuff-what-sugar-is-really-doing-to-your-body-whwpj55gmbc [accessed: 16 January 2022].

66 Gillespie, D., *The Sweet Poison Quit Plan: How to Kick the Sugar Habit and Lose Weight* (London: Penguin Books, 2010).

67 Taubes, G., *Good Calories, Bad Calories: Fats, Carbs and the Controversial Science of Diet and Health* (New York: First Anchor Books, 2007); Taubes, G., *Why We Get Fat and What to Do about It* (New York: Anchor Books, 2010); Taubes, *The Case Against Sugar*.

68 Appleyard, B., '18: how sugar got us in a sticky mess', *The Sunday Times*, 1 January 2017, https://www.thetimes.co.uk/article/18-how-sugar-got-us-in-a-sticky-mess-3l8l6s5oz [accessed: 3 January 2022].

69 Taubes, G., *Nobel Dreams: Power, Deceit and the Ultimate Experiment* (London: Random House, 1987); Taubes, G., *Bad Science: The Short Life and Weird Times of Cold Fusion* (London: Random House, 1993).

70 Blythman, J., 'The Case Against Sugar review – an unsweetened attack on diet myths', *The Observer*, 2 January 2017, https://www.theguardian.com/books/2017/jan/02/the-case-against-sugar-gary-taubes-review-compelling-attack-diet-myths [accessed: 3 January 2022].

71 Taubes, G., *The Case for Keto: The Truth about Low-Carb, High-Fat Eating* (London: Granta Publications, 2020).

72 Lustig, 'Sugar: the bitter truth'.

73 Lustig, R. and Gershen, C., *The Fat Chance Cookbook: More Than 100 Recipes Ready in under 30 Minutes to Help You Lose the Sugar and the Weight* (New York: Avery Publishing Group, 2014).

74 Lustig, R., *The Hacking of the American Mind: The Science behind the Corporate Takeover of Our Bodies and Brains* (New York: Avery, 2017).

75 Lustig, R., *Metabolical: The Truth about Processed Food and How it Poisons People and the Planet* (London: Yellow Kite Books, 2021).

76 Lustig, *Fat Chance: The Hidden Truth about Sugar, Obesity and Disease*, xiv.

77 Ibid., xiii.

Notes

78 Lustig is the fourth most frequently mentioned individual across the news-paper data. He comes after Action on Sugar chair Graham MacGregor, who is often asked to add commentary to sugar stories; UK Prime Minister David Cameron, whose prominence stems primarily from the drawn-out debates about the sugar tax; and in the top spot, celebrity chef Jamie Oliver (see Chapter 5).

79 See, for example, Atkins, R., *Dr Atkins New Diet Revolution* (London: Random House, 2003); Cordain, L., *The Paleo Diet: Lose Weight and Get Healthy by Eating the Foods You Were Designed to Eat*, revised edition (Boston, MA: Houghton Mifflin Harcourt, 2011); Perlmutter, D. and Loberg, K., *Grain Brain: The Surprising Truth about Wheat, Carbs, and Sugar – Your Brain's Silent Killer* (London: Yellow Kite Books, 2014).

80 The 2015 SACN report disputes this claim, concluding that there is insufficient evidence of specific harms associated with fructose. This marks a key point of rupture between the sugar-as-empty and sugar-as-toxic discourses.

81 Lustig, *Fat Chance: The Hidden Truth about Sugar, Obesity and Disease*, 21.

82 Taubes, G., 'Can sugar really give you cancer?', *Daily Mail*, 3 January 2017, https://www.dailymail.co.uk/health/article-4082450/Can-sugar-really-CANCER-Diet-author-reveals-smallest-trigger-health-problems-heart-disease-diabetes.html [accessed: 3 January 2022].

83 Murphy, M., *Sick Building Syndrome and the Problem of Uncertainty: Emvironmental Politics, Technoscience, and Women Workers* (Durham, NC, and London: Duke University Press, 2006), 168 (Kindle).

84 Hatch, *Blood Sugar: Racial Pharmacology and Food Justice in Black America*, 3.

85 Lustig, R., 'The science is in: the case for a sugar tax is overwhelming', *The Guardian*, 27 October 2015, https://www.theguardian.com/commentisfree/2015/oct/27/science-new-study-case-sugar-tax [accessed: 7 March 2022].

86 Lustig, *Fat Chance: The Hidden Truth about Sugar, Obesity and Disease*, 129.

87 Landecker, 'Food as exposure: nutritional epigenetics and the new metabolism'; Landecker, 'Postindustrial metabolism: fat knowledge.'

88 Landecker, 'Food as exposure: nutritional epigenetics and the new metabolism', 174.

89 Landecker, 'Postindustrial metabolism: fat knowledge', 496.

90 Taubes, *The Case Against Sugar*, 200.

91 Lustig, *Fat Chance: The Hidden Truth about Sugar, Obesity and Disease*, 7.

92 Barker, D., 'The foetal and infant origins of inequalities in health in Britain', *Journal of Public Health Medicine* 13 (1991): 64–68; Barker, D., 'Developmental origins of chronic disease', *Public Health* 126, no. 3 (2012): 185–189.

93 Schultz, L. C., 'The Dutch Hunger Winter and the developmental origins of health and disease', *PNAS* 107, no. 39 (2010): 16757–16758.

94 Taubes, *The Case Against Sugar*, 18.

95 Lustig, *Fat Chance: The Hidden Truth about Sugar, Obesity and Disease*, 79–80.

96 Yoshizawa, R. S., 'The Barker hypothesis and obesity: connections for transcisciplinarity and social justice', *Social Theory and Health* 10, no. 4 (2012): 1477; see also Warin, M., 'Material feminism, obesity science and the limits of discursive critique', *Body & Society* 21, no. 4 (2015): 48–76.

97 Guthman, *Weighing In: Obesity, Food Justice and the Limits of Capitalism*; Landecker, 'Food as exposure: nutritional epigenetics and the new metabolism', 179.

98 Lustig, *Fat Chance: The Hidden Truth about Sugar, Obesity and Disease*, 165.

99 Ibid., 164.

100 Yudkin, *Pure, White and Deadly: How Sugar is Killing Us and What We Can Do to Stop It*.

101 Ibid., 2.

102 Teicholz, *The Big Fat Surprise: Why Butter, Meat and Cheese Belong in a Healthy Diet*, 43.

103 Lustig, *Fat Chance: The Hidden Truth about Sugar, Obesity and Disease*, 115.

104 Yudkin, *Pure, White and Deadly: How Sugar is Killing Us and What We Can Do to Stop It*, 168.

105 Ibid., 188.

106 Ibid., 12.

107 Jordan-Young and Karkazis, *Testosterone: An Unauthorized Biography*, 10–11.

108 Lustig, *Fat Chance: The Hidden Truth about Sugar, Obesity and Disease*, xiv.

109 Ibid.

110 Epstein, S., *Impure Science: AIDS, Activism and the Politics of Knowledge* (Berkeley: University of California Press, 1996), 3.

111 Jauho, M., 'The social construction of competence: conceptions of science and expertise among proponents of the low-carbohydrate high-fat diet in Finland', *Public Understanding of Science* 25, no. 3 (2016): 332–345.

112 Taubes, *Why We Get Fat and What to Do about It*, xi.

113 Gillespie, *Sweet Poison: Why Sugar Makes Us Fat*, 194.

114 Lustig, *Fat Chance: The Hidden Truth about Sugar, Obesity and Disease*, 275.

115 Fraser, G., 'Sugar is poison. My heart attack has finally opened my eyes to the truth', *The Guardian*, 13 July 2017, https://www.theguardian.com/commentisfree/belief/2017/jul/13/sugar-is-poison-my-heart-attack-has-finally-opened-my-eyes-to-the-truth [accessed: 3 January 2022].

Chapter 2

1 Gillespie, *Sweet Poison: Why Sugar Makes Us Fat*, 96.
2 Gard, *The End of the Obesity Epidemic.*
3 Lambert, V., 'Sweet poison: why sugar is ruining our health', *The Daily Telegraph*, 11 December 2014, https://www.telegraph.co.uk/foodanddrink/healthyeating/9987825/Sweet-poison-why-sugar-is-ruining-our-health.html [accessed: 7 March 2022].
4 NHS Digital, *Statistics on Obesity, Physical Activity and Diet, England, 2020* (5 May 2020), https://digital.nhs.uk/data-and-information/publications/statistical/statistics-on-obesity-physical-activity-and-diet/england-2020/part-3-adult-obesity-copy [accessed: 7 March 2022]. Information from NHS Digital, licensed under the current version of the Open Government Licence.
5 Gard, *The End of the Obesity Epidemic*, 40.
6 Ibid., 45.
7 Ibid., 8.
8 Public Health England, *Sugar Reduction: The Evidence for Action*, 5.
9 Scarborough, P. et al., 'The economic burden of ill health due to diet, physical inacivity, smoking, alcohol and obesity in the UK: an update to 2006–07 NHS costs', *Journal of Public Health* 33, no. 4 (2011): 527–535.
10 House of Commons Health Committee, *Obesity: Third Report of the Session 2003–4* (London: House of Commons, 27 May 2004), 21, https://publications.parliament.uk/pa/cm200304/cmselect/cmhealth/23/2304.htm#a6 [accessed: 7 March 2022].
11 Foresight, *Tackling Obesity: Future Choices – Project Report*, Government Office for Science (London: Universities and Skills Department of Innovation, 2007), www.foresight.gov.uk [accessed: 1 November 2008].
12 Gard, *The End of the Obesity Epidemic*, 18.
13 Ibid., 15.
14 Ibid.
15 Department of Health and Social Care, *Tackling Obesity: Empowering Adults and Children to Live Healthier Lives* (London, 27 July 2020), https://www.gov.uk/government/publications/tackling-obesity-government-strategy/tackling-obesity-empowering-adults-and-children-to-live-healthier-lives [accessed: 7 March 2022].
16 Mann, T. et al., 'Medicare's search for effective obesity treatments', *American Psychologist* 62, no. 3 (2007): 220–233.
17 Pause, C., 'Borderline: the ethics of fat stigma in public health', *The Journal of Law, Medicine and Ethics* 45, no. 4 (2017): 510–517.
18 Gard, *The End of the Obesity Epidemic*, 25.
19 Boero, N., *Killer Fat: Media, Medicine and Morals in the American 'Obesity Epidemic'* (New Brunswick, NJ: Rutgers University Press, 2012), 94 (Kindle).

20 Campbell, D., 'Sugar and Britain's obesity crisis: the key questions answered', *The Guardian*, 23 October 2015, https://www.theguardian.com/society/2015/oct/23/sugar-britains-obesity-crisis-key-questions-answered [accessed: 16 January 2022].

21 Carlyle, 'The sweet stuff: what sugar is really doing to your body'.

22 Ahuja, A., 'The sugar-slashers are on the warpath', editorial, *The Daily Telegraph*, 4 February 2014, https://www.telegraph.co.uk/lifestyle/wellbeing/diet/10617229/The-sugar-slashers-are-on-the-warpath.html [accessed: 16 January 2022].

23 LeBesco, K., 'Neoliberalism, public health and the moral perils of fatness', *Critical Public Health* 21, no. 2 (2011): 153–164.

24 Boseley, S., 'Pressure grows for 20 tax on sugary drinks to fight childhood obesity', *The Guardian*, 30 November 2015, https://www.theguardian.com/society/2015/nov/30/sugary-drinks-tax-childhood-obesity-david-cameron [accessed: 16 January 2022].

25 Lustig, *Fat Chance: The Hidden Truth about Sugar, Obesity and Disease*, 75.

26 National Audit Office, *Tackling Obesity in England*, 55–56.

27 Boero, *Killer Fat: Media, Medicine and Morals in the American 'Obesity Epidemic'*, 546.

28 Rothblum, E. and Solovay, S., eds, *The Fat Studies Reader* (New York: New York University Press, 2009); Tomrley, C. and Kaloski Naylor, A., eds, *Fat Studies in the UK* (York: Raw Nerve Books, 2009); Cooper, C., 'Fat studies: mapping the field', *Sociological Compass* 4, no. 12 (2010): 1020–1034; Gard, M., Powell, D. and Tenorio, J., eds, *Routledge Handbook of Critical Obesity Studies* (London: Routledge, 2022).

29 Gard and Wright, *The Obesity Epidemic: Science, Morality and Ideology*.

30 Farrell, A. E., *Fat Shame: Stigma and the Fat Body in American Culture* (New York: New York University Press, 2011).

31 Jutel, A., 'The emergence of overweight as a disease entity: measuring up normality', *Social Science and Medicine* 63 (2006): 2268–2276; Burgard, D., 'Blinded by BMI', *Health at Every Size* 19, no. 1 (2005): 45–54; Monaghan, L. F., 'Body mass index, masculinities and moral worth: men's critical understandings of "appropriate" weight-for-height', *Sociology of Health and Illness* 29, no. 4 (2007): 584–609.

32 Greenhalgh, S., *Fat-Talk Nation: The Human Costs of America's War on Fat* (Ithaca, NY: Cornell University Press, 2015).

33 Bacon, L., *Health at Every Size: The Surprising Truth about Your Weight*, 2nd edition (Dallas, TX: BenBella Books, 2010).

34 Herndon, 'Collateral damage from friendly fire? Race, nation, class and the "war against obesity"'; Murray, S., *The 'Fat' Female Body* (Houndmills: Routledge, 2008); Strings, S., *Fearing the Black Body: The Racial Origins of Fat Phobia* (New York: New York University Press, 2019).

35   Cooper, C., *Fat Activism: A Radical Social Movement* (Bristol: HammerOn Press, 2016).

36   Lustig, *Fat Chance: The Hidden Truth about Sugar, Obesity and Disease*, 16.

37   Action on Sugar, 'Worldwide experts unite to reverse obesity epidemic by forming "Action on Sugar"'.

38   See, for example, Valverde, M., *Diseases of the Will: Alcohol and the Dilemmas of Freedom* (Cambridge: Cambridge University Press, 1998); Keane, H., *What's Wrong with Addiction?* (Melbourne: Melbourne University Press, 2002); Berridge, V., *Demons: Our Changing Attitudes to Alcohol, Tobacco & Drugs* (Oxford: Oxford University Press, 2013).

39   Keane, *What's Wrong with Addiction?*, 9.

40   American Psychiatric Assocation, *Diagnostic and Statistical Manual of Mental Disorders*, fifth edition (Arlington, VA: American Pscyhiatric Association, 2013).

41   Sedgwick, E. K., 'Epidemics of the Will', in *Tendencies* (Durham, NC: Duke University Press, 1993), 130–142.

42   See, for example, Volkow, N. D. and O'Brien, C. P., 'Issues for DSM-V: should obesity be included as a brain disorder?', *American Journal of Pyschiatry* 164, no. 5 (2007): 708–710; Avena, N. M. and Gold, M. S., 'Food and addiction – sugars, fats and hedonic overeating', *Addiction* 106, no. 7 (2011): 1214–1215; Gearhardt, A. N. et al., 'Can food be addictive? Public health and policy implications', *Addiction* 106, no. 7 (2011): 1208–1212; Rogers, P. J., 'Obesity – is food addiction to blame?', *Addiction* 106, no. 7 (2011): 1213–1214.

43   Courtwright, D. T., 'The NIDA brain disease paradigm: history, resistance and spinoffs', *Biosocieties* 5 (2010): 137–147.

44   Heim, D., 'Addiction: not just a brain malfunction', *Nature Reviews: Neuroscience* 507 (6 March 2014): 40.

45   Malika, N. M. et al., 'Low-income women's conceptualizations of food craving and food addiction', *Eating Behaviors* 18 (2015): 25–29.

46   Leckie, B., 'Sugar risk', *The Sun*, 16 August 2017, https://www.thescottish sun.co.uk/news/1429905/drug-drink-smoking-death-sugar-bill-leckie/ [accessed: 6 March 2022].

47   See also Fraser, S., 'Junk: Overeating and obesity and the neuroscience of addiction', *Addiction Research and Theory* 21, no. 6 (2013): 496–506.

48   Nelkin, D., *Selling Science: How the Press Covers Science and Technology*, revised edition (New York: W. H. Freeman and Company, 1995).

49   Lenoir, M. et al., 'Intense sweetness surpasses cocaine reward', *PLOS One* 8, no. e698 (2007): 1–10.

50   Lambert, 'Sweet poison: why sugar is ruining our health'.

51   Fraser, 'Junk: Overeating and obesity and the neuroscience of addiction'.

52 Law, 'Collateral realities'.

53 Lenoir et al., 'Intense sweetness surpasses cocaine reward', 1.

54 Ibid., 6.

55 Ibid., 1.

56 Ibid., 6.

57 Nelson, N. C., *Model Behaviour: Animal Experiments, Complexity and the Genetics of Psychiatric Disorders* (Chicago: University of Chicago Press, 2018), 4.

58 Avena, N. M., Rada, P. and Hoebel, B. G., 'Evidence for sugar addiction: behavioral and neurchemical effects of intermittent excess sugar intake', *Neuroscience and Biobehavioral Reviews* 32, no. 1 (2008): 20–39.

59 Ibid., 32.

60 DiNicolantonio, J. J., O'Keefe, J. H. and Wilson, W. L., 'Sugar addiction: is it real? A narrative review', *British Journal of Sports Medicine* 52 (2018): 910–918.

61 Davis, N., 'Is sugar really as addictive as cocaine? Scientists row over effect on body and brain', *The Guardian*, 25 August 2017, https://www.theguardian.com/society/2017/aug/25/is-sugar-really-as-addictive-as-cocaine-scientists-row-over-effect-on-body-and-brain [accessed: 16 January 2022].

62 Mansey, K. and Ungoed-Thomas, J., 'Sweet but deadly', *The Sunday Times*, 29 December 2013, https://www.thetimes.co.uk/article/sweet-but-deadly-h6opff97873 [accessed: 17 January 2022].

63 Erlichman, J., 'Supersize vs undersize: food portions and obesity', *The Guardian*, 18 February 2013, https://www.theguardian.com/society/2013/feb/18/supersize-undersize-food-portions-obesity [accessed: 17 January 2022].

64 Westwater, M. L., Fletcher, P. C., and Ziauddeen, H., 'Sugar addiction: the state of the science', *European Journal of Nutrition* 55, supplement 2 (2016): S55–69.

65 Davis, 'Is sugar really as addictive as cocaine? Scientists row over effect on body and brain'.

66 Mayes, C., *The Biopolitics of Lifestyle: Foucault, Ethics and Health Choices* (London: Routledge, 2016).

67 Colquhoun, D., 'DC's improbable science', blog, 2006–2022, www.dcscience.net [accessed: 7 March 2022].

68 Renton, A., 'The demon drink: war on sugar', *The Observer*, 8 August 2013, https://www.theguardian.com/lifeandstyle/2013/aug/04/demon-drink-war-on-sugar [accessed: 17 January 2022].

69 Smyth, C., 'Lansley ridicules claims that sugar is the new tobacco', *The Times*, 10 January 2014, https://www.thetimes.co.uk/article/lansley-ridicules-claims-that-sugar-is-the-new-tobacco-6wfz5t08r7g [accessed: 7 March 2022].

70   Gard and Wright, *The Obesity Epidemic: Science, Morality and Ideology*, 17.

71   Woods, J., 'Why I'm backing Jamie Oliver over his sugar tax', *The Daily Telegraph*, 22 October 2015, https://www.telegraph.co.uk/news/poli tics/11947641/Why-Im-backing-Jamie-Oliver-over-his-sugar-tax.html [accessed: 7 March 2022].

72   Birrell, I., 'We must tax sugar before Britain eats itself to death', *Daily Mail*, 19 September 2014, https://www.dailymail.co.uk/news/article-2761683/ We-MUST-tax-sugar-Britain-eats-death-His-dad-Tate-Lyle-executive-IAN-BIRRELL-believes-food-industry-needs-taken-on.html [accessed: 17 January 2022].

73   Lustig, *Fat Chance: The Hidden Truth about Sugar, Obesity and Disease*, 210–211.

74   Stearns, *Fat History: Bodies and Beauty in the Modern West*; Schwartz, H., *Never Satisfied: A Cultural History of Diets, Fantasies and Fat* (New York: The Free Press, 1986); de la Peña, *Empty Pleasures: The Story of Artificial Sweeteners from Saccharin to Splenda*.

75   Cooper, *Fat Activism: A Radical Social Movement*.

76   Johnston, P., 'Is a fat tax the only way to combat our growing epidemic of obesity?', *The Daily Telegraph*, 8 August 2015, https://www.telegraph.co.uk/ news/nhs/11808059/Is-a-fat-tax-the-only-way-to-combat-our-growing-epid emic-of-obesity.html [accessed: 15 February 2022].

77   See, for example, Charles, N. and Kerr, M., *Women, Food and Families: Power, Status, Love and Anger* (Manchester: Manchester University Press, 1988); Cairns, K. and Johnston, J., *Food and Femininity* (London: Bloomsbury, 2015).

78   Herndon, 'Collateral damage from friendly fire? Race, nation, class and the 'war against obesity'.

79   Knight, C., '"If you're not allowed to have rice, what do you have with your curry?" Nostalgia and tradition in low-carbohydrate diet discourse and practice', *Sociological Research Online* 16, no. 2 (2011): 4.

80   Harjak, H., 'Would your grandmother have eaten it? Sarah Wilson on wellness fads', *The Guardian*, 1 June 2017, https://www.theguardian.com/ guardian-masterclasses/guardian-masterclass-blog/2017/jun/01/would-your-grandmother-have-eaten-it-sarah-wilson-on-wellness-fads [accessed: 17 January 2022].

81   Gard and Wright, *The Obesity Epidemic: Science, Morality and Ideology*, chapter 3.

82   Barron, C. et al., *Barriers to Play and Recreation for Children and Young People with Disabilities* (Warsaw: de Gruyter Open, 2017).

83   Landecker, 'Food as exposure: nutritional epigenetics and the new metabolism', 190.

84   Cordain, *The Paleo Diet: Lose Weight and Get Healthy by Eating the Foods You Were Designed to Eat*, 3.

85 Noakes, T., Proudfoot, J. and Creed, S.-A., *The Real Meal Revolution: The Radical, Sustainable Approach to Healthy Eating* (London: Robinson, 2015), 14.

86 Yudkin, *Pure, White and Deadly: How Sugar is Killing Us and What We Can Do to Stop It*, 8–9.

87 Lustig, *Fat Chance: The Hidden Truth about Sugar, Obesity and Disease*, 129.

88 Yudkin, *Pure, White and Deadly: How Sugar is Killing Us and What We Can Do to Stop It*, 10.

89 Cleave, T. L., *The Saccharine Disease: Conditions Caused by the Taking of Refined Carbohydrate Such as Sugar and White Flour* (Bristol: J. Wright, 1974); Dufty, W., *Sugar Blues* (New York: Hachette Book Group, 1975).

90 Knight, C., '"An alliance with Mother Nature": natural food, health and morality in low-carbohydrate diet books', *Food and Foodways* 20, no. 2 (2012): 102–122.

91 Cordain, *The Paleo Diet: Lose Weight and Get Healthy by Eating the Foods You Were Designed to Eat*, 10.

92 Knight, C., '"We can't go back a hundred million years"', *Food, Culture and Society* 18, no. 3 (2015): 441–461.

93 Zuk, M., *Paleofantasy: What Evolution Really Tells Us about Sex, Diet and How We Live* (New York: W.W. Norton and Company, 2013), 271.

94 Gard and Wright, *The Obesity Epidemic: Science, Morality and Ideology*, 109.

95 Cordain, L. et al., 'Plant-animal subsistence ratios and macronutrient energy estimations in worldwide hunter-gatherer diets', *American Journal of Clinical Nutrition* 71 (2000): 691.

96 Zuk, *Paleofantasy: What Evolution Really Tells Us about Sex, Diet and How We Live*, 115.

97 Milton, K., 'Hunter-gatherer diets – a different perspective', *American Journal of Clinical Nutrition* 71 (2000): 665–667.

98 Lustig, *Fat Chance: The Hidden Truth about Sugar, Obesity and Disease*, 105.

Chapter 3

1 Change4Life, 'SugarSwaps', 4 January 2019, https://www.youtube.com/watch?v=PWE_UMno5P8 [accessed: 19 March 2019].

2 Lafrance, M., Lafrance, S., and Norman, M. E., 'Life lessons: learning about what it means to be fat in the North American mass media', *Cultural Studies <—> Critical Methodologies* 15, no. 5 (2015): 350–360.

3 Halse, C., 'Bio-citizenship: virtue discourses and the birth of the bio-citizen', in *Biopolitics and the 'Obesity Epidemic': Governing Bodies*, ed. J. Wright and V. Harwood (London: Routledge, 2009), 45–59; Rail, G. and Jette, S., 'Reflections on biopedagogies and/of public health: on bio-others, rescue

missions and social justice', *Cultural Studies <—> Critical Methodologies* 15, no. 5 (2015): 327–336.

4   Halse, 'Bio-citizenship: virtue discourses and the birth of the bio-citizen', 47.

5   Jones, E., *Goodbye Sugar: Hello Weight Loss, Great Skin, More Energy and Improved Mood* (Dublin: Gill & Macmillan, 2015), 111.

6   Action on Sugar, 'Up to 25 teaspoons of sugar per serving: equivalent to ≈ 3 cans of Coca Cola', 17 February 2016, www.actiononsugar.org/surveys/2016/hot-flavoured-drinks/ [accessed: 15 February 2020].

7   Evans, P., 'THOU SHALT NOT SIN (unless you've paid the tax)', *The Sunday Times*, 20 March 2016, https://www.thetimes.co.uk/article/thou-shall-not-sin-unless-youve-paid-the-tax-l5fbsrndb [accessed: 23 January 2022].

8   Lafrance, Lafrance, and Norman, 'Life lessons: learning about what it means to be fat in the North American mass media', 352.

9   Saguy, A. and Almeling, R., 'Fat in the fire? Science, the news media and the "obesity epidemic"', *Sociological Forum* 23, no. 1 (2008): 53–83.

10 Cooper, C., 'Headless fatties', January 2007, http://charlottecooper.net/fat/fat-writing/headless-fatties-01-07 [accessed: 20 January 2022].

11 Jordan-Young and Karkazis, *Testosterone: An Unauthorized Biography*, 11.

12 Evans, 'THOU SHALT NOT SIN (unless you've paid the tax)'.

13 Jones, D., 'Fatty latte: 16 times more sugar than doughnut in chains' drinks', *The Sun*, 17 February 2016 (print edition).

14 Brignall, M., 'The cafes serving drink with 25 teaspooons of sugar per cup', *The Guardian*, 16 Feburary 2016, https://www.theguardian.com/business/2016/feb/17/cafe-chains-selling-drinks-25-teaspoons-sugar-starbucks-costa-coffee [accessed: 23 January 2022].

15 Callow, C., 'Of course Starbucks' drinks are full of sugar. Go to a proper coffee shop instead.', *The Daily Telegraph*, 17 February 2016, https://www.telegraph.co.uk/food-and-drink/drinks/of-course-starbucks-drinks-are-full-of-sugar-go-to-a-proper-coff/ [accessed: 23 January 2022].

16 Fielding-Singh, P., *How the Other Half Eats: The Untold Story of Food and Inequality in America* (New York: Little, Brown Spark, 2021), 4.

17 Warin and Zivkovic, *Fatness, Obesity and Disadvantage in the Australian Suburbs: Unpalatable Politics*, 3398.

18 Campbell, D., 'Half of fizzy drinks have more sugar in one can than adult daily limit', *The Guardian*, 15 November 2016, https://www.theguardian.com/lifeandstyle/2016/nov/15/half-of-fizzy-drinks-have-more-sugar-in-one-can-than-adult-daily-limit [accessed: 23 January 2022].

19 Hashem, K. M. et al., 'Cross sectional survey of the amount of sugar and energy in cakes and biscuits on sale in the UK for the evaluation of the sugar-reduction programme', *British Medical Journal Open* 8 (2018): e019075.

20 Holland, M., 'How to stop your Battenberg being a health risk', *The Guardian*, 6 August 2018, https://www.theguardian.com/lifeandstyle/shortcuts/2018/aug/06/how-to-stop-your-battenburg-being-a-health-risk [accessed: 23 January 2022].

21 Leake, J., 'Battenberg's sugar content branded a public health risk', *The Sunday Times*, 5 August 2018, https://www.thetimes.co.uk/article/battenbergs-show-stopping-sugar-content-branded-a-public-health-risk-wrdbhmok2 [accessed: 23 January 2022].

22 Pike, M. R., 'How unhealthy are your favourite treats?', *Daily Mail*, 5 August 2018, https://www.dailymail.co.uk/femail/food/article-6028725/Nutritionist-reveals-shocking-sugar-content-Battenberg-cakes.html [accessed: 23 January 2022].

23 Yates-Doerr, E., *The Weight of Obesity: Hunger and Global Health in Postwar Guatemala* (Oakland: University of California Press, 2015), 140 (Kindle).

24 Mansey, K. and Ungoed-Thomas, J, '"Natural" food has more sugar than Coca-Cola', *The Sunday Times*, 5 May 2013, https://www.thetimes.co.uk/article/natural-food-has-more-sugar-than-coca-cola-26h272692t8 [accessed: 23 January 2022].

25 Brignall, 'The cafes serving drink with 25 teaspooons of sugar per cup'.

26 Mendick, R., 'Supermarket ready meals contain double as much sugar as a can of Coca-Cola', *The Sunday Telegraph*, 24 October 2015, https://www.telegraph.co.uk/news/health/news/11952743/Supermarket-ready-meals-contain-double-as-much-sugar-as-can-of-Coca-Cola.html [accessed: 23 January 2022].

27 Graham-Leigh, E., *A Diet of Austerity: Class, Food and Climate Change* (Winchester: Zero Books, 2015), 665 (Kindle).

28 Groves, J., 'Families told to slash sugar intake by HALF', *Daily Mail*, 17 July 2015, https://www.dailymail.co.uk/health/article-3164626/Families-warned-Slash-sugar-intake-half-Report-warns-obesity-epidemic-cripple-NHS-unless-levels-reduced.html [accessed: 23 January 2022].

29 Knapton, S., 'Breakfast biscuits contain unhealthy levels of sugar, nutritionists warn', *The Daily Telegraph*, 18 June 2016, https://www.telegraph.co.uk/science/2016/06/18/breakfast-biscuits-contain-unhealthy-levels-of-sugar-nutritionis/ [accessed: 23 January 2022].

30 Francis, M., 'How your "healthy" porridge could have more sugar than a bowl of FROSTIES', *MailOnline*, 16 September 2014, https://www.dailymail.co.uk/health/article-2756927/Porridge-sugar-Frosties.html [accessed: 23 January 2022].

31 Siddique, 'Sugar should be no more than 5% of daily calories, say nutrition experts'.

32 Smithers, R., 'High street meal deals "can contain up to 30 teaspoons of sugar"', *The Guardian*, 31 October 2017, https://www.theguardian.com/society/2017/oct/31/high-street-lunch-meal-deals-can-contain-up-to-30-teaspoons-of-sugar [accessed: 23 January 2022].

33 Hashem, K. M., 'Is Battenberg a health risk?', 2018, www.actiononsugar.org/news-centre/surveys/2018/2018/is-battenberg-a-health-risk.html [accessed: 23 September 2020].

34 Ibid.

35 Action on Sugar, 'Cakes and biscuits', news release, 26 July 2018, www.actiononsugar.org/surveys/2018/cakes-and-biscuits/#d.en.751316 [accessed: 13 March 2022].

36 Hashem, 'Is Battenberg a health risk?'

37 Holland, 'How to stop your Battenberg being a health risk'.

38 Action on Sugar, 'Fruit snacks', news release, 16 September 2020, https://www.actiononsugar.org/news-centre/press-releases/2020/experts-call-for-honest-labelling-on-so-called-healthy-fruit-snacks-loaded-with-sugars-and-misleading-claims.html [accessed: 13 March 2022].

39 Ibid.

40 Ibid.

41 Mansey and Ungoed-Thomas, '"Natural" food has more sugar than Coca-Cola'.

42 Saunders, 'The sugar trap: part one'.

43 Wilson, B., *Swindled: From Poison Sweets to Counterfeit Coffee – the Dark History of Food Cheats* (London: John Murray, 2009).

44 Carpenter, 'Life without sugar: one family's 30-day challenge'.

45 Saunders, 'The sugar trap: part one'.

46 Lustig, R., 'Sugar is the "alcohol of the child", yet we let it dominate the breakfast table', *The Guardian*, 4 January 2017, https://www.theguardian.com/commentisfree/2017/jan/04/sugar-alcohol-child-breakfast-diabetes-liver-disease-corporate [accessed: 23 January 2022].

47 Wollaston, S., 'Jamie's Sugar Rush review: Jamie Oliver is great – I'd put him in charge of the country', *The Guardian*, 4 September 2015, https://www.theguardian.com/tv-and-radio/2015/sep/04/jamies-sugar-rush-jamie-oliver [accessed: 23 January 2022].

48 Ursell, A., 'How much sugar is in your booze?', *The Sun*, 4 February 2014 (print edition).

49 Jupes, O., 'As a dentist, I hate sugar. But I don't want kids scared off it with horror packaging', *The Guardian*, 28 June 2017, https://www.theguardian.com/commentisfree/2017/jun/28/dentist-hate-sugar-kids-scared-health-warnings [accessed: 23 January 2022].

50 Lustig, *Fat Chance: The Hidden Truth about Sugar, Obesity and Disease*, 114.

51 Jordan-Young and Karkazis, *Testosterone: An Unauthorized Biography*, 11.

52 Noon, R., 'Goodbye Mr Cube', *History Today* 51, no. 10 (2001): 40–41.

53 Barrett, D. and Calvi, N., *The Sugar Girls: Tales of Hardship, Love and Happiness in Tate and Lyle's East End* (London: Harper Collins, 2012), 118.

54 Saner, E., "'Does the criticism affect me? Yes, massively": Jamie Oliver's war on childhood obesity', *The Guardian*, 29 April 2018, https://www.theguardian.com/lifeandstyle/2018/apr/29/jamie-oliver-criticism-affect-me-childhood-obesity [accessed: 23 January 2022].

55 See, for example, Brookes and Baker, *Obesity in the News: Language and Representation in the Press*, chapter 3.

56 Hoyle, A., 'My "healthy" family are eating the equivalent of 215 Krispy Kreme doughnuts every WEEK', *The Mail on Sunday*, 25 October 2015 (print edition).

57 The online version of this article did not include this comment, which appears to have been edited out after the print edition: https://www.dailymail.co.uk/femail/article-3288029/Oh-sugar-healthy-family-eating-equivalent-215-Krispy-Kremes-WEEK-One-mother-s-shockingly-sugary-meal-diary-converted-doughnuts.html [accessed: 13 March 2022].

58 Change4Life, 'Jamelia gets Sugar Smart', (5 January 2016), https://youtu.be/jlG246SIrtU [accessed: 12 March 2022].

59 Ursell, A., 'Sugar app told me why my kids had tooth decay', *The Sun*, 16 February 2016 (print edition).

60 McCaffrey, J., 'Would you feed your kids this much sugar?', *The Sun*, 9 July 2017 (print edition).

61 Ibid.

62 Lustig, 'Sugar is the "alcohol of the child", yet we let it dominate the breakfast table'.

63 Carpenter, 'Life without sugar: one family's 30-day challenge'.

64 Scientific and Advisory Committee on Nutrition, *Carbohydrates and Health*, 17.

65 Action on Sugar, 'Children's juices', news release, 11 November 2014, www.actiononsugar.org/surveys/2014/childrens-juices/#d.en.751324 [accessed: 20 October 2020].

66 Saunders, 'The sugar trap: part one'.

67 Lustig, 'The science is in: the case for a sugar tax is overwhelming'.

68 Carpenter, 'Life without sugar: one family's 30-day challenge'.

69 Maxted, A., 'Did banning sugar turn my kids into sweet little angels?', *The Daily Telegraph*, 26 February 2015, https://www.telegraph.co.uk/foodanddrink/foodanddrinkadvice/11375030/Did-banning-sugar-turn-my-kids-into-sweet-little-angels.html [accessed: 23 January 2022].

70 Hoyle, 'My "healthy" family are eating the equivalent of 215 Krispy Kreme doughnuts every WEEK'.

71 Poulter, S., "'Healthy" veg crisps with equivalent of 8 spoons of sugar – more than 6 chocolate digestives', *Daily Mail*, 6 May 2017, https://www.dailymail.co.uk/news/article-4478854/Vegetable-crisps-equivalent-EIGHT-spoons-sugar.html [accessed: 23 January 2022].

Notes

72 Yates-Doerr, *The Weight of Obesity: Hunger and Global Health in Postwar Guatemala*, 71.

73 See, for example, Bordo, S., *Unbearable Weight: Feminism, Western Culture and the Body* (Berkeley, Los Angeles and London: University of California Press, 1993).

74 Maxted, 'Did banning sugar turn my kids into sweet little angels?'

75 McCaffrey, 'Would you feed your kids this much sugar?'

76 Ibid.

77 Ibid.

Chapter 4

1 Gillespie, *The Sweet Poison Quit Plan: How to Kick the Sugar Habit and Lose Weight*, 105.

2 Lichterman, P., 'Self-help reading as thin culture', *Media, Culture and Society* 14, no. 3 (1992): 421–447.

3 Grodin, D., 'The interpreting audience: the therapeutics of self-help book reading', *Critical Studies in Mass Communication* 8, no. 4 (1991): 404–420.

4 Jones, *Goodbye Sugar: Hello Weight Loss, Great Skin, More Energy and Improved Mood*; Wilson, S., *I Quit Sugar: Your Complete 8-Week Detox Program and Cookbook* (London: Bluebird, 2014).

5 O'Neill, 'Pursuing "wellness": considerations for media studies', 629.

6 DeFigio, D., *Beating Sugar Addiction for Dummies* (Hoboken, NJ: John Wiley and Sons, Inc., 2013).

7 McKenna, P., *Get Control of Sugar Now! Great Choices for your Health Future* (London: Transworld Publishers, 2016); Carr, A., *Good Sugar, Bad Sugar: Eat Yourself Free from Sugar and Carb Addiction* (London: Arcturus, 2018).

8 Carr, A., 'Allen Carr's Easyway', 2022, https://www.allencarr.com [accessed: 30 January 2022].

9 McKenna, P., 'Paul McKenna', 2022, https://www.paulmckenna.com [accessed: 30 January 2022].

10 Starker, S., *Oracle at the Supermarket: The American Preoccupation with Self-Help Books* (New Brunswick, NJ, and Oxford: Transaction Publishers, 1989), 9.

11 Gillespie, *The Sweet Poison Quit Plan: How to Kick the Sugar Habit and Lose Weight*; Goran, M. I. and Ventura, E. E., *Sugarproof: The Hidden Dangers of Sugar that Are Putting Your Child's Health at Risk and What You Can Do* (New York: Avery, 2020).

12 Goran and Ventura, *Sugarproof: The Hidden Dangers of Sugar that Are Putting Your Child's Health at Risk and What You Can Do*, xi.

13 Gillespie, *The Sweet Poison Quit Plan: How to Kick the Sugar Habit and Lose Weight*, 4.

14 Mowbray, N., *Sweet Nothing: Why I Gave Up Sugar and How You Can Too* (London: Orion, 2014); Schaub, E., *Year of No Sugar: A Memoir* (Naperville, IL: Sourcebooks, Inc., 2014).

15 Styvertsen, T. and Enil, G., 'Digital detox: media resistance and the promise of authenticity', *Convergence: The International Journal of Research into New Media Technologies* 26, nos. 5–6 (2019): 1269–1283.

16 Mowbray, *Sweet Nothing: Why I Gave Up Sugar and How You Can Too*, 17.

17 Ibid., 302.

18 Goran and Ventura, *Sugarproof: The Hidden Dangers of Sugar that Are Putting Your Child's Health at Risk and What You Can Do*, 206.

19 Mowbray, *Sweet Nothing: Why I Gave Up Sugar and How You Can Too*, 9.

20 McKenna, *Get Control of Sugar Now! Great Choices for Your Health Future*, 16–20.

21 Ibid., 56.

22 Schaub, *Year of No Sugar: A Memoir*, 141.

23 Murray, S., '(Un/be)coming out? Rethinking fat politics', *Social Semiotics* 15, no. 2 (August 2005): 154.

24 Gillespie, *The Sweet Poison Quit Plan: How to Kick the Sugar Habit and Lose Weight*, 52.

25 McKenna, *Get Control of Sugar Now! Great Choices for Your Health Future*, 189.

26 Slimming World, 'Slimming World: taste the freedom', 2022, https://www.slimmingworld.co.uk [accessed: 30 January 2022].

27 Cairns, K. and Johnston, J., 'Choosing health: embodied neoliberalism, post-feminism and the do-diet', *Theory and Society* 44, no. 2 (2015): 153–175.

28 DeFigio, *Beating Sugar Addiction for Dummies*, 67.

29 Mowbray, *Sweet Nothing: Why I Gave Up Sugar and How You Can Too*, 17.

30 Jones, *Goodbye Sugar: Hello Weight Loss, Great Skin, More Energy and Improved Mood*, 41.

31 Gillespie, *The Sweet Poison Quit Plan: How to Kick the Sugar Habit and Lose Weight*, 6.

32 Ibid., 9.

33 Mowbray, *Sweet Nothing: Why I Gave Up Sugar and How You Can Too*, 15.

34 Carr, *Good Sugar, Bad Sugar: Eat Yourself Free from Sugar and Carb Addiction*, 248–249.

35 Jones, *Goodbye Sugar: Hello Weight Loss, Great Skin, More Energy and Improved Mood*, 44–47.

36 Gillespie, *The Sweet Poison Quit Plan: How to Kick the Sugar Habit and Lose Weight*, 43.

37 DeFigio, *Beating Sugar Addiction for Dummies*, 272, 273.

38 Carr, *Good Sugar, Bad Sugar: Eat Yourself Free from Sugar and Carb Addiction*, 40, 129.

39 Slimming World, 'Slimming World: taste the freedom'.

40 McGee, M., *Self-Help, Inc. Makeover Culture in American Life* (Oxford: Oxford University Press, 2005), 160.

41 DeFigio, *Beating Sugar Addiction for Dummies*, 2.

42 Goran and Ventura, *Sugarproof: The Hidden Dangers of Sugar that Are Putting Your Child's Health at Risk and What You Can Do*, 203.

43 Mowbray, *Sweet Nothing: Why I Gave Up Sugar and How You Can Too*, 45.

44 Giraud, E., *Veganism: Politics, Practice and Theory* (London: Bloomsbury, 2021).

45 Goran and Ventura, *Sugarproof: The Hidden Dangers of Sugar that Are Putting Your Child's Health at Risk and What You Can Do*, 108.

46 DeFigio, *Beating Sugar Addiction for Dummies*, 49.

47 McGee, *Self-Help, Inc. Makeover Culture in American Life*, 17.

48 Mowbray, *Sweet Nothing: Why I Gave Up Sugar and How You Can Too*, 16–17.

49 Jones, *Goodbye Sugar: Hello Weight Loss, Great Skin, More Energy and Improved Mood*, 29.

50 Mowbray, *Sweet Nothing: Why I Gave Up Sugar and How You Can Too*, 74.

51 Ibid., 87.

52 Cairns and Johnston, 'Choosing health: embodied neoliberalism, post-feminism and the do-diet', 163.

53 Schaub, *Year of No Sugar: A Memoir*, 272.

54 Goran and Ventura, *Sugarproof: The Hidden Dangers of Sugar that Are Putting Your Child's Health at Risk and What You Can Do*, xiii.

55 Ibid., viii–x.

56 DeFigio, *Beating Sugar Addiction for Dummies*, 123.

57 Ibid., 122.

58 Ibid., 167.

59 Carr, *Good Sugar, Bad Sugar: Eat Yourself Free from Sugar and Carb Addiction*, 92.

60 Wilson, *I Quit Sugar: Your Complete 8-Week Detox Program and Cookbook*, 1.

61 Jones, *Goodbye Sugar: Hello Weight Loss, Great Skin, More Energy and Improved Mood*, xvi.

62 Wilson, *I Quit Sugar: Your Complete 8-Week Detox Program and Cookbook*, 31.

63 McKenna, *Get Control of Sugar Now! Great Choices for Your Health Future*, 87.

64 Wilson, *I Quit Sugar: Your Complete 8-Week Detox Program and Cookbook*, 26.

Notes

65 Goran and Ventura, *Sugarproof: The Hidden Dangers of Sugar that Are Putting Your Child's Health at Risk and What You Can Do*, xvi.

66 McKenna, *Get Control of Sugar Now! Great Choices for Your Health Future*, 122.

67 Carr, *Good Sugar, Bad Sugar: Eat Yourself Free from Sugar and Carb Addiction*, 93.

68 Wilson, *I Quit Sugar: Your Complete 8-Week Detox Program and Cookbook*, 13.

69 Carr, *Good Sugar, Bad Sugar: Eat Yourself Free from Sugar and Carb Addiction*, 136.

70 Jones, *Goodbye Sugar: Hello Weight Loss, Great Skin, More Energy and Improved Mood*, 41.

71 Gillespie, *The Sweet Poison Quit Plan: How to Kick the Sugar Habit and Lose Weight*, 115.

72 Ibid., 69.

73 Schaub, *Year of No Sugar: A Memoir*, 255.

74 Ibid., 261.

75 Gillespie, *The Sweet Poison Quit Plan: How to Kick the Sugar Habit and Lose Weight*, 77.

76 See, for example, Guthman, J., 'Fast food/organic food: reflexive tastes and the making of "yuppie chow"', *Social and Cultural Geography* 4, no. 1 (2003): 45–58; Naccarato, P. and LeBesco, K., *Culinary Capital* (London: Berg, 2012).

77 Rimke, H. M., 'Governing citizens through self-help literature', *Cultural Studies* 14, no. 1 (2000): 61–78.

78 Jones, *Goodbye Sugar: Hello Weight Loss, Great Skin, More Energy and Improved Mood*, 43.

79 DeFigio, *Beating Sugar Addiction for Dummies*, 106.

80 Ibid., 110.

81 Carr, *Good Sugar, Bad Sugar: Eat Yourself Free from Sugar and Carb Addiction*, 243–244.

82 McKenna, *Get Control of Sugar Now! Great Choices for Your Health Future*, 122.

83 Carr, *Good Sugar, Bad Sugar: Eat Yourself Free from Sugar and Carb Addiction*, 244.

84 McGee, *Self-Help, Inc. Makeover Culture in American Life*, 145.

85 Ibid., 15.

86 Jones, *Goodbye Sugar: Hello Weight Loss, Great Skin, More Energy and Improved Mood*, 33–34.

87 DeFigio, *Beating Sugar Addiction for Dummies*, 93.

88 Jones, *Goodbye Sugar: Hello Weight Loss, Great Skin, More Energy and Improved Mood*, 34.

89 DeFigio, *Beating Sugar Addiction for Dummies*, 89.

90 McKenna, *Get Control of Sugar Now! Great Choices for Your Health Future*, 127.

91 Mowbray, *Sweet Nothing: Why I Gave Up Sugar and How You Can Too*, 281.

92 Ibid., 271-2.

93 See, for example, Backett-Milburn, K. C. et al., 'Food, eating and taste: parents' perspectives on the making of the middle class teenager', *Social Science and Medicine* 71 (2010): 1316-1323; Johnson and Baumann, *Foodies: Democracy and Distinction in the Gourmet Foodscape*; Wills, W. et al., 'The framing of social class distinctions through family food and eating practices', *The Sociological Review* 59, no. 4 (2011): 725-740.

94 Mowbray, *Sweet Nothing: Why I Gave Up Sugar and How You Can Too*, 86.

95 Ibid., 282.

96 Evans, B., Colls, R. and Hörschelmann, K., '"Change4Life for your kid": embodied collectives and public health pedagogy', *Sport, Education and Society* 16, no. 3 (2011): 335.

97 DeFigio, *Beating Sugar Addiction for Dummies*, 23.

98 Jones, *Goodbye Sugar: Hello Weight Loss, Great Skin, More Energy and Improved Mood*, xiv, 14, 22.

99 Ibid., xv.

100 Ibid., 15.

101 See Cherry, S., 'The ontology of a self-help book: a paradox of its own existence', *Social Semiotics* 18, no. 3 (2008): 337-348.

102 Throsby, K., 'Happy re-birthday: weight loss surgery and the "new me"', *Body & Society* 14, no. 1 (2008): 117-133.

103 Jones, *Goodbye Sugar: Hello Weight Loss, Great Skin, More Energy and Improved Mood*, 39.

104 DeFigio, *Beating Sugar Addiction for Dummies*, 122.

105 McKenna, *Get Control of Sugar Now! Great Choices for Your Health Future*, 34.

106 McGee, *Self-Help, Inc. Makeover Culture in American Life*, 43.

107 McKenna, *Get Control of Sugar Now! Great Choices for Your Health Future*, 138.

108 Gillespie, *The Sweet Poison Quit Plan: How to Kick the Sugar Habit and Lose Weight*, 161.

109 McGee, *Self-Help, Inc. Makeover Culture in American Life*, 42.

110 Jones, *Goodbye Sugar: Hello Weight Loss, Great Skin, More Energy and Improved Mood*, 36.

111 Ibid., 37.

Chapter 5

1 *Jamie's Sugar Rush,* directed by V. Cooper (Channel 4, 3 September 2015), https://www.youtube.com/watch?v=7psynBdrZnA [accessed: 1 March 2022].

2 Buckton, C. H. et al., 'A discourse network analysis of UK newspaper coverage of the "sugar tax" debate before and after the announcement of the Soft Drinks Industry Levy', *BMC Public Health* 19, article 490 (2019): 7.

3 Sustain, *How the Sugary Drinks Tax Was Won* (London: Sustain, 2018), 15, https://www.sustainweb.org/publications/how_the_sugary_drinks_tax_was_won/ [accessed: 21 January 2021].

4 See, for example, Warin, M., 'Foucault's progeny: Jamie Oliver and the art of governing obesity', *Social Theory and Health* 9, no. 1 (2011): 24–40; Crawshaw, P., 'Governing at a distance: social marketing and the (bio)politics of responsibility', *Social Science and Medicine* 75 (2012): 200–207.

5 *That Sugar Film*, directed by D. Gameau (Madman Production Company, 2014), DVD.

6 Hollows, J. and Jones, S., '"At least he's doing somethiing": moral entrepreneurshihp and individual responsibiilty in Jamie's Ministry of Food', *European Journal of Cultural Studies* 13, no. 3 (2010): 307–322.

7 Karp, P., 'Jamie Oliver urges Australia to "pull your finger out" and implement sugar tax', *The Guardian*, 17 March 2016, https://www.theguardian.com/australia-news/2016/mar/17/jamie-oliver-urges-australia-to-pull-your-finger-out-and-implement-sugar-tax [accessed: 6 February 2022].

8 *Fed Up*, directed by S. Soechtig (Atlas Films, 2014), DVD.

9 *Sugar Coated*, directed by M. Hozer (The Cutting Factory, 2015), https://vimeo.com/ondemand/sugarcoated/136276681?autoplay=1 [accessed: 14 March 2022].

10 Oliver, J., *Jamie's Sugar Manifesto* (2015), https://cdn.jamieoliver.com/sugar-rush/pdf/FINALJamiesSugarManifesto.pdf [accessed: 15 March 2022].

11 *Super Size Me*, directed by M. Spurlock (Hart Sharp Video, 2004), DVD.

12 Gameau, D., *That Sugar Book: This Book Will Change the Way You Think about 'Healthy' Food* (Sydney: Macmillan, 2015).

13 Gameau, D., *That Sugar Movement* (2022), https://thatsugarmovement.com [accessed: 1 February 2022].

14 Royal College of Surgeons of England, 'Shocking 24% increase in tooth extractions performed on children aged 0–4 in the last decade', news release, 21 March 2017, https://www.rcseng.ac.uk/news-and-events/media-centre/press-releases/child-tooth-extractions-24-per-cent/ [accessed: 6 February 2022].

15 Bodkin, H., 'Rise in removals of rotting milk teeth fuelled by children's sugary diet', *The Daily Telegraph*, 21 March 2017, https://www.telegraph.

co.uk/news/2017/03/21/rise-removals-rotting-milk-teeth-fuelled-childrens-sugary-diet/ [accessed: 6 February 2022].

16 Spencer, B., 'Sugar-addict children who need every tooth removed', *Daily Mail*, 15 April 2016 (print edition).

17 Healthwatch England and British Dental Association, *The 2021 Spending Review and the Future of NHS Dentistry* (2021), https://www.bda.org/news-centre/press-releases/Documents/bda-healthwatch-letter-spending-review-future-of-nhs-dentistry-21-oct-21.pdf [accessed: 13 March 2022].

18 Galloway, D., McAlpine, K. B. and Harris, P., 'From Michael Moore to JFK Reloaded: towards a working model of interactive documentary', *Journal of Media Practice* 8, no. 3 (2007): 325–339.

19 Barnes, C., 'Mediating good food and moments of possibility with Jamie Oliver: problematising celebrity chefs as talking labels', *Geoforum* 84 (2017): 169–178.

20 Deakin University, 'Should we take *That Sugar Film* with a grain of salt?', news release, 5 March 2015, https://www.deakin.edu.au/about-deakin/news-and-media-releases/articles/should-we-take-that-sugar-film-with-a-grain-of-salt [accessed: 1 February 2022].

21 Solomon, H., *Metabolic Living: Food, Fat and the Absorption of Illness in India* (Durham, NC, and London: Duke University Press, 2016), 4471 (Kindle).

22 Ibid., 4478.

23 Gameau, *That Sugar Book: This Book Will Change the Way You Think about 'Healthy' Food*, 14.

24 Ibid., 49.

25 Kelly, J., Oliva, D. and Jesudason, S., *Indigenous 'Yarning Kidneys'* (Melbourne: Kidney Health Australia, University of Adelaide, 2018), https://kidney.org.au/uploads/resources/Adelaide-Yarning-Kidneys-Consultation-Report.pdf [accessed: 14 March 2022].

26 In *That Sugar Book*, Gameau attributes a slightly revised version of this statement to Leonard Burton, a male dialysis patient: 'Before we had bush tucker, then the white man came and he brought lollies and biscuits.'

27 See, for example, Lopez, O. and Jacobs, A., 'In a town with so little water, Coca-Cola is everywhere. So is diabetes', *The New York Times*, 14 July 2018, https://www.nytimes.com/2018/07/14/world/americas/mexico-coca-cola-diabetes.html [accessed: 14 March 2022]; Tuckman, J. and Bagnoli, D., 'Coca-Cola country in southern Mexico – a photo essay', *The Guardian*, 15 November 2019, https://www.theguardian.com/world/2019/nov/15/coca-cola-country-in-southern-mexico-photo-essay [accessed: 14 March 2022].

28 Leer, J. and Kjær, K. M., 'Strange culinary adventures: stranger fetishism in *Jamie's Italian Kitchen* and *Gordon's Great Escape*', *Food, Culture and Society* 18, no. 2 (2015): 309–327.

Notes

29 Otto, M., *Teeth: The Story of Beauty, Inequality and the Struggle for Oral Health in America* (New York: The New Press, 2017), 180–181.

30 Elmore, B. J., *Citizen Coke: The Making of Coco-Cola Capitalism* (New York: W. W. Norton & Company, 2015).

31 Saner, '"Does the criticism affect me? Yes, massively": Jamie Oliver's war on childhood obesity'.

32 Bell, D., Hollows, J. and Jones, S., 'Campaigning culinary documentaries and the responsibilization of food crises', *Geoforum* 84 (2017): 179–187.

33 Cooper, 'Headless fatties'.

34 Guthman, 'Fast food/organic food: reflexive tastes and the making of "yuppie chow"', 46.

35 Wollaston, 'Jamie's Sugar Rush review: Jamie Oliver is great – I'd put him in charge of the country'.

36 'Jamie Oliver for Chief Medical Officer', *The Lancet* 365 (2005): 1282.

37 Saner, '"Does the criticism affect me? Yes, massively": Jamie Oliver's war on childhood obesity'.

38 Gameau, *That Sugar Book: This Book Will Change the Way You Think about 'Healthy' Food*, 6.

39 Ibid.

40 Ouellette, L., 'Reality TV gives back: on the civic functions of reality entertainment', *Journal of Popular Film and Television* 38, no. 2 (2010): 66–71.

41 Boseley, S., 'Jamie Oliver's Sugar Rush: a crusade to save Britain's health', *The Guardian*, 27 October 2015, https://www.theguardian.com/lifeand style/2015/aug/27/jamie-oliver-sugar-rush-channel-4-crusade-save-britain-health [accessed: 6 February 2022].

42 Health Committee, 'Childhood obesity strategy' (19 October 2015), https://parliamentlive.tv/Event/Index/9824c8bb-2610-45bc-8257-bbf05a338e13 [accessed: 6 February 2022].

43 Cornelson, L. et al., 'Change in non-alcoholic beverage sales following a 10-pence levy on sugar-sweetened beverages within a national chain of restaurants in the UK', *Journal of Epidemiology and Community Health* 71, no. 11 (2017): 1107–1112.

44 Garavelli, D., 'Sugar tax could save a generation of Scots', *The Times*, 1 July 2015, https://www.thetimes.co.uk/article/sugar-tax-could-save-a-genera tion-of-scots-dombjc53nqw [accessed: 14 March 2022].

45 Gameau, *That Sugar Book: This Book Will Change the Way You Think about 'Healthy' Food*, 46.

46 Ibid., 47.

47 Throsby, K., '"You can't be too vain to gain if you want to swim the Channel": marathon swimming and the construction of heroic fatness', *International Reivew for the Sociology of Sport* 50, no. 9 (2013): 769–784; Throsby, K., *Immersion: Marathon Swimming, Embodiment and Identity*, New Ethnographies (Manchester: Manchester University Press, 2016).

Notes

48 LeBesco, K., 'Situating fat suits: blackface, drag and the politics of performance', *Women & Performance: A Journal of Feminist Theory* 15, no. 2 (2005): 231–242.

49 Hendry, M., 'Bru deserve it: Jamie Oliver branded "lettuce shagger" by Irn Bru fans as his Glasgow and Edinburgh restaurants are axed along with 20 others across the UK', *The Scottish Sun*, 21 May 2019, https://www.thescot tishsun.co.uk/news/4270054/jamie-oliver-administration-scots-irn-bru-restaurants-pizza/ [accessed: 6 February 2022].

50 Gordon, B., 'The sugar tax has brough out the snob in all of us', *The Daily Telegraph*, 19 March 2016, https://www.telegraph.co.uk/health-fitness/nutri tion/bryony-gordon-the-sugar-tax-has-brought-out-the-snob-in-all-of-u/ [accessed: 6 February 2022].

51 Jackson, P., '"Go home Jamie": reframing consumer choice', *Social and Cultural Geography* 17, no. 6 (2016): 753–757.

52 Saner, '"Does the criticism affect me? Yes, massively": Jamie Oliver's war on childhood obesity'.

53 Rainey, S., 'Celebrity chefs: are they making us ill?', *The Daily Telegraph*, 25 April 2013, https://www.telegraph.co.uk/foodanddrink/healthyeating/10015342/Celebrity-chefs-are-they-making-us-ill.html [accessed: 6 February 2022].

54 Johnson, J. and Goodman, M. K., 'Spectacular foodscapes: food celebrities and the politics of lifestyle mediation in an age of inequality', *Food, Culture and Society* 18, no. 2 (2015): 205–222.

55 Slocum, R. et al., '"Properly, with love, from scratch": Jamie Oliver's food revolution', *Radical History Review* 2011, no. 110 (2011): 1780–1791.

56 Gameau, *That Sugar Book: This Book Will Change the Way You Think about 'Healthy' Food*, 6.

57 Ibid., 153, 190.

58 Ibid., 138.

59 Ibid., 76.

60 McKenna, *Get Control of Sugar Now! Great Choices for Your Health Future*, 76.

61 Gameau, *That Sugar Book: This Book Will Change the Way You Think about 'Healthy' Food*, 183, 155.

62 Barnes, 'Mediating good food and moments of possibility with Jamie Oliver: problematising celebrity chefs as talking labels'.

63 Goodman, M. K., Johnson, J. and Cairns, K., 'Food, media and space: the mediated biopolitics of eating'.

64 Rojek, C., '"Big citizen" celanthropy and its discontents', *International Journal of Cultural Studies* 17, no. 2 (2014): 124–141; Piper, N., 'Jamie Oliver and cultural intermediation', *Food, Culture and Society* 18, no. 2 (2015): 245–264.

65 Health Committee, 'Childhood obesity strategy'.

Notes

66 Health and Social Care Committee, *Childhood Obesity* (1 May 2018), https://www.parliamentlive.tv/Event/Index/14fd35da-3f7f-4207–886d-904fb87fd b03 [accessed: 6 February 2022].

67 Bell, Hollows and Jones, 'Campaigning culinary documentaries and the responsibilization of food crises'.

68 Saner, '"Does the criticism affect me? Yes, massively": Jamie Oliver's war on childhood obesity'.

69 Kidd, P., 'Once more unto the breach with Jamie in the battle of sugar hill', *The Times*, 20 October 2015, https://www.thetimes.co.uk/article/once-more-unto-the-breach-with-jamie-in-the-battle-of-sugar-hill-fg69l6zhcxp [accessed: 6 February 2022].

70 Campbell, D. and Mason, R., 'David Cameron faces pressure to back sugar tax', *The Guardian*, 22 October 2015, https://www.theguardian.com/society/2015/oct/22/david-cameron-faces-pressure-to-back-sugar-tax [accessed: 6 February 2022].

71 Mostrous, A., 'Fizzy drinks giant pays millions to diet experts', *The Times*, 9 October 2015, https://www.thetimes.co.uk/article/fizzy-drinks-giant-pays-millions-to-diet-experts-78cfc36znmc [accessed: 6 February 2022].

72 Smyth, C., Sylvester, R. and Thomson, A., 'Senior Tory urges PM to think again on sugar tax', *The Times*, 24 October 2015, https://www.thetimes.co.uk/article/senior-tory-urges-pm-to-think-again-on-sugar-tax-h6lns8j75br [accessed: 19 March 2022].

73 Crace, J., 'Sugar, fat and junk nibbles on the Hugh and Jamie show', *The Guardian*, 1 May 2018, https://www.theguardian.com/politics/2018/may/01/sugar-fat-junk-obsesity-uk-hugh-jamie-parliament-health-committee [accessed: 6 February 2022].

74 Saner, '"Does the criticism affect me? Yes, massively": Jamie Oliver's war on childhood obesity'.

75 Naik, A., 'Did Jamie Oliver really put school dinners on the agenda? An examination of the role of the media in policy making', *The Political Quarterly* 79, no. 3 (2008): 426–433.

76 Fitzpatrick, A., *A Children's Future Fund: How Food Duties Could Provide Money to Protect Children's Health and the World They Grow Up In* (London: Sustain, January 2013), https://www.sustainweb.org/publications/a_childrens_future_fund/ [accessed: 14 March 2022].

77 Gameau, *That Sugar Book: This Book Will Change the Way You Think about 'Healthy' Food*, 188.

Chapter 6

1 Evans, 'THOU SHALT NOT SIN (unless you've paid the tax)'.

2 Osborne, G., 'Budget 2016: George Osborne's speech' (16 March 2016),

https://www.gov.uk/government/speeches/budget-2016-george-osbornes-speech [accessed: 14 February 2022].

3   March 2016 has the second highest number of newspaper articles in the dataset (beaten only by October 2015), making the release of the PHE report and the subsequent introduction of the sugar tax linchpin events in the contemporary story of sugar in the UK.

4   See, for example, Bray, G. A., Nielsen, S. J. and Popkin, B. M., 'Consumption of high fructose corn syrup in beeverages may play a role in the epidemic of obesity', *American Journal of Clinical Nutrition* 79, no. 4 (2004): 537–543; Nielsen, S. J. and Popkin, B. M., 'Changes in beverage intake between 1977 and 2001', *American Journal of Preventive Medicine* 27, no. 3 (2004): 205–210; Vartanian, L. R., Schwawrtz, M. B. and Brownell, K. D., 'Effects of soft drink consumption on nutrition and health: a systematic review and meta-analysis', *American Journal of Public Health* 97, no. 4 (2007): 667–675.

5   Popkin, B. M. and Ng, S. W., 'Sugar-sweetened beverage taxes: lessons to date and the future of taxation', *PLOS Medicine* 18, no. 1 (2021): e1103412.

6   See, for example, World Health Organization, *Taxes on Sugar Drinks: Why Do It?* (Geneva: World Health Organization, 2017), http://apps.who.int/iris/bitstream/handle/10665/260253/WHO-NMH-PND-16.5Rev.1-eng.pdf [accessed: 15 March 2022].

7   Sánchez-Pimiento, T. G. et al., 'Sugar sweetened beverages are the main sources of added sugar intake in the Mexico population', *Journal of Nutrition* 146, no. 9 (2016): S1888–1896.

8   Agren, D., 'Benefits of Mexican sugar tax disputed as congress approves cut', *The Guardian*, 26 October 2015, https://www.theguardian.com/world/2015/oct/22/benefits-of-mexican-sugar-tax-disputed-as-congress-approves-cut [accessed: 15 February 2022].

9   Batis, C. et al., 'First year evaluation of Mexico's tax on nonessential energy-dense foods: an observational study in an urban environment', *PLOS Medicine* 13, no. 7 (2016): e10767336; Colchero, M. A. et al., 'In Mexico, evidence of sustained consumer response two years after implementing a sugar-sweetened beverage tax', *Health Affairs* 36, no. 3 (2017): 564–571; Colchero, M. A. et al., 'Beverage purchases from stores in Mexico under the excise tax on sugar sweetened beverages: observational study', *British Medical Journal* 352 (2016): h6704.

10 Colchero et al., 'Beverage purchases from stores in Mexico under the excise tax on sugar sweetened beverages: observational study'.

11 Colchero, M. A. et al., 'Beverage sales in Mexico before and after implementation of a sugar sweetened beverage tax', *PLOS One* 11, no. 9 (2016): 301636463.

12 Ng, S. W. et al., 'Did high sugar-sweetened beverage purchasers respond differently to the excise tax on sugar-sweetened beverages in Mexico?',

Notes

Public Health Nutrition 22, no. 4 (2019): 750–756, https://doi.org/10.1017/S136898001800321X.

13 Sánchez-Romero, L. M. et al., 'Projected impact of Mexico's sugar-sweetened beverage tax policy on diabetes and cardiovascular disease: a modellng study', *PLOS Medicine* 13, no. 11 (2016): e1002158.

14 Basto-Abreu, A. et al., 'Cost-effectiveness of the sugar-sweetened beverage excise tax in Mexico', *Health Affairs* 38, no. 11 (2019): 1824–1831.

15 Macaskill, M., 'Sugar tax "best way" to beat obesity', *The Sunday Times*, 1 May 2016, https://www.thetimes.co.uk/article/sugar-tax-is-best-way-to-beat-obesity-9sb72ppsf [accessed: 15 February 2022].

16 Rosenberg, T., 'How one of the most obese countries on earth took on the soda giants', *The Guardian*, 3 November 2015, https://www.theguardian.com/news/2015/nov/03/obese-soda-sugar-tax-mexico [accessed: 15 February 2022].

17 See, for example, Brandes, S., 'Sugar, colonialism and death: on the origins of Mexico's day of the dead', *Comparative Studies in Society and History* 39, no. 2 (1997): 270–299; Montoya, M. J., *Making the Mexican Diabetic: Race, Science and the Genetics of Inequality* (Berkeley: University of California Press, 2011); Roberts, D., *Fatal Invention: How Science, Politics, and Big Business Re-Create Race in the Twenty-First Century* (New York: The New Press, 2011).

18 See, for example, Kersh, R., 'Of nannies and nudges: the current state of US obesity policymaking', *Public Health* 129, no. 8 (2015): 1083–1091; Magnusson, R. S., 'Case studies in nanny state name-calling: what can we learn?', *Public Health* 129, no. 8 (2015): 1074–1082; Coggan, J., *The Nanny State Debate: A Place Where Words Don't Do Justice* (London: Faculty of Public Health, 2018).

19 Gault, A., 'Tax the biscuit', *The Sun*, 18 March 2016 (print edition).

20 Dathan, M. et al., 'The sugar tax backlash: Osborne's new levy could force up price of diet drinks and even bottles of water, say critics', *Daily Mail*, 18 March 2016, https://www.dailymail.co.uk/news/article-3497105/Sugar-tax-INCREASE-sugar-intake-sweetest-drinks-attract-tax-gram-experts-warn-tear-apart-George-Osborne-s-flagship-Budget-measure.html [accessed: 15 March 2022].

21 Ramanauskas, B., 'Why sugar taxes are a bad idea', news release, 6 April 2019, https://www.taxpayersalliance.com/why_sugar_taxes_are_a_bad_idea [accessed: 15 February 2022].

22 Elliott, C., '"Big Food" and "gamified products": promotion, packaging and the promise of fun', *Critical Public Health* 25, no. 3 (2015): 348–360.

23 Boseley, S., 'How Britain got so fat', *The Guardian*, 21 June 2014, https://www.theguardian.com/society/2014/jun/21/how-britain-got-so-fat-obese [accessed: 15 February 2022].

24 Garavelli, 'Sugar tax could save a generation of Scots'.

Notes

25 Davies, S. C., *Annual Report of the Chief Medical Officer, 2018 Health 2040 – Better Health within Reach* (London: Department of Health and Social Care, 21 December 2018), https://www.gov.uk/government/publications/chief-medical-officer-annual-report-2018-better-health-within-reach [accessed: 15 February 2022].

26 For example, Spencer, B., 'UK's top doctor demands string of new taxes on chocolates and crisps to tackle child obesity as she brands herself "chief nanny"', *Daily Mail*, 21 December 2018, https://www.dailymail.co.uk/health/article-6518511/Britains-doctor-calls-new-taxes-salt-sugar.html [accessed: 15 February 2022].

27 Public Health England, '10 year olds in the UK have consumed 18 years' worth of sugar', news release, 2 January 2019, https://www.gov.uk/government/news/10-year-olds-in-the-uk-have-consumed-18-years-worth-of-sugar [accessed: 15 February 2019].

28 Smyth, C., 'Children eat three times as much sugar as they should', *The Times*, 2 January 2019, https://www.thetimes.co.uk/article/children-eat-three-times-as-much-sugar-as-they-should-3zgdbdkg2 [accessed: 15 February 2022].

29 Young, S., 'BBC Radio 4 host Nick Robinson accused of being "sexist" live on air by Professor Dame Sally Davies', *The Independent*, 7 February 2019, https://www.independent.co.uk/life-style/nick-robinson-radio-4-sally-davies-sexist-interview-bbc-radio-4-children-smartphones-a8767236.html [accessed: 15 February 2022].

30 Birrell, 'We must tax sugar before Britain eats itself to death'.

31 Farquharson, K., 'Nanny knows best when it comes to choccy', *The Times*, 22 January 2016, https://www.thetimes.co.uk/article/nanny-knows-best-when-it-comes-to-choccy-hm7rnpg7529 [accessed: 16 February 2022].

32 Rosenberg, 'How one of the most obese countries on earth took on the soda giants'.

33 See, for example, Brownell, K. D. and Warner, K. E., 'The perils of ignoring history: Big Tobacco played dirty and millions died. How similar is Big Food?', *Millbank Quarterly* 87, no. 1 (2009): 259–294; Oreskes, N. and Conway, E. M., *Merchants of Doubt: How a Handful of Scientists Obscured the Truth on Issues from Tobacco Smoke to Global Warming* (London: Bloomsbury, 2010); Wiist, W. H., 'The corporate playbook, health and democracy: the snack food and beverage industry's tactics in context', in *Sick Societies: Responding to the Global Challenge of Chronic Disease*, ed. D. Stuckler and K. Siegel (Oxford: Oxford University Press, 2011), 204–216; Campbell, N. et al., 'How are frames generated? Insights from the industry lobby against the sugar tax in Ireland', *Social Science and Medicine* 264 (2020), https://doi.org/10.1016/j.socscimed.2020.113215; Nestle, *Unsavory Truth: How Food Companies Skew the Science of What We Eat*.

Notes

34 Oreskes and Conway, *Merchants of Doubt: How a Handful of Scientists Obscured the Truth on Issues from Tobacco Smoke to Global Warming*.

35 Llewellyn Smith, J., 'John Yudkin: the man who tried to warn us about sugar', *The Sunday Telegraph*, 17 February 2014, https://www.telegraph.co.uk/lifestyle/wellbeing/diet/10634081/John-Yudkin-the-man-who-tried-to-warn-us-about-sugar.html [accessed: 15 March 2022].

36 Ibid.

37 Rainey, S., 'All aboard the sugar bandwagon', *Daily Mail*, 29 November 2015, https://www.dailymail.co.uk/news/article-3338770/The-Coca-Cola-truck-touring-Britain-s-fattest-towns-plying-children-free-drinks.html [accessed: 15 February 2022].

38 Scrinis, G., 'Ultra-processed foods and the corporate capture of nutrition', *British Medical Journal* 371 (2020): m4601.

39 Nestle, *Unsavory Truth: How Food Companies Skew the Science of What We Eat*, 5.

40 See, for example, Law, J., *Big Pharma: How the World's Biggest Drug Companies Control Illness* (London: Constable, 2006); Goldacre, B., *Bad Pharma: How Drug Companies Mislead Doctors and Harm Patients* (London: Fourth Estate, 2012); Healy, D., *Pharmageddon* (Berkeley: University of California Press, 2012).

41 Martin, A., 'The sugar tsars "in bed" with confectionery giants', *Daily Mail*, 19 January 2014, https://www.dailymail.co.uk/news/article-2542367/The-sugar-tsars-bed-confectionery-giants-Five-members-committee-tasked-battling-obesity-epidemic-worryingly-close-ties.html [accessed: 15 February 2022].

42 Ungoed-Thomas, J. and Barrett, S., 'Diabetes UK's £500,000 tie-up with sugar giant', *The Sunday Times*, 25 November 2018, https://www.thetimes.co.uk/article/diabetes-uks-500–000-tie-up-with-sugar-giant-wmh5mjtqk [accessed: 15 February 2022].

43 Boseley, S., 'Sugar intake must come down, says WHO – but UK likely to resist', *The Guardian*, 7 September 2013, https://www.theguardian.com/lifeandstyle/2013/sep/07/sugar-diet-who-uk-experts [accessed: 15 February 2022].

44 Ungoed-Thomas, J. and Mansey, K., 'Sugar watchdog works for Coca-Cola', 19 January 2014, https://www.thetimes.co.uk/article/sugar-watchdog-works-for-coca-cola-fjdsgt5cjmj [accessed: 15 February 2022].

45 Mostrous, 'Fizzy drinks giant pays millions to diet experts'.

46 Nestle, *Unsavory Truth: How Food Companies Skew the Science of What We Eat*, 158.

47 Nestle, M., 'Corporate funding of food and nutrition research: science or marketing?', *Journal of the American Medical Association Internal Medicine* 176, no. 1 (2016): 13.

48 Nestle, *Unsavory Truth: How Food Companies Skew the Science of What We Eat*, 5.

49 Department of Health, *The Public Health Responsibility Deal* (London: Department of Health, 2011), 3, https://extranet.who.int/nutrition/gina/ sites/default/filesstore/GBR%202011%20The%20Public%20Health%20 Responsibility%20Deal.pdf [accessed: 15 March 2022].

50 Department of Health and Social Care, 'Public Health Responsibility Deal announces new pledge', news release, 26 March 2012, https://www.gov.uk/ government/news/public-health-responsibility-deal-announces-new-food- pledge [accessed: 14 February 2022].

51 Boseley, S. and Campbell, D., 'Food industry playing for time on regula- tion, says obesity expert', *The Guardian*, 19 February 2013, https://www.the guardian.com/society/2013/feb/18/food-industry-regulation-obesity-expert [accessed: 15 February 2022].

52 See, for example, Knai, C. et al., 'Has a public–private partnership resulted in action on healthier diets in England? An analysis of the Public Health Responsibility Deal food pledges', *Food Policy* 54 (2015): 1–10; Panjwani, C. and Caraher, M., 'The Public Health Responsibility Deal: brokering a deal for public health, but on whose terms?', *Healthy Policy* 114, no. 2 (2014): 163–173; Gilmore, A. B., Savell, E. and Collin, J., 'Public health corporations and the new responsibility deal: promoting partnerships with vectors of disease', *Journal of Public Health* 33, no. 1 (2011): 2–4.

53 Public Health England, *Sugar Reduction and Wider Reformulation Programme: Report on Progress towards the First 5% Reduction and Next Steps* (London: Public Health England, May 2018), https://assets.publish ing.service.gov.uk/government/uploads/system/uploads/attachment_data/ file/709008/Sugar_reduction_progress_report.pdf [accessed: 16 March. 2022].

54 Boseley, S., 'Time to stockpile Irn-Bru? How the sugar tax will change our favourite drinks', *The Guardian*, 2 April 2018, https://www.theguardian. com/lifeandstyle/2018/apr/02/time-to-stockpile-irn-bru-how-sugar-tax- change-nations-favourite-drinks [accessed: 16 March 2022].

55 Butler, S., 'Coca-Cola and other soft drinks firms hit back at sugar tax plan', *The Guardian*, 17 March 2016, https://www.theguardian.com/business/2016/ mar/17/coca-cola-hits-back-at-sugar-tax-plan [accessed: 15 February 2016].

56 Boseley, S., 'Sugar tax could prevent obesity in over 4 million people, chari- ties say', *The Guardian*, 19 February 2016, https://www.theguardian.com/ society/2016/feb/19/sugar-tax-could-prevent-obesity-in-almost-4-million- people-charities-say [accessed: 16 March 2022].

57 Campbell et al., 'How are frames generated? Insights from the industry lobby against the sugar tax in Ireland', 5.

58 Smithers, R., 'Co-op to remove 100 m teaspoons of sugar with own brand squash range', *The Guardian*, 20 June 2014, https://www.theguardian.com/

business/2014/jun/20/co-op-sugar-squash-range-supermarket-obesity-dia
betes#comment-37216486 [accessed: 15 February 2022].

59 Malnick, E., 'Food firms sidestep pledge on sugar', *The Sunday
Telegraph*, 31 May 2014, https://www.telegraph.co.uk/foodanddrink/
foodanddrinknews/10866839/Manufacturers-fail-to-reduce-sugar-despite-
healthy-eating-pledge-Telegraph-finds.html [accessed: 15 February 2022].

60 Scrinis, G., 'Reformulation, fortification and functionalization: big food
corporations' nutritional engineering and marketing strategies', *Journal of
Peasant Studies* 43, no. 1 (2016): 17–37.

61 Boseley, S., 'Sugar content cuts to Lucozade and Ribena leave campaigners
unimpressed', *The Guardian*, 22 January 2013, https://www.theguardian.
com/business/2013/jan/22/sugar-content-lucozade-ribena-cut [accessed:
15 February 2022].

62 Boseley, S., 'Saturated fat to be cut in chocolate products, makers pledge',
The Guardian, 26 October 2013, https://www.theguardian.com/lifeand
style/2013/oct/26/saturated-fat-cut-pledge [accessed: 15 February 2022].

63 Knapton, S., 'San Pellegrino has more sugar than Coke', *The Daily
Telegraph*, 12 June 2014, https://www.telegraph.co.uk/news/science/science-
news/10893554/Upmarket-fizzy-drinks-contain-more-sugar-than-Coca-
Cola.html [accessed: 15 February 2015].

64 Boseley, 'Sugar content cuts to Lucozade and Ribena leave campaigners
unimpressed'.

65 Thompson, A., 'Junk food firms fail miserably to meet a sugar reduction
target set by Government to cut child obesity', *Daily Mail*, 22 May 2018,
https://www.dailymail.co.uk/health/article-5757595/Juice-milkshake-man
ufacturers-urged-slash-sugar-calories-popular-drinks.html [accessed:
15 February 2018].

66 Briggs, A. et al., 'Overall and income specific effect on prevalence of overweight and obesity of 20% sugar sweetened drink tax in UK: econometric
and comoparative risk assessment modelling study', *British Medical Journal*
347 (2013): f6189.

67 Birrell, 'We must tax sugar before Britain eats itself to death'.

68 Bhimjiyani, A. and Knuchel-Takano, A., *Short and Sweet: Why the
Government Should Introduce a Sugary Drinks Tax* (London: Cancer
Research UK, February 2016), https://bit.ly/35VuqQc [accessed: 16 March
2022].

69 HM Treasury, 'Soft Drinks Industry Levy comes into effect', news release,
5 April 2018, https://www.gov.uk/government/news/soft-drinks-industry-
levy-comes-into-effect [accessed: 9 July 2018].

70 Public Health England, 'Third year of industry progress to reduce sugar
published', news release, 7 October 2020, https://www.gov.uk/government/
news/third-year-of-industry-progress-to-reduce-sugar-published [accessed:
14 February 2022].

Notes

71 Public Health England, *Sugar Reduction: Report on Progress between 2015 and 2019* (London: Public Health England, 2020), https://assets.publishing. service.gov.uk/government/uploads/system/uploads/attachment_data/file/ 984282/Sugar_reduction_progress_report_2015_to_2019–1.pdf [accessed: 16 March 2022].

72 Teng, A. M. et al., 'Impact of sugar-sweetened beverage taxes on purchases and dietary intake: systematic review and meta-analysis', *Obesity Reviews* 20 (2019): 1187–1204.

73 Griffith, R. et al., *The Evidence on the Effects of Soft Drink Taxes* (Institute of Fiscal Studies, 2019), https://ifs.org.uk/uploads/BN255-the-evidence-on-the-effects-of-soft-drink-taxes.pdf [accessed: 16 March 2022].

74 Gračner, T., Marquez-Padilla, F. and Hernandez-Cortes, D., 'Changes in weight-related outcomes among adolescents following consumer price increases of taxed sugar-sweetened beverages', *Journal of the American Medical Association Pediatric* 176, no. 2 (2022): 150–158.

75 Pickles, K., 'Sugary breakfast cereals must be treated in the same way as fizzy drinks to fight childhood obesity, warns the head of the NHS', *Daily Mail*, 3 July 2018, https://www.dailymail.co.uk/news/article-5911573/Cut-sugar-breakfast-cereals-warns-head-NHS.html [accessed: 15 February 2022].

76 Bhimjiyani and Knuchel-Takano, *Short and Sweet: Why the Government Should Introduce a Sugary Drinks Tax*.

77 Bødker, M. et al., 'The rise and fall of the world's first fat tax', *Health Policy* 119, no. 6 (2015): 737–742.

78 Osborne, 'Budget 2016: George Osborne's speech'.

79 HM Treasury, 'Soft Drinks Industry Levy comes into effect'.

80 Fitzpatrick, *A Children's Future Fund: How Food Duties Could Provide Money to Protect Children's Health and the World They Grow Up In*.

81 Sustain, 'Hundreds of millions of pounds of sugary drinks tax money not being allocated to improve children's healthy diets, breaking government promise', news release, 12 January 2021, https://www.sustainweb.org/news/jan21-refreshingsdil/ [accessed: 14 February 2022].

82 'Javid admits Treasury has swallowed sugar tax cash', *The Grocer*, 7 September 2019, https://www.proquest.com/docview/2305521135 [accessed: 14 February 2022].

83 Renton, A., 'The sugar tax is a great idea. Why not go after processed foods next?', *The Observer*, 20 March 2016, https://www.theguardian.com/commentisfree/2016/mar/20/sugar-tax-good-idea-go-after-processed-foods-next [accessed: 15 February 2016].

84 Health Committee, 'Childhood obesity strategy'.

85 Smyth, C., 'Sugar tax cuts fizzy drinks sales', *The Times*, 7 January 2016, https://www.thetimes.co.uk/article/sugar-tax-cuts-fizzy-drink-sales-mjlcqs nlsk5 [accessed: 15 February 2022].

86 Saner, '"Does the criticism affect me? Yes, massively": Jamie Oliver's war on childhood obesity'.

87 Health Committee, 'Childhood obesity strategy'.

Chapter 7

1 See, for example, O'Hara, M., *Austerity Bites* (Bristol: Policy Press, 2015); Garthwaite, *Hunger Pains: Life inside Foodbank Britain*; Cooper and Whyte, *The Violence of Austerity*; Evans, B. M. and McBride, S., eds, *Austerity: The Lived Experience* (Toronto: University of Toronto Press, 2017); Ryan, F., *Crippled: Austerity and the Demonization of Disabled People* (London: Verso, 2019).

2 Hochlaf, D., Quilter-Pinner, H. and Kibasi, T., *Ending the Blame Game: The Case for a New Approach to Public Health and Prevention* (Institute of Public Policy Research, 2019), https://www.ippr.org/files/2019-06/public-health-and-prevention-june19.pdf [accessed: 16 February 2022].

3 Alston, P., *Visit to the United Kingdom of Great Britain and Northern Ireland: Report of the Special Rapporteur on Extreme Poverty and Human Rights* (Human Rights Council, United Nations General Assembly, 23 April 2019), 5, https://documents-dds-ny.un.org/doc/UNDOC/GEN/G19/112/13/PDF/G1911213.pdf?OpenElement [accessed: 16 February 2022].

4 Booth, R., 'UN report compares Tory welfare policies to creation of work-houses', *The Guardian*, 22 May 2019, 6, https://www.theguardian.com/politics/2019/may/22/un-report-compares-tory-welfare-reforms-to-crea tion-of-workhouses [accessed: 16 February 2022].

5 Clarke, J. and Newman, J. 'The alchemy of austerity', *Critical Social Policy* 32, no. 3 (2012): 299–319.

6 Tyler, *Revolting Subjects: Social Abjection and Resistance in Neoliberal Britain*.

7 Graham-Leigh, *A Diet of Austerity: Class, Food and Climate Change*; Forth, C., *Fat: A Cultural History of the Stuff of Life* (London: Reaktion Books Ltd, 2019).

8 Graham-Leigh, *A Diet of Austerity: Class, Food and Climate Change*, 374.

9 See, for example, de Benedictus, S., '"Feral" parents: austerity parenting under neoliberalism', *Studies in the Maternal* 4, no. 2 (2012): 1–21; Tyler, *Revolting Subjects: Social Abjection and Resistance in Neoliberal Britain*; Allen, K. et al., 'Welfare queens, thrifty housewives and do-it-all mums', *Feminist Media Studies* 15, no. 6 (2015): 907–925; Jensen, T. and Tyler, I, '"Benefits broods": the cultural and politlcal crafting of anti-welfare com-monsense', *Critical Social Policy* 35, no. 4 (2015): 470–491.

10 Jensen and Tyler, '"Benefits broods": the cultural and politlcal crafting of anti-welfare commonsense'.

11 Thaler, R. and Sunstein, C. R., *Nudge: Improving Decisions about Health, Wealth and Happiness* (London: Penguin, 2009).

12 Action on Sugar, 'Call for ban on excessively high sugar and calorie milkshakes sold in high street and restaurant food chains', news release, 13 November 2018, www.actiononsugar.org/news-centre/press-releases/2018/call-for-ban-on-excessively-high-sugar-and-calorie-milkshakes-sold-in-high-street-resta urants--fast-food-chains-.html [accessed: 18 October 2019].

13 Larbi, M., 'Not so sweet: call for BAN on "grotesquely sugar milkshakes" could hit Toby Carvery, Pizza Hut and McDonald's', *The Sun*, 13 November 2018, https://www.thesun.co.uk/fabulous/7726420/sugar-milkshake-possi ble-ban-toby-carvery-pizza-hut-mcdonalds/ [accessed: 16 February 2022].

14 Beagan et al., *Acquired Tastes: Why Families Eat the Way They Do.*

15 Gault, 'Tax the biscuit'.

16 Dathan, M., 'SUGAR TAX AXED: Boris Johnson rules out sugar taxes as part of his post coronavirus battle against obesity', *The Sun*, 15 July 2020, https://www.thesun.co.uk/news/12134748/boris-axe-sugar-tax-obesity-battle/ [accessed: 16 March 2022].

17 Williams, L., 'After The Sun's disgusting "scrounger" awards, it's time to recognise the biggest injustices of the benefits system', *The Independent*, 19 January 2015, https://www.independent.co.uk/voices/comment/after-sun-s-disgusting-scrounger-awards-it-s-time-recognise-biggest-injustices-benefits-system-9982983.html [accessed: 18 February 2022].

18 Evans and McBride, *Austerity: the Lived Experience.*

19 Clarke and Newman, 'The alchemy of austerity', 302.

20 Johnston, 'Is a fat tax the only way to combat our growing epidemic of obe-sity?'

21 Ibid.

22 Foster, P., 'American way: it is time to curb the American sugar rush', *The Sunday Telegraph*, 15 November 2014, https://www.telegraph.co.uk/news/worldnews/northamerica/usa/11233057/American-Way-It-is-time-to-curb-the-great-American-sugar-rush.html [accessed: 18 February 2022].

23 Jensen, T., *Parenting the Crisis: The Cultural Politics of Parent-Blame* (Bristol: Policy Press, 2018).

24 Osborne, G., 'George Osborne's speech to the Conservative Party Conference in full', *The Guardian*, 4 October 2010, https://www.theguardian.com/politics/2010/oct/04/george-osborne-speech-conservative-conference [accessed: 19 December 2022].

25 Graham-Leigh, *A Diet of Austerity: Class, Food and Climate Change*, 198.

26 Fitzpatrick, *A Children's Future Fund: How Food Duties Could Provide Money to Protect Children's Health and the World They Grow Up In*, 2.

27 See, for example, Batis et al., 'First year evaluation of Mexico's tax on nones-sential energy-dense foods: an observational study in an urban environment'; Colchero et al., 'Beverage sales in Mexico before and after implementation of

Notes

a sugar sweetened beverage tax'; Colchero et al., 'In Mexico, evidence of sustained consumer response two years after implementing a sugar-sweetened beverage tax'; Colchero et al., 'Beverage purchases from stores in Mexico under the excise tax on sugar sweetened beverages: observational study'.

28 Campbell, D., 'Sugar tax: financially regressive but progressive for health?', *The Guardian*, 18 March 2016, https://www.theguardian.com/society/2016/mar/18/sugar-tax-financially-regressive-but-progressive-for-health [accessed: 18 February 2022].

29 Smyth, C., 'Boris close to backing tax on sugar', *The Times*, 22 October 2015, https://www.thetimes.co.uk/article/boris-close-to-backing-tax-on-sugar-nvvbrnvtdoz [accessed: 18 February 2022].

30 Iacobucci, G., 'Public health leaders slam Boris Johnson over "sin tax" review', *British Medical Journal* 366 (2019): l4451.

31 Kamm, O., 'The critics have got it wrong – a sugar tax will hit the sweet spot', *The Times*, 2 June 2016, https://www.thetimes.co.uk/article/the-critics-have-got-it-wrong-a-sugar-tax-will-hit-the-sweet-spot-fqk2v7rfw [accessed: 18 February 2022].

32 See, for example, Clarke and Newman, 'The alchemy of austerity'; Levitas, R., 'The just's umbrella: austerity and the big society in coalition policy and beyond', *Critical Social Policy* 32, no. 3 (2012): 320–342.

33 Jensen, *Parenting the Crisis: The Cultural Politics of Parent-Blame*.

34 Renton, 'The sugar tax is a great idea. Why not go after processed foods next?'

35 Health and Social Care Committee, *Childhood Obesity*.

36 Marmot, M., *The Health Gap: The Challenge of an Unequal World* (London: Bloomsbury, 2015).

37 Department of Health and Social Care, 'New obesity strategy unweiled as country urged to lose weight to beat coronavirus (COVID-19) and protect the NHS'.

38 Hunter, D. J., 'Trying to "protect the NHS" in the United Kingdom', *New England Journal of Medicine* 383 (2020): e183.

39 Graham-Leigh, *A Diet of Austerity: Class, Food and Climate Change*, 112.

40 Evans, D., 'Thrifty, green or frugal: reflections on sustainable consumption in a changing economic climate', *Geoforum* 42, no. 5 (2011): 551–552.

41 *Kirstie: Keep Crafting and Carry On*, Channel 4, 2020, https://www.channel4.com/programmes/kirstie-keep-crafting-and-carry-on [accessed: 13 March 2022]; *Jamie: Keep Cooking and Carry On*, Channel 4, 2020, https://www.channel4.com/programmes/jamie-keep-cooking-and-carry-on [accessed: 13 March 2022]; Martin, J., 'Keep crafting and carry on: nostalgia and domestic cultures in the crisis', *European Journal of Cultural Studies* 24, no. 1 (2021): 358–364.

42 Hatherley, O., 'Lash out and. cover up: austerity nostalgia and ironic authoritarianism in recession Britain', *Radical Philosophy* 157 (2009): 2–7.

43 Allen et al., 'Welfare queens, thrifty housewives and do-it-all mums', 912.

44 Wincott, A., 'The allotment in the restaurant: the paradox of foodie auster-ity and changing food values', in *Hard Times Today: Austerity, Myth and Popular Culture*, ed. P. Bennett and J. A. McDougall (Abingdon: Routledge, 2017), 28–41.

45 Action on Sugar (@actiononsugar), 'If you're a fan of pre-made pasta sauce make it go further and reduce your sugar intake by mixing in tinned toma-toes #SugarAwarenessWeek #5aday', 18 November 2018, https://twitter. com/actiononsugar/status/1064150732935450624?s=20&t=BbQkSAf5OdZ9 ETCLAqxIVg [accessed: 18 February 2022].

46 Action on Sugar (@actiononsugar), 'Day 1 of #SugarAwarenessWeek! Take up the challenge to cut down, by switching half your sugary cereal with a lower sugar variety you can save around 6g of sugar! That's nearly 2 teaspoons', 12 November 2018, https://twitter.com/actiononsugar/status/ 1061910835021406208?s=20&t=BbQkSAf5OdZ9ETCLAqxIVg [accessed: 18 February 2018].

47 Jensen, *Parenting the Crisis: The Cultural Politics of Parent-Blame*, chapter 5.

48 Martin, 'Keep crafting and carry on: nostalgia and domestic cultures in the crisis'.

49 Wincott, 'The allotment in the restaurant: the paradox of foodie austerity and changing food values'.

50 Evans, 'Thrifty, green or frugal: reflections on sustainable consumption in a changing economic climate'.

51 Evans, B. M. and McBride, S., 'Introduction: manufacturing the common sense of austerity', in *Austerity: The Lived Experience*, ed. B. M. Evans and S. McBride (Toronto: University of Toronto Press, 2017), 19.

52 Allen et al., 'Welfare queens, thrifty housewives and do-it-all mums', 914.

53 Graham-Leigh, *A Diet of Austerity: Class, Food and Climate Change*, 458.

54 See, for example, Gill, R. and Orgad, S., 'The amazing bounce-backable woman: resilience and the psychological turn in neoliberalism', *Sociological Research Online* 23, no. 2 (2018): 477–495; Littler, J., *Against Meritocracy: Culture, Power and Myths of Mobility* (London: Routledge, 2018).

55 Metzl, 'Introduction: why against health?', 2.

56 For Popkin's publications, see, for example, Colchero et al., 'Beverage pur-chases from stores in Mexico under the excise tax on sugar sweetened bever-ages: observational study'; Popkin and Ng, 'Sugar-sweetened beverage taxes: lessons to date and the future of taxation'.

57 Boseley, S., 'First US sugar tax sees soft drinks sales fall by almost 10% study shows', *The Guardian*, 18 April 2017, https://www.theguardian.com/soci ety/2017/apr/18/first-us-sugar-tax-sees-soft-drink-sales-fall-by-almost-10-study-shows [accessed: 18 February 2022].

58 Stone, J., 'Tory MPs block plan to extend free school meals over the holi-days', *The Independent*, 21 October 2020, https://www.independent.co.uk/

Notes

news/uk/politics/free-school-meals-vote-marcus-rashford-boris-johnson-holidays-b1209118.html [accessed: 18 February 2022].

59 Murphy, S., 'Free school meals: the Tory MPs defending refusal to support campaign', *The Guardian*, 25 October 2020, https://www.theguardian.com/education/2020/oct/25/free-school-meals-uk-marcus-rashford-conservative-mps-defend-ministers-refusal-to-u-turn [accessed: 18 February 2022].

60 Martin, J., 'Jack Monroe and the cultural politics of the austerity celebrity', *European Journal of Cultural Studies* 25, no. 4 (2021): 1156–1173, https://doi.org/10.1177%2F13675494211030938.

61 Fraser, 'Sugar is poison. My heart attack has finally opened my eyes to the truth'.

62 Goran and Ventura, *Sugarproof: The Hidden Dangers of Sugar that Are Putting Your Child's Health at Risk and What You Can Do*, chapter 10.

63 Mowbray, *Sweet Nothing: Why I Gave Up Sugar and How You Can Too*, 147.

64 Sassatelli, R., 'The political morality of food: discourses, contestation and alternative consumption', in *Qualities of Food: Alternative Theoretical and Empirical Approaches*, ed. M. Harvey, A. McMeeckin and A. Warde (Manchester: Manchester University Press, 2004), 176–191; Graham-Leigh, *A Diet of Austerity: Class, Food and Climate Change*.

65 Giraud, *Veganism: Politics, Practice and Theory*, 156.

66 McKenna, *Get Control of Sugar Now! Great Choices for Your Health Future*, 139–140.

67 Goran and Ventura, *Sugarproof: The Hidden Dangers of Sugar that Are Putting Your Child's Health at Risk and What You Can Do*, 265.

68 Ibid., 264.

69 Shotwell, A., *Against Purity: Living Ethically in Compromised Times* (Minneapolis: University of Minnesota Press, 2016), 3.

70 Ibid., 4.

71 Ibid., 8–9.

72 DeFigio, *Beating Sugar Addiction for Dummies*, 155.

73 Carr, *Good Sugar, Bad Sugar: Eat Yourself Free from Sugar and Carb Addiction*, 189.

74 Ibid., 244.

75 Jones, *Goodbye Sugar: Hello Weight Loss, Great Skin, More Energy and Improved Mood*, 39.

76 DeFigio, *Beating Sugar Addiction for Dummies*, 154.

77 Goran and Ventura, *Sugarproof: The Hidden Dangers of Sugar that Are Putting Your Child's Health at Risk and What You Can Do*, 199.

78 Wilson, *I Quit Sugar: Your Complete 8-Week Detox Program and Cookbook*, 51.

79 Goran and Ventura, *Sugarproof: The Hidden Dangers of Sugar that Are Putting Your Child's Health at Risk and What You Can Do*, 265.

80 Shotwell, *Against Purity: Living Ethically in Compromised Times*, 121.

Chapter 8

1 Fielding-Singh, *How the Other Half Eats: The Untold Story of Food and Inequality in America*, 127.

2 Saguy and Almeling, 'Fat in the fire? Science, the news media and the "obesity epidemic"', 77.

3 Denis, G., 'Death by chocolate: the sugar-fuelled diabetes surge in South Asia', *The Guardian*, 2 March 2015, https://www.theguardian.com/global-development-professionals-network/2015/mar/02/diabetes-india-south-asia-type-2 [accessed: 28 February 2022].

4 Solomon, *Metabolic Living: Food, Fat and the Absorption of Illness in India*, 4494.

5 Ibid., 4515.

6 Department of Health, *Change4Life Marketing Strategy: In Support of Healthy Weight, Healthy Lives* (London: Department of Health, April 2009), 22, https://fdocuments.net/document/change4life-marketing-strategy-april09.html [accessed: 16 March 2022].

7 Gillespie, *The Sweet Poison Quit Plan: How to Kick the Sugar Habit and Lose Weight*, 176.

8 Department of Health, *Change4Life Marketing Strategy: In Support of Healthy Weight, Healthy Lives*, 26.

9 Lustig, *Fat Chance: The Hidden Truth about Sugar, Obesity and Disease*, 85–86.

10 Fielding-Singh, *How the Other Half Eats: The Untold Story of Food and Inequality in America*, chapter 15.

11 Lustig, *Fat Chance: The Hidden Truth about Sugar, Obesity and Disease*, 86.

12 Strings, *Fearing the Black Body: The Racial Origins of Fat Phobia*, 203.

13 Lustig, *Fat Chance: The Hidden Truth about Sugar, Obesity and Disease*, 3.

14 Ibid., 105.

15 Ibid., 209.

16 Eaton, S. B. and Konner, M., 'Paleolithic nutrition: a consideration of its nature and current implications', *New England Journal of Medicine* 312, no. 5 (1985): 285.

17 Ibid.

18 See, for example, Daschuk, J., *Clearing the Plains: Disease, Politics of Starvation and the Loss of Aboriginal Life* (Regina, Saskatchewan: University of Regina Press, 2013).

19 See, for example, Washington, H., *Medical Apartheid: The Dark History of Medical Experimentation on Balck Americans form Colonial Times to the Present* (New York: Anchor Books, 2006); Montoya, *Making the Mexican Diabetic: Race, Science and the Genetics of Inequality*; Roberts, *Fatal Invention: How Science, Politics, and Big Business Re-Create Race in the Twenty-First Century*.

20 Taubes, *The Case Against Sugar*, 11–12.

21 Gillespie, *Sweet Poison: Why Sugar Makes Us Fat*, 16.

22 Neel, J., 'Diabetes mellitus: a "thrifty" geneotype rendered detrimental by "progess"?', *American Journal of Human Genetics* 14, no. 4 (1962): 354.

23 Fee, M., 'Racializing narratives: obesity, diabetes and the 'aboriginal' thrifty genotype', *Social Science and Medicine* 62 (2006): 2290.

24 Yates-Doerr, *The Weight of Obesity: Hunger and Global Health in Postwar Guatemala*, 40.

25 Guthman, J. and DuPuis, E. M., 'Enbodying neoliberalism: economy, culture and the politics of fat', *Environment and Planning D: Society and Space* 24, no. 3 (2006): 432. In the early seventeenth century, Spanish colonists called them the Pima Indians rather than the name they used for themselves: Akimel O'oodham.

26 Taubes, *The Case Against Sugar*, 212. See also Taubes, *Good Calories, Bad Calories: Fats, Carbs and the Controversial Science of Diet and Health*; Taubes, *Why We Get Fat and What to Do about It*.

27 Taubes, *Good Calories, Bad Calories: Fats, Carbs and the Controversial Science of Diet and Health*, 235–327.

28 Taubes, *Why We Get Fat and What to Do about It*, 23.

29 Ibid., 20.

30 Russell, F., 'The Pima Indians', in *Twenty-Sixth Annual Report of the Bureau of Ethnology, 1904–1905* (Washington DC: Bureau of American Ethnology, 1908), 17–389.

31 Taubes, *Why We Get Fat and What to Do about It*, 20.

32 Russell, 'The Pima Indians', 66.

33 Ibid., 69.

34 Smith-Morris, C., *Diabetes among the Pima: Stories of Survival* (Tucson: University of Arizona Press, 2006) (Kindle).

35 Moran-Thomas, A., *Traveling with Sugar: Chronicles of a Global Epidemic* (Oakland: University of California Press, 2019), 1005 (Kindle).

36 Ibid., 4332.

37 Ibid., 4453.

38 Smith-Morris, *Diabetes among the Pima: Stories of Survival*, 2143.

39 Yates-Doerr, *The Weight of Obesity: Hunger and Global Health in Postwar Guatemala*, 48.

40 Moran-Thomas, *Traveling with Sugar: Chronicles of a Global Epidemic*, 4487.

41 See, for example, Charles and Kerr, *Women, Food and Families: Power, Status, Love and Anger*; DeVault, M. L., *Feeding the Family: The Social Organisation of Caring as Gendered Work*, Women in Culture and Society (Chicago: University of Chicago Press, 1991); Beagan et al., *Acquired Tastes: Why Families Eat the Way They Do*; Cairns and Johnston, *Food and Femininity*; Bowen, Brenton and Elliott, *Pressure Cooker: Why Home*

Notes

Cooking Won't Solve Our Problems and What We Can Do about It; Fielding-Singh, *How the Other Half Eats: The Untold Story of Food and Inequality in America.*

42 Earle, C., 'Hidden risks in a spoon of sugar: AS THREE FAMILIES' FOOD DIARIES REVEAL SHOCKING RESULTS', *The Sun*, 14 February 2017 (print edition).

43 Mansey, K, '"Five-a-day" foods packed with sugar', *The Sunday Times*, 12 January 2014 [accessed: 16 March 2022].

44 Knapton, S., 'Sugar does not make children hyperactive, claims psychologist', *The Daily Telegraph*, 7 June 2015, https://www.telegraph.co.uk/news/science/science-news/11657719/Sugar-does-not-make-children-hyperactive-claims-psychologist.html [accessed: 1 March 2022].

45 Schenker, S., 'I'm raising sons sugar-free, and here's how you can too', *The Daily Telegraph*, 27 March 2017, https://www.telegraph.co.uk/family/parenting/raising-sonssugar-free-can/ [accessed: 15 March 2022]; print edition 1, 'Could you raise a sugar free family?', *The Daily Telegraph*, 27 March 2017, 19, 21.

46 Schaub, *Year of No Sugar: A Memoir*, 266.

47 Gameau, *That Sugar Book: This Book Will Change the Way You Think about 'Healthy' Food*, 14.

48 Ibid., 194.

49 Griffiths, S., 'Sweet on you. Jamie Oliver's latest campaign is a tax on sugar – and advising parents how to limit our intake at home', *The Sunday Times*, 1 November 2015, https://www.thetimes.co.uk/article/sweet-on-you-mmp38ohf2b9 [accessed: 1 March 2022].

50 Fielding-Singh, *How the Other Half Eats: The Untold Story of Food and Inequality in America*, 139.

51 Hollows, J., 'Oliver's Twist: leisure, labour and domestic masculinity in "The Naked Chef"', *International Journal of Cultural Studies* 6, no. 2 (2003): 229–248.

52 Erlichman, J., *Addicted to Food: Understanding the Obesity Epidemic* (London: Guardian Books, 2013), 349 (Kindle).

53 Spring, B. et al., 'Abuse potential of carbohydrates for overweight carbohydrate cravers', *Psychopharmacology* 197 (2008): 637–647.

54 In order, ibid.; Corsica, J. A. and Pelchat, M. L., 'Food addiction: true or false?', *Current Opinion in Gastroenterology* 26 (2010): 165–169; Blumenthal, D. M. and Gold, M. S., 'Neurobiology of food addiction', *Current Opinion in Clinical Nutrition and Metabolic Care* 13 (2010): 359–365.

55 Carlyle, 'The sweet stuff: what sugar is really doing to your body'.

56 Gillespie, *The Sweet Poison Quit Plan: How to Kick the Sugar Habit and Lose Weight*, 120.

57 Lupton, D., *Food, the Body and the Self* (London: Sage, 1996; repr. 1998), 109.

58 Ibid.

Notes

59 Gillespie, *The Sweet Poison Quit Plan: How to Kick the Sugar Habit and Lose Weight*, 124.

60 Cooke, R., 'Sweetness and blight: the mounting case against sugar', *The Guardian*, 16 January 2017, https://www.theguardian.com/society/2017/jan/16/case-against-sugar-sweetness-and-blight-rachel-cooke [accessed: 2 March 2022].

61 Department of Health, *Change4Life Marketing Strategy: In Support of Healthy Weight, Healthy Lives*.

62 Crawford, 'Health as a meaningful social practice', 419.

63 Southam, H., 'Sugar was making me unwell, so I gave it up overnight', *The Daily Telegraph*, 8 March 2014, https://www.telegraph.co.uk/foodanddrink/healthyeating/10684836/Sugar-was-making-me-unwell-so-I-gave-it-up-overnight.html [accessed: 17 March 2022].

64 Guthman, 'Too much food and too little sidewalk? Problematizing the obesogenic environment thesis', 154.

65 Kirkland, A., 'The environmental account of obesity: a case for feminist skepticism', *Signs* 36, no. 2 (2011): 477.

66 Mason, R., 'David Cameron calls on obese to accept help or risk losing benefits', *The Guardian*, 14 February 2015, https://www.theguardian.com/politics/2015/feb/14/david-cameron-obese-addicts-accept-help-risk-losing-benefits [accessed: 28 February 2022].

67 Kirkland, 'The environmental account of obesity: a case for feminist skepticism', 477.

68 Department of Health, *Healthy Weight, Healthy Lives: Consumer Insight Summary* (London: Department of Health, 2008), https://lx.iriss.org.uk/sites/default/files/resources/Healthy.pdf [accessed: 17 March 2022].

69 Ibid., 49.

70 Department of Health, *Change4Life: Three Year Social Marketing Strategy* (London: Department of Health, 13 October 2011), 31, https://assets.publishing.service.gov.uk/government/uploads/system/uploads/attachment_data/file/213719/dh_130488.pdf [accessed: 20 March 2022].

71 Kirkland, 'The environmental account of obesity: a case for feminist skepticism', 476.

72 Ibid., 474.

73 Ibid., 476.

74 Warin and Zivkovic, *Fatness, Obesity and Disadvantage in the Australian Suburbs: Unpalatable Politics*, 3272.

75 OPAL provided A$ 40 million over a ten-year period from 2008 to 2018.

76 Warin and Zivkovic, *Fatness, Obesity and Disadvantage in the Australian Suburbs: Unpalatable Politics*, 3272–3282.

77 See, for example, Beagan et al., *Acquired Tastes: Why Families Eat the Way They Do*; Fielding-Singh, *How the Other Half Eats: The Untold Story of Food and Inequality in America*.

Notes

78 See, for example, Daniel, C., 'Economic constraints on taste formation and the true cost of healthy eating', *Social Science and Medicine* 148 (2016): 34–41; Daniel, C., 'Is healthy eating too expensive? How low-income parents evaluate the cost of food', *Social Science and Medicine* 248 (2020): 112823.

79 Department of Health, *Change4Life Marketing Strategy: In Support of Healthy Weight, Healthy Lives*, 20.

80 Fielding-Singh, *How the Other Half Eats: The Untold Story of Food and Inequality in America*, 253.

81 Ibid., 114.

82 Ibid., 118.

83 Kirkland, 'The environmental account of obesity: a case for feminist skepticism', 474.

84 Guthman, *Weighing In: Obesity, Food Justice and the Limits of Capitalism*, 193.

Conclusion

1 Landecker, 'Food as exposure: nutritional epigenetics and the new metabolism', 168.

2 Guthman, *Weighing In: Obesity, Food Justice and the Limits of Capitalism*.

3 Briggs, C. L. and Mantini-Briggs, C., *Stories in the Time of Cholera: Racial Profiling during a Medical Nightmare* (Berkeley: University of California Press), 327.

Index

Index

fructose 26, 39–43, 47, 89, 108, 142, 220

Gameau, Damon
  coloniality 133–134
  masculinity 217
  self-experimentation 128, 140–143
  spectacle 128–131
  see also non-expert expert; Oliver, Jamie; *That Sugar Film*
Gillespie, David 36, 45, 47, 53, 96, 104–108, 114, 121, 139–140, 206, 219–220
Guthman, Julie 138, 211, 223, 229, 236

headless fatties 78, 137
healthism 9, 235
heart disease 5, 7, 40, 43, 53–54, 75, 160, 186, 206
hidden-sugar shock 20, 76–77, 79–82, 84–85, 87–88, 91, 97, 99–100, 116, 166, 179
hunter-gatherer 66, 72, 205, 209–210

Jamie's Sugar Rush 21, 124–125, 127, 130, 132, 138, 141, 143, 147–148, 154, 195, 202, 232
Johnson, Boris 12, 34, 51, 181, 186, 188

Keys, Ancel 5–6, 43–44

lifestyle 2, 5, 51, 59, 103–104, 183, 190, 208, 210, 224
  dietary 15
  diseases 160
  healthy 206, 225
  sedentary 28
  sugar-free 101
low-carb 37, 39, 92
  dieters 45
  diets 71
  evangelists 44, 72

low-carbohydrate 7, 68–70, 96
  see also low-carb
Lustig, Robert 9, 38–46 *passim*, 54, 63, 66, 71, 94, 206–207

MacGregor, Graham 64, 78, 79, 215
metabolic syndrome 40, 63, 106, 110
  see also metabolism
metabolism 25, 27, 32, 46
  post-industrial 40–41
  see also metabolic syndrome
Mexico 127, 134–136, 207
  sugar tax 153–154, 171, 185, 195
modernity 113, 154, 205, 207, 211–212
molecularisation 8–10, 235
mortified mother 92–93, 98–99, 116, 122, 214–215
Mowbray, Nicole 104–105, 107, 109–111, 117, 197

nanny state 152, 155–158, 174
National Health Service 23, 50, 130, 158
  see also NHS
National Obesity Forum 157, 171
Nestle, Marion 26, 161–162
NCDs *see* non-communicable diseases
NHS 34, 50–52, 130, 183, 186
  protect the 188
  see also National Health Service
NOF *see* National Obesity Forum
non-communicable diseases 2, 26, 47, 152, 187
non-expert expert 21, 126, 143, 145
nostalgia 20, 65–69, 71, 73, 94, 191, 229
  austerity 190
  see also paleo-nostalgia
nutricentric 17, 87, 109, 232, 233
nutritional science 2, 7, 33–34, 37, 43, 84, 105
nutritionism 26, 91
  see also nutritionist paradigm
nutritionist paradigm 8, 27
  see also nutritionism

Index

Index

Taubes, Gary 35, 37, 39–42, 45,
  210
  see also metabolism; Pima
That Sugar Film 21, 37, 125–128, 138,
  148, 217
tobacco
  addiction 57, 59, 63–64
  industry 127, 159
  regulation 151
  sugar is the new 2, 18, 56–57, 59,
  63–65

type 2 diabetes 40, 45, 49, 53–54, 75,
  141, 173, 202
  see also alcohol; drugs

welfare state 1, 176, 182–183, 186
wellness 26, 101, 103–104, 110, 112,
  224
WHO 26, 29–30, 32, 35
World Health Organization 25–26, 95

Yates-Doerr, Emily 83, 97, 211, 213